P9-DNC-995

Praise for *Allah, Liberty and Love*

"Irshad Manji once again shows herself to be a Muslim reformist of outstanding courage. Hers is the unwavering conviction that all religions, including Islam, fulfill their timeless moral precepts through universal love, freedom and reason. To understand how these virtues can be allied with Allah and the Quran—not in theory, but in our messy real world—you must read this book."

—N. J. Dawood, translator of *The Koran* (Penguin Classics)

"As a reporter, I have witnessed the impact of Irshad Manji's work on young Muslims in the Middle East. By listening to their ideas about how to use emerging technologies to circumvent state censors, Manji has reached a new generation of Arab activists and helped raise their democratic aspirations."

—Katherine Zoepf, journalist and Schwartz Fellow at the New America Foundation

"*Allah, Liberty and Love* is illuminating and liberating. While escaping her assassins, Irshad Manji fearlessly speaks truth to power. In so doing, she wisely points to the new heaven and hell—right here on Earth."

—Shohreh Aghdashloo, star of *The Stoning of Soraya M*

Also by Irshad Manji

Risking Utopia: On the Edge of a New Democracy

The Trouble with Islam Today:
A Muslim's Call for Reform in Her Faith

THE COURAGE TO RECONCILE
FAITH AND FREEDOM

IRSHAD MANJI

ALLAH, LIBERTY AND LOVE

Free Press

New York   London   Toronto   Sydney

Free Press
A Division of Simon & Schuster, Inc.
1230 Avenue of the Americas
New York, NY 10020

Copyright © 2011 by Mosaic Media, Inc.

All rights reserved, including the right to reproduce this book or portions thereof
in any form whatsoever. For information address Free Press Subsidiary Rights
Department, 1230 Avenue of the Americas, New York, NY 10020.

First Free Press hardcover edition June 2011

FREE PRESS and colophon are trademarks of Simon & Schuster, Inc.

For information about special discounts for bulk purchases,
please contact Simon & Schuster Special Sales at
1–866–506–1949 or business@simonandschuster.com.

The Simon & Schuster Speakers Bureau can bring authors to your live event.
For more information or to book an event contact the Simon & Schuster Speakers
Bureau at 1-866-248-3049 or visit our website at www.simonspeakers.com.

Designed by Carla Jayne Jones

Manufactured in the United States of America

1   3   5   7   9   10   8   6   4   2

Library of Congress Cataloging-in-Publication Data
Manji, Irshad.
Allah, liberty and love : the courage to reconcile faith and freedom / Irshad Manji.
    p. cm.
1. Islam.   2. Liberty of conscience (Islam)   3. Muslims—Conduct of life.   I. Title.
BP161.3.M363 2011
297.5'677—dc22   2011003846

ISBN 978-1-4516-4520-0
ISBN 978-1-4516-4522-4 (ebook)

DEAR MARIANNE —

In memory of my grandmother, "Leila Liberty"

YOU GO, GIRL!
(AS MY MOTHER
ONCE TOLD ME...)
LOVE,

Joshua
Z

CONTENTS

AUTHOR'S NOTE

Allah is the Arabic name for God—the universally shared God of liberty and love. Not exactly the perception that many people have of Allah, I realize. But as I'll strive to show, God loves me enough to give me choices and the liberty to make them. In turn, I am to love God's other children enough to have faith in their ability to make choices. Love, then, obliges me to do two things at once: champion freedom for more than just myself and challenge powermongers who steal choices from you and me. In these topsy-turvy times, the link between liberty and love has to be explored with clarity. As I'll show, my ebullient relationship with Allah helps me do that.

Clarity requires reason, which invariably leads to the question, "How can you know God exists?" I can't know. I believe. I acknowledge this up front so as not to insult the intelligence of agnostic and atheist readers. Still, I'll also show that the best way to respect everybody's intelligence is by having faith in our potential to become agents of change in this life rather than sit on our hands in fatalistic anticipation of some hereafter. Through my faith in the creative capacity of individuals, I hope to speak respectfully to nonbelievers as much as to believers.

In fact, individuals of various creeds have shaped my thinking, so let me say a few words about sources. Over the past decade, among the most high-impact teachers I've had are the Muslims and non-Muslims who engaged with me directly—whether at events, on Facebook or by email. With deep gratitude, I've woven a lot of them into this book. In the main, I've cited only first names or none at all. And when I've been aware of danger to my correspondents, I've changed their names.

So much additional research has gone into *Allah, Liberty and Love* that printing the footnotes would add an absurd number of pages. To make the book readable and affordable, as well as to avoid killing more trees, I've posted all the footnotes on my website, irshadmanji.com. I also use the footnotes to flesh out a number of my points. Please visit this section of my site if you're curious to learn more about anything you've just read.

Finally, at the back of the book, I provide a list of recommended readings—some of which still blow my mind. May they inspire as much as inform you.

INTRODUCTION

FROM ANGER TO ASPIRATION

On a chilly afternoon in February 2007, I arrived in Texas for the first time ever. Houston's Rice University had invited me to speak about my book *The Trouble with Islam Today: A Muslim's Call For Reform in Her Faith*. En route to the interfaith center, my host and I discussed (what else?) science. We marveled at the theory that physicists have come up with to explore a world beyond the material, and we exulted in the fact that "superstring theory," like a spiritual quest marinated in mystery, has its doubters as well as its defenders. A short while later, in a state-of-the-art auditorium named for Shell Oil, I stood before rows of people who reflected a Bible Belt throbbing with diversity: Muslims, Christians, Jews, Buddhists, polytheists, atheists and—Lord love us all—misfits.

Jazzed by what he witnessed, my host pushed the envelope of diversity and introduced me as the Muslim to whom Oprah Winfrey, an African American, had given her Chutzpah Award—*chutzpah* being the Yiddish word for courage bordering on craziness. The audience laughed. Timidly. Everyone could feel the apprehension. Writing about the need for change in Islam doesn't win you points for diplomacy, not even in Texas. I consider myself a truth-teller, but many in the crowd feared a flamethrower.

"I'm here to have a conversation," I assured them—a conversation "about a very different story of Islam." We all knew the Islam that jumped out of our headlines: an unholy trinity of bombings, beheadings and blood. We also knew that, according to moderate Muslims, Islam means "peace." Anybody could have given this audience more of the same, but that's never been my mission. The story I would tell, I promised, "revolves around a really big idea that I believe has the capacity to change the world for good."

That idea is *ijtihad*—Islam's own tradition of dissenting, reasoning and reinterpreting. For non-Muslims in my audience, I pronounced it carefully: *ij-tee-had*. It comes from the same root as *jihad*, "to struggle," but unlike violent struggle, ijtihad is about struggling to understand our world by using our minds. Which implies exercising the freedom to ask questions—sometimes uncomfortable ones. I spoke about why all of us, Muslim and not, need ijtihad. Burning a hole in my back pocket was an email from Jim, one of my American readers. "The message of ijtihad, of questioning, speaks to more than just Muslims," he enthused. "Throw away the confines of political correctness and discuss, debate, challenge and learn. A brown Muslim woman inspiring a white Christian man. Isn't freedom great?"

I was about to be reminded just how great freedom is. The evening saw its share of questions for me: What about the ills of the West? Will it be women who kick-start reform in Islam? How do you use ijtihad to beat the terrorists? At the end of the night a Muslim student quietly made his way over and told me that only when he attended university in the United States did he hear about ijtihad. "Why," he wondered, "aren't we taught about this Islamic tradition in our madrassas?" I directed him to the part of my book in which I addressed his question. He thanked me and turned away. In mid-motion, the young Muslim stopped to ask me another question: "How do I get your chutzpah?"

———————

Over the past eight years, I've had hundreds of conversations like this. They've taken me on a surreal journey that's culminated in the book you're holding now. Let me back up.

On the morning of September 11, 2001, I was in Toronto, conducting my first meeting as the executive producer of a TV channel dedicated to spirituality. I had no idea about the World Trade Center attacks until the meeting wrapped up and I returned to an office of stunned colleagues hunched over TV sets. Soon after, I wrote a newspaper editorial about why we Muslims can no longer point fingers at non-Muslims to explain away our dysfunction. For too long we'd broken faith with chapter 13, verse 11, of the Qur'an: "God does not change the condition of a people until they change what is inside themselves." It's a 13:11 solution to a 9/11 abomination.

My editorial, "A Muslim Plea for Introspection," triggered such a flood of response that publishers wanted to make it a full-fledged book. I had to decide if I'd give up my dream job to pour my heart into something that Muslims might not be ready to hear: questions. As I had asked my madrassa teacher in Vancouver twenty years earlier, Why can't I take Christians and Jews as friends? Why can't a woman lead prayer? Why should I avoid examining the Qur'an and understanding it? Isn't this all a recipe for corruption? Before 9/11, not a single person seemed to care.

I followed my conscience, writing *The Trouble with Islam Today* as an open letter to fellow Muslims. The trouble, I argued, is more than the militants; even mainstream Muslims have curdled Islamic faith into an ideology of fear. Evidently, the questions I posed touched a raw nerve. When the book came out in September 2003 in my country of Canada, it hit number one, and within months it also became a bestseller in the United States. One by one, European countries released their translations, followed by the world's largest Muslim country, Indonesia.

Despite the glamour of international attention, I'd actually embarked on what the Qur'an calls "the uphill path." I found myself confronting a vice president of Iran about the atrocity of stoning women to death. Pakistan's Pervez Musharraf instructed me to "Sit down!" because he didn't appreciate my inquiry about his human rights record. The political leader of a terrorist group, Islamic Jihad, ran me out of Gaza when he couldn't locate any justification in the Qur'an for the violent tactics that he insisted were "everywhere" in Islam's scripture.

Truth is, though, my most memorable exchanges have been with everyday people. The book tour evolved into a global conversation, taking me to all the countries of North America and western Europe, many in eastern Europe and some in the Middle East, as well as India, Australia and Indonesia, where stern Muslim puritans and a spunky Muslim transsexual showed up at my book party. (More about that later.)

In the United States alone, I visited forty-four states, engaging with fans and foes in libraries, restaurants, theaters, classrooms, gymnasiums, chapels and temples. No mosques, however. All invitations by Muslims hit the roadblock of mosque leaders who regarded me as a rabble-rouser. Still, Muslims attended each of my public events. Many came to jeer, but many others came to find solace in the fact that someone was saying what *they* wanted to say, yet felt they couldn't. A reader named Ayesha summed it up when she emailed, "Millions think like you but are afraid to go public with their views for fear of persecution." I heard her: Some days I received so much hate mail that I had to dance like Muhammad Ali to take the pounding and sustain the meaning.

Ayesha's email is featured on my website, irshadmanji.com. Every couple of weeks I posted several new messages, along with my replies. My site burgeoned into a hub of debate, connecting me to what people of vastly different beliefs thought and felt about reform in Islam—and about why I couldn't take the backlash too personally. "I've been reading the postings on your website," Jonathan wrote. "Even if you are everything your critics say you are—an infidel, blaspheming, self-hating, mind-poisoning, money-grubbing, Zionist dyke (have I omitted anything?), it would still not follow that your ideas have no merit." He quoted the twelfth-century Jewish philosopher Maimonides, who was himself influenced by free-thinking Muslims: "Truth does not become more true by virtue of the fact that the entire world agrees with it, or less so even if the whole world disagrees with it." My reply to Jonathan? "Yeah, but you're just a self-hating, mind-poisoning, money-grubbing, dyke-loving Jew. Enough said."

I took the death threats seriously when they contained specifics, proving that my opponents had planned out their execution fantasies. Those emails I forwarded to the police. Counterterrorism experts advised me against using a cell phone because ill-wishers could easily exploit the technology to track me down. And for a time I had a bodyguard. He was cute, to boot. But I let him go early on because young Muslims would be watching how I handled the consequences of going public with my questions, and I didn't want them assuming that the only way to survive is to hire round-the-clock protection.

The decision to drop 24-hour security opened up communication with young Muslims—and opportunities for change. My inbox overflowed with messages from the Middle East, asking me when

I'd be getting the book translated into Arabic so a new generation of reformers could share it with their friends. I'd love to, I replied, but name one Arab publisher that will distribute a book like this. A lot of the kids wrote back, "So what?" They encouraged me to post an Arabic translation on my website, which they could download free of charge. (They were young but they weren't born yesterday.) I thought, "How sassy. How subversive. How can I not go for it?"

In 2005, I uploaded the Arabic translation to my site at no cost to readers. The following year a number of democracy activists waved me down in the streets of Cairo. "Are you Irshad?" they asked. In most cases—security still being an issue—I said yes. At which point they told me they'd been reading the book online. On another occasion I sat with a journalist who'd seen photocopies of the translations being passed around by Arab youth, which inspired me to offer the same access to readers in Iran, where the book is banned. So far, the multiple online translations have been downloaded more than two million times.

———

Inside the trenches, something was happening inside *me*. As I witnessed an intense thirst for reform among Muslims, I felt myself maturing from anger to aspiration. I remember one such moment: Hamza, a Canadian teenager with Pakistani parents, implored me in an email "not to leave Islam" because "we really need people like you." But, he prodded, "sometimes you criticize Islam too much. Perhaps you could endorse the open-minded, forward-looking Islam more." I embraced his challenge; it showed faith in my capacity to grow.

PBS approached me about shooting a documentary based on my book, and I counteroffered: Let's not focus on the trouble with Islam, but on what there is to love about Islam—from the perspective of a dissident. Among other places, my crew and I filmed in Yemen. There, we interviewed Osama bin Laden's former body-guard, who proudly announced the hope that his five-year-old son, Habib, would one day be a martyr. I was yanked back into dismay. Over the course of filming, moderate Muslims too evaded my basic question: What are we doing to restore faith with that glorious pas-sage in the Qur'an, "God does not change the condition of a people until they change what is inside themselves"? For all that I love about Islam, I couldn't reconcile myself to certain Muslim practices.

Faith Without Fear, my documentary, premiered in April 2007. I took it on the road, meeting yet more people who told me that they struggle with the cultures, traditions and power structures that fence in their own religious experiences. Although Muslims have been in the spotlight since 9/11, it's not as if other communities are sitting pretty. I listened to Christians, Jews, Hindus and Sikhs who'd resolved to leave their narrowing folds—until being energized by the fight of Muslim reformers.

Those discussions compelled me to think more about the differ-ence between faith and dogma. Faith doesn't forbid exploration. It's dogma that does. Dogma, by definition, is threatened by questions, while faith welcomes questions because it trusts that God, being magisterial, can handle them. That's a God whose grace can be felt by curious individuals everywhere.

Then an agnostic friend introduced me to the concept of "moral courage," a phrase that I'd never heard. Robert F. Kennedy described moral courage as the willingness to speak truth to power within your community for the sake of a greater good. Moral cour-age allows each of us to tap our consciences, to replace conformity with individuality and to draw closer to the Source that created us by coming to know ourselves. It dawned on me how necessary moral courage is for anybody who wants to live with wholeness—

integrity—whether within a religious tradition or outside of religion altogether.

Scholars at New York University picked up on the point about integrity. After my film screening at the Robert F. Wagner Graduate School of Public Service, the dean asked if I'd consider launching the Moral Courage Project with her. We would teach individuals how to speak up in a world that often wants to shut us up. In 2008, I became founding director of the Moral Courage Project. Once I settled into New York, led my first class and caught my breath, I turned to the next chapter of this journey: linking my mission of reform among Muslims with the universal message of moral courage for us all.

————

Surrounded by boxes of emails, handwritten letters from the public and notes that I'd scribbled to myself over the years, I sifted and sorted. Patterns surfaced. Muslims feared dishonoring their families and God if they honestly admitted what they believed. Non-Muslims feared being dishonored as bigots if they voiced their questions about what's happening in the name of Islam.

The result was a collective, culturally sensitive muteness in the face of heinous crimes. The murders, for example, of "dishonorable" women and girls in the Middle East, in Europe, in Asia and increasingly in North America are born of culture, not religion. But in a multicultural world, culture has become something of a god—even among secular people. Out of misplaced reverence for multiculturalism, too many of us perpetuate deadly silences.

Such injustices ate away at me. How can we be indifferent to flagrant abuses of power while defining that indifference as sensitivity? Where's the compass to guide us out of this lie? And what's the greater good as people from a breathtaking spectrum of cultures try to live together? Messages from my readers helped me connect the dots.

Wrote Helene: "You encourage Christians like me to look at Islamic society with compassion and understanding instead of fear and anger. I will now be able to speak my opinions without that huge amount of guilt about feeling intolerant, knowing that I have weighed the sides carefully and thoughtfully. We can all be instruments of change." I then zeroed in on an email from Zahur, who predicted that Muslim reformers "will teach the West how precious freedom of expression is for a healthy and functioning society. Ask the Iranian youth how they feel about that."

Reflecting on their mutual love of freedom, I flashed back to disturbing scenes from my journey. On the campuses of Western universities, good-hearted non-Muslims whispered that they wanted to support my mission but felt they had no right to get involved. At the same places, Islam-supremacists felt far more free than liberal Muslims to champion their interpretations of the Qur'an. "This is nuts," I recalled mumbling to myself. "Freedom-haters appreciate their freedoms enough to use them for the purpose of stifling others. How can the rest of us let them get away with it?"

That, I realized, is a moral courage challenge for our era. Muslims and non-Muslims who live in democracies have to develop the spine to expand individual liberty, not stunt it, because without the freedom to think and express there can be no integrity of the self or integration of society.

I threw myself into research about how previous movements for freedom had succeeded. Martin Luther King, Jr., came alive for this Muslim girl, as did some of his teachers: the philosopher Socrates, the theologian Reinhold Niebuhr, the novelist Lillian Smith, who campaigned to reform a culture of "honor" in the U.S. South, the source of long-standing racial segregation. I also learned about

Islam's Gandhi. (Yes, there is one! I'll tell you his story, which can be a lodestar for us.)

These and other agents of moral courage spurred my thinking about the big questions I've heard from people of every background and creed: Why should I risk my reputation to tell my truth? How do I deal with community disapproval? What's God got to do with any of it?

Even our failing economy reinforced the new direction of this journey. Ordinary folks, their financial security shattered in spite of minding their own business, began to protest that change can't be left exclusively to Wall Street insiders. After all, insiders seek to preserve their status. Exactly. This insight also applies to Islam, a global religion whose internal dynamics affect countless lives outside the religion. This is everybody's business. Muslims and non-Muslims need each other to widen the circle of the free.

———————

In 2010, an ugly debate broke out over the proposed Islamic center and mosque near Ground Zero in New York City. The toxic politics that pits all of Islam against all of the West has roiled Europe for years; with that toxicity traveling to America, I'm receiving more hate mail. Muslim reformers have long been in the crosshairs of Islam-supremacists, but now their most vocal adversaries—Islam-bashers—are targeting reformers like me simply for remaining Muslim. "Islam is a mass-murdering Fascist ideology and you are an ignorant, barbaric, backward Mohammedan," goes an email that typifies our climate. In an emotional environment where individuals congeal into tribes, moral courage sometimes seems a pipe dream.

That's why the time is right for this book. Moral courage is urgently needed, and it starts with love. But to be truly courageous, love needs to be accompanied by questions. Today, free societies face dilemmas that demand gutsy thinking. How, for example, can we produce pluralists, people who tolerate multiple perspectives, without producing relativists, people who fall for anything because they stand for nothing? Democracies have to raise such questions, not squelch them for fear that their citizens are incapable of maturing.

If you believe as I do that our shared God gives us the grace to grow, then we're eminently capable of dealing with questions. To steady myself, I rely on two touchstones of Allah's grace. First, almost every chapter of the Qur'an opens by praising God as "the compassionate and merciful," not the capricious and malicious. Second, the Qur'an has three times as many verses urging Muslims to think than verses promoting blind worship. Combine the scripture's appeal to use my mind with its affirmation of God as supreme benevolence, and I've got a path to reconciling Allah, liberty and love.

I want to show that you too can live faithfully free—whatever your faith. Since 9/11, many of you have shaped my journey, and the growing I've done brings me to seven lessons for living with moral courage, presented in the book you're about to read. I offer these lessons with the hope that even more of you will join me in one of the signature reform efforts of our age. Along the way, you'll learn how to transform high defenses about "the Other" and low expectations of ourselves into the opposite—higher expectations of ourselves and lower defenses about the Other. You'll build the courage to ask questions of your own communities. And you'll discover the God that loves those questions. God could be your conscience, or your Creator, or the joyous integration of both, known as integrity.

1

SOME THINGS ARE MORE
IMPORTANT THAN FEAR

Can you just imagine my life without you? Can you just imagine?"

Can you imagine hearing that from your own mother? Can you imagine watching her beg you to tone down your call for moderate Muslims to speak out against the destructive extremists? We're at the dining room table, floral teacups before us but barely touched. Mum can't swallow right now. "I live with my heart in my throat every day," she gently reminds me. She looks as if she could vomit. Thank God for me that her heart is blocking her throat.

When she falls silent, her mouth remains slightly open, as if ready to refute whatever my head might marshal in feeble defense. And my defense does feel feeble, because the issue here isn't winning a debate with my mother. It's abiding by the universal law that children are supposed to bury their parents, not the other way around.

Years ago Mum had advised me, "Whatever you do, don't anger Allah." Can you imagine having to wonder if a just and loving God is furious with you because violent ideologues might make you break the parents-must-die-first rule? Talk about a double whammy. I won't lie to my mother, so when she asks about the latest death threats, I answer. "What about the new ones?" Mum whispers. "What do they say?" I tell her that one of them ends, "This is your last warning."

Can you imagine your mother developing any measure of calm when you insist that cowering in fear only hands the enemies of humanity more power than they already have? That they can give you their last warning but you refuse to give them the last word? I don't expect my mother to agree. What I expect from her is faith—not so much that I'll live another day, since longevity isn't guaranteed to any of us; faith, instead, that if I'm offed tomorrow, I'll go with my conscience fully and ferociously alive.

Lesson one: *Some things are more important than fear.*

———

It's remarkable that Salman Rushdie has outlived the Ayatollah Khomeini. On February 14, 1989, Khomeini harnessed the murder machine of the Islamic Republic of Iran to promise death to Rushdie, author of *The Satanic Verses*. But the novelist ran afoul of more than the world's most notorious cleric. During a public conversation in New York City to mark the twentieth anniversary of "the fatwa," Rushdie told me about the reaction of one family member: "I had an uncle who was a general in the Pakistani army. I hated his guts, but there he was. He hated mine too."

"Normal family dysfunction," I interjected. "You get it everywhere."

"Well, actually, not so normal," Rushdie corrected me. "After the Khomeini fatwa, he took out an ad in the newspaper to say, essentially, we never liked [Salman] anyway."

Rushdie's story brings to mind something that an educated relative of mine had said to me a couple of years earlier. "Do you still live at the same place?" he asked.

2

"Yes," I replied.

"So maybe the security threat isn't that real. I mean, it looks like Muslims haven't targeted you enough."

I like this man—he's been good to my mother when she's most needed the support. But, as Rushdie would agree, Muslim uncles say the darnedest things.

Risking the disapproval of our families ranks among the biggest fears of Muslims. While that's true for everybody, it's even more so for Muslims. Our culture of honor, as I'll soon explain, makes us believe that we must protect our families from shame before claiming dignity for ourselves. Put bluntly, individual dignity doesn't exist without the acceptance of your community. No wonder I receive messages like these from Muslims who live in the East and the West:

I read your book on the Internet and you are right, we need a wake-up call. I was born in north Iraq. My family have become citizens of the United Arab Emirates. I am this century's child and I will live the way life is now, not in ancient times. . . . Muslims are locked in their rules. It will take more people like you and me to unlock the iron wall. I was going to tell the world my feeling, but I love my family and I don't want to ruin their life. —Alya

I look at other Muslims and ask them if they have any doubts about Islam. They all reply "no" without any hesitation. Is there something wrong with me? Why is it that everyone else seems to accept what they were taught? I'm so frustrated at this point that I can't help but cry about it. All I'd like is some time away from the religion so I can find myself without outside influences.

But to do that, I would have to forsake my family. They would never speak to me again if I were to take the path that I wish to take. Every time I even ask them questions, I get yelled at, get told not to question, or get an explanation that comes directly from the Qur'an. I can never tell them that in order for me to believe those explanations, I would need to have unquestioned belief in the Qur'an itself. After so many years, I'm at the breaking point. If you have any advice at all, it would be appreciated.   —Yasmin

Many of the questions on your website address Muslim and non-Muslim couples. I was in a relationship of that sort. But it is ended now because I realize there is no hope. The only hope is if I leave my family, and family is too important to do that to. . . . I'm the type of person who hides a lot of my own feelings for my family. How do I become the person I want to be? Or the person I am, but am too scared to let out?   —Phirdhoz

I am a Muslim and am aspiring to be a writer. My mother is a Christian and my father is a Muslim. Therefore, I've grown up accustomed to nasty stares from other Muslims. As the days go by, however, I find myself torn between being an advocate for reform in Islam and completely dropping my religion. As if Muslims did not take enough crap from non-Muslims and it wasn't a constant struggle to distinguish yourself from a terrorist, it seems we also have to face the judgments of our fellow Muslims.

Sometimes, I have moments of weakness when I feel it's just not worth it anymore; these people cannot be changed. But the soul-searching calls to prayer and soul-soothing surahs [chapters] of the Qur'an that I recite daily are a part of me that I love. Currently, I am dealing with adversity within my own family. All these older aunts and uncles always have something to criticize. They talk behind your back because they are sooo self-righteous. Is there any way, in your experience, to make them see things from a different perspective and maybe even show compassion?   —Elizabeth

My hometown is Solo, Central Java. This is also the home of the Indonesian Mujahideen Council, a radical Islamist organization. Since 2005, I have been participating in a youth group to promote Islamic reform and plural-

4

ism. We do this by distributing publications to many universities. A couple of years ago, we tried to organize a seminar on pluralism and received phone calls saying they would send hundreds of Allah's soldiers to stop us.

My family is also very conservative. They will send me threatening letters whenever I get my work published. Recently, I was highly disappointed by a relative who is a local imam. He became involved in one of the terrorist groups. He is now in jail, leaving a wife and son without proper care. What kind of jihad is that? But no matter how conservative they are, I love my family and I want them to love me for what I believe. I often find myself giving up when I face my father. Then I lie. I don't speak my mind. I don't want to hurt him and I don't want him to hurt me because I don't want to hate him. So how do I use my freedom of speech? —Sakdiyah

I responded to them all that before you decide you can't upset your family, think about one of the most overlooked verses in the Qur'an: "Believers! Conduct yourselves with justice and bear true witness before God, even if it be against yourselves, your parents, or your relatives" (4:135). That's a call for honesty, no matter who's offended by it. How could traditional family members argue with the Qur'an? They wouldn't go there. But they'll always concoct excuses to belittle the point made by such a verse, which is why citing passages isn't enough ballast for speaking truth to power within the Muslim family—or community. Suspicions about reform-minded Muslims will persist, so each of us has to grapple with Yasmin's question: *Is there something wrong with me?*

In a way, there is. You care about Islam. You feel pain precisely because you pay attention to the integrity of your faith. Your conscience counts, and that's an open invitation to hurt. If Alya, Yasmin, Phirdhoz, Elizabeth and Sakdiyah didn't care, then by definition they'd lapse into apathy. That's probably the case with many of their family and friends, as it is with more than a few of mine. The irony is, religious types pronounce reform-minded Muslims unfaithful, and yet we might be more consumed with faith—because of our haunting questions—than believers who have no questions at all.

That said, there *is* something we shouldn't care so much about: the approval of other mortals. If they don't tolerate our curiosity, why should closed minds enjoy the power to define our dignity? As I recall asking my own mother (for whom blood relations once meant everything), "If so-and-so wasn't family, would I respect her enough to want her as a friend?" Sultan Abdulhameed, a teacher with the Muslim Reform Movement in New York, knows where I'm coming from. In his redemptive series of essays *The Quran and the Life of Excellence*, he cautions against turning your family into your deity: "If we let the superstitions and prejudices of our ancestors dictate to us, we ascribe authority to something other than God, who wants us to live consciously and take responsibility for our lives."

Mushy? Not to a God-conscious reformer named Martin Luther King, Jr. Even before he faced off against white segregationists, King had to challenge the abrasive prejudices of his father, a spellbinding Christian minister and dominant figure in Atlanta, Georgia. The historian Taylor Branch writes that Daddy King tried "to prevent his son from joining a new interracial council of students from Atlanta's white and Negro colleges, arguing that M.L. should stay among his own and not risk 'betrayals' from the white students. King thought this was absurd."

Years later, as a civil rights leader, King had to choose between his father and his conscience. It was nearing Easter weekend, 1963. Activists had been slapped with an injunction not to march in Birmingham, Alabama, quite possibly the most incorrigible stronghold of racism in the United States at that time. Would King follow the law and obey the injunction? The dilemma glared. At the same table, upping the ante of guilt, duty and respect, sat his father, who made no secret of the fact that he wanted his son back at church on one of the most festooned weekends in the Christian calendar. King retreated to another room for prayer. When he emerged, he didn't need to say a word. According to Branch, "The fact that he came out in blue jeans is announcing that 'I'm not going to the services with the flowers and the anthems and the great choirs. I'm going somewhere in blue jeans,' which meant jail."

———————

In too many Muslim households today, parents demand robotic respect—to the point where their children censor themselves as a habit. But we've just seen from the letters of young Muslims that self-censorship doesn't foster peace of mind. If the "religion of peace" is observed with countless consciences secretly churning in turmoil, there's no peace to speak of. There's also no faith. There's only dogma. At that point, the question is not whether the law demands obedience; the question is whether the law *deserves* obedience. We know where King would have stood on this. In his jeans.

Every reform-minded Muslim will have to risk backlash to widen the path of Islam. Muslims deem Islam "the straight path"—a simple and clear code of living. But the straight path can also be "the wide path," connecting us to the God that's bigger than biological family, larger than local community, more transcendent than the international Muslim tribe.

Muslims are monotheists. To be a monotheist, you must accept that Allah knows the full truth and that we human beings don't. Nor, as monotheists, may we play the role of Allah. Recognizing God's infinite wisdom means acknowledging our own limited wisdom and therefore letting a thousand flowers bloom. So it's an act of faith to create societies in which we can disagree with each other

7

without physical harm from one another. Anything less undermines the Almighty's mandate as final judge and jury. To devote myself to one God is to defend liberty.

In widening the path of Islam, the stakes are high—but so is the payoff. Given how entwined the globe has become, a reformed Muslim mind-set could make life better for most inhabitants of God's green Earth. I'm reminded of this by Ahmadollah, an artist who emailed me from Egypt three years before his country's January 2011 uprising for freedom:

although i am traditional muslim and committed so much with five prayers a day i wont decide to kill you immediately. ☺ your book make me ask some facts and open my mind to try that bad thing called free thinking. for example why the media in egypt shows israel as the evil enemy? you know, ariel sharon's son in jail while gamal mubarak rides government cars with a huge security? why really a young egyptian engineer fly away and hits himself to the walls of world trade center and what was the message he was trying to say and what kind of education pushed him do such stupid thing?

the problem i believe is we r living in continually suppressed-thinking state. I mean we egyptians have right to shout loud in a football game but we doesn't have right to protest against any political or religious affair. Do you know that a girl was arrested because she made a group on the facebook calling for strike? and famous journalist was jailed because he said that mubarak is maybe, maybe, ill because he doesn't show up at a recent ceremony?

As we know by now, Ahmadollah wasn't exaggerating. When I traveled to Egypt in May 2006, banners preached openness, yet the place reeked of authoritarianism. That week in Cairo, President Mubarak's hired henchmen pummeled democracy activists in the streets. I could appreciate Ahmadollah's desperation when he ended his message to me: "oh irshad sometimes I dare to ask—while I am hiding in dark—is there a hope for us?"

I believe there is hope. I believe it not only because Egyptians have shown themselves capable of a bottom-up revolt for political liberty, but also because of subtle signals that reveal a thirst for religious liberty. A self-described "Sharia law student" at Cairo's Al-Azhar University wrote to me with a pledge: "i will be a reformist scholar and i will support lesbians and gays."

Can we pause here for a moment? Think about the intellectual will and moral muscle it takes to go your own way at the College of Sharia within Al-Azhar University, the most respected school in the Sunni Muslim world. God help him. This student, who signed his name and whom I feel obliged to protect by not including it, understood just how stacked the odds are:

i'm studying at one of the greatest Islamic universities but yet no one are using his mind or the critical creative thinking, i can't say what i think, feel or want about hijab, jews, etc. if i say what i think i will be accused to be a kafer [unbeliever] then my family will get hurt or my family will hurt me. the best that can happen is a dear friend will listen to me. i have decided that i will support you any way i go and i will not read the Qor'an and Sunnah [Prophet Muhammad's reported words and deeds] as i used to read them before. . . . i really need your support and i want you to know that i as a future Imam InshAllah [God willing] support you.

We who love freedom owe him a debt because his success will help secure freedom beyond his own borders. Those of us lucky enough to be in open societies have a responsibility to recognize what this young man does: that some things are more important than fear. It's a lesson for which I've got zest and gratitude.

9

My family and I are refugees from Uganda. General Idi Amin, the military dictator, expelled us along with hundreds of thousands of other Muslims. We settled near Vancouver. Our Canadian port of entry was Montreal. The immigration agent on duty had no formal reason to care about us, but she engaged with my mother anyway. "Why do you want to live in Montreal?" she asked *en français*.

Mum grew up in the Belgian Congo and spoke French. "Why do we want to live in Montreal?" she replied, buying time. "Well, Montreal begins with the letter M, and our family's name begins with the letter M, so maybe God thinks we will fit nicely together."

Sensing my mother's distress, the agent assured her that this wasn't intended to be an interrogation. "It's just that I'm looking at your three daughters," she said, "and I realize they're all dressed for tropical weather. Madame Manji, have you ever seen snow?"

Still assuming this to be a pretext for denying us entry, my mother exclaimed, "No, but I can't wait to see snow!"

"Then you've come to the right country," the agent confirmed. "But with your permission, I'd like to send you and your girls to the closest thing we have to a mild climate." A few stamps of the paperwork later, we flew to the other side of Canada—to Vancouver.

Some would cast this immigration agent as a shrewd arbiter of cheap immigrant labor, yet I think she was more complex than a cartoon cutout. By exploring what else we might need—peace, sure, but also fleece—she bucked an ice-cold bureaucracy, invited the scrutiny of peers and quite possibly jeopardized her job. For me, her minuscule act of taking the time to ask compassionate questions has become an instructive moment. In an open society, the individual matters. So do her choices.

More than three decades on, I still wake up thanking God that as a refugee I wound up in a part of the world where I can fulfill much if not most of my potential. Gratitude is the essence of my relationship with Allah. Which is why I have to chuckle when I'm assailed as a *kafir* or *kuffar* (spelled in various ways, as you'll see). This word describes both an unbeliever and somebody who's ungrateful to God—neither of which applies to me. Beyond giving thanks, I ask Allah to help me be worthy of my citizenship in an open society, because the freedom to make my future bigger than my past is a treasure I didn't earn.

When my mother, my sisters and I stepped onto the precious soil of Canada, we were gifted freedom. None of us begged for it, took up arms for it or remotely struggled for it. Freedom got handed to us with our raincoats in Vancouver. Now I feel obliged to use this gift to reinforce the dignity of those who don't yet enjoy freedom of thought, conscience or expression. Like the Al-Azhar student who fears being tagged a kafir, I'm choosing to ask questions. Unlike him, I can ask them *out loud*. That's when questions become useful to my society and not just to my inner dialogue.

It pains me to see people in relatively free and democratic countries bump along as if their freedom to choose is an abstraction divorced from daily life. A month before 9/11, I decided to leave my position as an on-air personality at what was then Toronto's hippest TV channel. Having been there for three years and achieved what I'd envisioned doing, I accepted a post as executive producer of a digital channel about spirituality. The dot-com bubble had burst by then, making the launch of anything digital a fragile venture. So I figured that any congratulations from my colleagues would be about seizing this opportunity. Instead, friends pulled me aside, as though sensing corporate cops hot on their heels, to tell me again and again, "You're so brave for leaving."

"What do you mean?" I asked each of them. They all responded with a rendition of "I'm sick of how they treat me here." My next question (asked out loud): "Then why do you stay?"

The answers astounded me, coming from young, single people without children and, for the most part, without mortgages. "Cachet," said one, echoing many more. "Everybody out there wants to work here. This job gives me self-respect." Forget the obvious sermon about the true origins of self-respect: I want to make a different point. For my pampered friends at the impossibly cool TV station—the one that made them feel less than cool every day—the test of courage was nothing more than to exit. They could have done it without drama. Anybody who actually did qualified as a hero, which made the refugee in me bristle. Although I smiled at their excuses and wished them well, I admit that I felt contempt for just how spoiled, soft and insecure we, the beneficiaries of the open society, had become. Why was the act of leaving a lousy job considered so courageous when you had only yourself to feed?

But I now have empathy for my old colleagues because the challenge of teaching courage has hit home. At New York University, I've explained to my students that by "courage," I mean speaking your truth. I've then given them concrete incentives to display courage within the safe confines of my classroom: The syllabus for my course states that their grades will depend in part on the frequency and quality of their challenges to me.

Time and again, I've reminded students that sincerely pushing back on my assumptions and conclusions isn't only permissible, it's advisable, because telling me why I might be wrong could vault them into grade-A territory. So much for enlightened self-interest. The number of times I've had to dangle this carrot, only to receive hesitant assurances that "they get it," followed by silences that suggest they really don't, tipped me off to deeper issues here.

I've invited my students to help me fathom why speaking their truths seems so palpably tough to realize. Independently of each other, they've emphasized that they associate the classroom with passivity, having come of age in educational environments teeming with computers and video screens but denuded of the sense that they're allowed to use their keyboards for anything audacious.

Listen to this conversation with one of the most promising young men I know in New York City. I approached him about blogging for a campaign to combat human rights abuses of women in Iran.

> He: You want *me* to blog?
> Me: Sure. You're a serious thinker and you care about justice. This is an opportunity to express your ideas.
> He: I'm not sure I can.
> Me: Why not?
> He: I don't know what's going to be used against me.

Here's a twenty-something who worked his way out of a crime-riddled neighborhood to a perch as a dean's assistant and plans to enter law school. He and I have compared research about leadership—among the reasons I know he's thoughtful. Yet his ability to share those thoughts is hobbled by worry about which of his words will inadvertently set someone off. In short: What will "they" think of me?

> Me: Everything can be used against you. Always. But do you honestly believe that silence will protect you? If everything can be used against you, then so can inaction. Reflect on that, read the blog and let me know if you'll come aboard. It's your choice entirely.

Eventually, he did join the human rights campaign as a blogger. A few months later, he introduced me to research showing that in American history the most accomplished black leaders didn't work themselves into a lather about who would say what about them. My on-the-spot excitement at hearing this had less to do with his research than with his growth—and, through his, mine.

Let me give this generation of students a break: The fear of being judged didn't begin with them. In the 1960s, the psychologist Stanley Milgram conducted a battery of experiments about why people conform to authority—or, more accurately, to the abuse of authority. Does personality drive reckless obedience, as the conventional wisdom went? Or might it have more to do with the circumstances of the situation? The first subjects Milgram tested were students at Yale University. Every last one of his recruits administered what they believed to be electrical shocks, some of severe voltage, to fellow human beings merely because a man in a lab coat ordered them to do so. Milgram's entire sample of Ivy Leaguers succumbed to authoritarianism. As a result, he had to look beyond the university for a more representative sample of people, including some who would think for themselves.

Nor is the problem confined to youth. Most investment executives and economists discarded independent thinking in the run-up to the 2008 global economic meltdown. If they had doubts about stocks, housing or credit, very few let on. As a former senior vice president at Lehman Brothers put it, "Anyone at our level who had a different view from senior management would find themselves going somewhere else quick. You are not paid to rock the boat." But when that boat capsized, his income sank and pulled down the paychecks of many more. And by then they had nowhere else to go—"quick" or otherwise.

A certain thread connects the young Muslims who clam up in their family homes and the Wall Street moguls who shut themselves down in their investment houses. Death isn't top of mind for them. Ridicule is.

———

I know the feeling. *The Trouble with Islam Today* inspired (or incited) an entire website's worth of mockery from fellow Muslims. For the moment, I'm going to exhale and share some of the funnier exchanges:

We should just kick your ass as far as hell and then see the flames eat your living flesh. You're as bogus as hell so don't come up with your stupid books about Islam.
—Mo

Let me get this straight, Mo. I'm as bogus "as hell," but my ass should be kicked "to hell"—which, by your account, is a "bogus" destination. Want to try again?

Hello Miss Liberated Feminist Lesbian Irshad. I am an educated Muslim who is a moderate and yet I feel you have some fantasies for fame and greed. Here's a good title for you to think about for your future books: "How I can fool the West into thinking that homosexuality is acceptable in Islam." Here is another one: "How to sell yourself to the devil." I will not buy your book! Unless you want to send it free to me. I could use it in my fireplace.

P.S. My next door neighbors are Lesbians and we respect each other immensely, so try another spin in your rebuttal.
—S.R.

Salaams Liberated Neighbor. Thanks for your engaging email—and for the new book titles. I'll certainly take them into consideration as I continue racking up my riches and fending off book publishers who want more, more, more from me and my un-Islamic morality. Thanks, also, for offering to burn my book if I send you a free copy. I've thought long and hard about whether to oblige and my decision is . . . (drum roll please) . . . Nah. You see, I'm just too greedy for profits to give you a freebie. Why deny my greed? Since I'm calling for honesty in this book, I'd better lead by example. Nonetheless, enjoy your neighbors. I'm sure they're lovely ladies. I only hope they realize how lovely you are.

Ex-sister Irshad: What is your partner's religion? Jew?   —Anonymous

I met my partner at an Anglican church, where I attended services as part of my research for a new TV program. Prompted by your question, I've asked her to level with me about her religion. I've demanded the truth. She responded, "Just call me Shlomo." I'm still coping.

You are offending 98.9% of the true Muslims in the world. Islam is not a hard religion to understand and I don't need to read your book to understand what is wrong with it. Nothing is wrong with Islam. I will agree that many, many Muslim individuals and societies today are confused or are manipulating the teachings of Islam to achieve a personal or political agenda. You remind me of the extreme right of Islam who condone killing people indiscriminately, but you are on the extreme left. Your book comes off as a product with no academic value, to be bought by curious housewives who watch CNN all day. Please don't cover a topic that you have no business covering. Write a book on fashion or something else.   —Anonymous

First, am I to censor myself because you are offended? Suppose I told you that I'm offended by the fact that you're offended. By your logic, you have an obligation to stay quiet because I'm offended. Will you? Second, how did you determine that 98.9% of true Muslims in this world are offended by me? Why not 98.7% Or 99.1%? Please cite your sources, as I do with every claim I make in my thoroughly un-academic book. Finally, I appreciate your suggestion to write about fashion. I can see a title now—*The Cardinals' Sin: What Drab Catholic Clergy Can Learn About Dressing for Success from Pious Wahhabi Housewives Who Sport Prada, Gucci and Bling Beneath their Burqas.* As you know, I'm not very skilled at composing inoffensive book titles, so if you've got a better one to propose (as others already have), fire away. Meanwhile, here I come, *Cosmo*.

You say you're a Muslim. I suggest you change that to "non-practicing disobedient Muslim." You really should check the ruling on getting your hair cut like that.
—Shauaib

I've reviewed Fashion Fatwa #4866 and it simply states, "It is haram to use hair gel that contains traces of alcohol. Bacon bits, however, are halal, as they will be caught between the gelled spikes of hair and thereby not seep into the scalp, inshAllah."

Let me start by saying how useful your book really is. I found that it is, in fact, much cheaper to use as toilet paper than your average TP packages. Although, I do have a complaint: the pages are a bit rough in certain areas and I have sensitive skin. Then a wonderful idea crossed my mind. You would definitely sell more books if the book came with a moisturizer . . . Please tell me that you will at least think about this. I guarantee that it would do some good to your sales, although many would prefer traditional methods of hygiene. As for your image, there is not much I can say or suggest to improve that. Hiring a publicist might be useful (or firing your current one). Good luck and keep writing.
—Falaha

Greetings Rough Buns! Regarding my image problem, I'm not the one describing my bathroom habits to the world. But I am relieved (so to speak) that your bowel movements seem regular. That means you're picking up my book regularly, too. "Bottom" line: I'll never need a publicist as long as I have you.

Comic relief enriches the soul. I don't mean that defensively. Derision emboldens me to be clear about why I believe what I believe—and whether I should believe it at all. In this way, even caustic critics are allies in my evolution. They repeatedly teach me that some things are more important than fear. Their pen is my zen.

———————

People who act on their moral courage will always encounter disapproval. To have moral courage is to challenge conformity within our own tribes—be they religious, cultural, ideological or professional—and to do so for a more universal good.

The fact that the phrase "moral courage" even exists says something consoling: No matter how marooned I might feel, no matter how deranged mainstream Muslims tell me I am, no matter how often non-Muslims assure me that Islam is inherently fascist and I'm tilting at windmills, I can lean on a contrarian tradition. Leadership literature recognizes moral courage because others have adopted this approach to be true to their consciences while lifting up their communities from within. I'm not alone—and I never have been.

Still, choosing to confront intimidation, insult and injury from one's "own" can sound like an impossible idea. In 1966, Robert F. Kennedy exhorted South African students to defeat apartheid, the legislated segregation of whites and blacks. Atoning for his own country's race-based firewalls, Kennedy confessed, "Few men are willing to brave the disapproval of their fellows, the censure of their colleagues, the wrath of their society. Moral courage is a rarer commodity than bravery in battle or great intelligence. Yet it is the one essential, vital quality for those who seek to change the world which yields most painfully to change."

Moral courage rises above other virtues because there's no wound deeper than that of being ostracized by your people. Humans consistently take the bait of blaming others. And, damn, does it feel good. When you indict others, you can wear your rage as a badge of tribal credibility. "Look at me," you're advertising, "as I stand up for 'us' against 'them.' I know where I belong." Watch the accolades pour forth. But if you expose the injustices perpetrated by your own people, the security blanket of instant belonging disappears. Now how will you know who you are?

Welcome to one of the most liberating opportunities of our time: waking up from "identity politics." It's the politics that reduce individuals to mascots of the communities with which we identify—Muslim, Christian, Jewish, feminist, queer, banker, Bollywood fan, you name it. Wherever there's an orthodoxy, there's an enshrined identity and a set of precepts for representing it "correctly." We saw these politics at play in the email exchanges with my funnier critics. But the laughs that I hope they produced shouldn't distract us from understanding that even sincere people indulge:

I disagree with the title of your book. It should have been *The Trouble with Muslims*. Just because Muslims do hateful and hurtful things doesn't mean that it is part of Islam's teaching. If the Qur'an's message is misinterpreted, it is no fault of Islam. —Shawn

Had I called my book *The Trouble with Muslims*, the professional lobbyists who pawn themselves off as Muslim "representatives" would have accused me of hate-mongering against an "identifiable group." Imagine the lawsuits. My dissident derrière would have been in court several times over. Great—if you're in this strictly for book sales. I'm not. I'm in this to help Muslims realize our right and responsibility to think.

How in the hell can you still call yourself a Muslim? Who do you represent? I'm a Muslim woman. I don't cover my hair and I'm married to an American who doesn't practice Islam, but he thinks Muslims are the best people in the whole wide world, and he wishes that Christians would have the same morals as Arabs have. All the problems in the Middle East are because of Israel. I'm a Palestinian refugee since 1968. Me and my family are scattered everywhere. Why can't you say anything to help the Palestinians? I know we are the best nation that Allah has chosen. May Allah help us from people like you and Bin Laden.   —Mona

I'm not surprised that you accuse me of neglecting Palestinians. In our politically polarized environment, if you point out (as I do) that Israelis and Arabs share culpability for the plight of Palestinians, then you're anti-Palestinian if not anti-Muslim. The reason? You haven't declared Israel to be the sole oppressor. I don't buy it, Mona. Neither do many Palestinians, who are as angry with the corruption of their "leaders" as they are with the military presence of the IDF. Both occupations need to end.

Take a cue from Dr. Eyad Serraj, founder of the Gaza Community Mental Health Program. According to him, "We Arabs and Palestinians need a lot of self-criticism" for "a tribal structure in which dissent is seen as treason." That tribal structure, he tells me, is why "we have not yet developed a state of citizenry, within all the Arab countries, in which people are equal before the law." So, Mona, I leave you with a few questions: 1) Can "all the problems of the Middle East" really be pinned on Israel? 2) Don't you sound like a zealous Zionist when you insist that Allah has "chosen" Arabs as the best nation? 3) Do you see why I'm not rankled that you consider me a lousy Muslim?

What you neglect to address is how Muslims can interact with other cultures and the larger world without losing their unique identity. Some Muslims have a fear of losing themselves to Western culture.   —Bongo

The key word here is "fear." Islamic civilization laid the ground work for the European Renaissance. Doesn't this suggest that the dichotomy between "Islam" and the "the West" is artificial?

I have nothing against the fact that you expressed your views about Islam. But people who do not know what Islam was pre– September 11 may hold your book as the truth about it and not care to learn all the other aspects of our great religion. You should stress more the main positive characteristics of Islam before continuing with the negative aspects in order to educate a society where people are hungry for knowledge about Muslims. As people continue to stare at us, or try to run over us with their cars (which has recently happened to me), I would like you to realize that your book may be contributing hardship to the lives of your Muslim brothers and sisters. You are not exempt from what many people believe about Muslims. You are still one of us. —Anonymous

Thanks for the warning. But have you bothered to read my book? If so, then you'll know that I emphasize what was once positive, pluralistic and progressive about Islam: ijtihad, our own tradition of independent thinking. We Muslims can rediscover it if we care—and dare. Which brings me to the basic contradiction of your argument. On the one hand, you say that society is "hungry for knowledge about Muslims." On the other hand, you speculate that people will stop reading once they've finished my book. If people are hungry, then why would they treat my book as the last word in learning about Islam? You give me far too much power and you give the public far too little credit.

Three pieces of advice: One, those who try to mow you down with their cars are criminals; report them to the police—for everybody's sake. Two, recognize that in assuming non-Muslims to be infantile, you're stereotyping them as much as you worry that they're stereotyping you. Revealing, isn't it, that even though you feel victimized, you're exercising the power to frame others as you imagine them to be? Three, have more faith in your fellow human beings, just as you would have them do for you.

I am writing from Iraq. You may feel that you have done a very brave and great job in your book, but it may be no more than what the mullahs and extremists would have done, namely, further distorting Islam. Once and for all, Muslims are NOT to be identified with Islam. If you are bad and you are a Marxist, it doesn't mean that Marx was bad. —Nizar

Muslims are not to be identified with Islam? That's patently illogical. I agree that the theory of Islam, like the theory of Marxism, differs from what most of their practitioners do. But theory has limited value if it doesn't translate into behavior. The truth is, Islam is whatever we Muslims make of it. If Muslims have nothing to do with Islam, then we can't rescue Islam from corruption. Your approach holds out no hope. Fortunately, Prophet Muhammad had other ideas. He was reportedly asked, "What is religion?" And he reportedly replied, "Religion is the way we conduct ourselves toward others." By that definition, how we Muslims behave is Islam.

Why do you call yourself a Muslim? We really don't need an itch on our asses. Please affiliate yourself with some other religion. I'm sure the Christians would embrace a lesbian with open arms. —Siddique

You're right about one thing. Many Christians have embraced me. It's the illiberal ones who spurn my advances, and for the same reason you do: the fact that I'm a lesbian who challenges literalism. Don't you see what this means, Siddique? You have something in common with the Christians whom you despise! God, I love building bridges.

But I think you're mistaken about something else. You say that Muslims don't need an itch on our asses. Actually, every society, culture and religion needs gadflies—stubborn Socratic critters who pick away at the herd mentality by asking uncomfortable questions out loud. Consider Martin Luther King, Jr. He was accused by fellow clergymen (those damned Christians again) of creating needless tension.

MLK's response? "I must confess that I am not afraid of the word 'tension.' I have earnestly opposed violent tension but there is a type of constructive, nonviolent tension which is necessary for growth. Just as Socrates felt it was necessary to create a tension in the mind so that individuals could rise from the bondage of myths and half-truths to the unfettered realm of creative analysis and objective appraisal, so we must see the need for having non-violent gadflies to create the kind of tension in society that will help men rise from the dark depths of prejudice and racism to the majestic heights of understanding and brotherhood."

Christians galore didn't want an itch on their asses—and yet, they needed one. The time has come, Siddique, for Muslims to do some serious scratching.

Notice the repeated assumption by these readers that I have to hew to acceptable thoughts, attitudes and approaches. I need to represent others before I can speak for myself. That's not for my integrity; it's for their identity. Developing the individuality to speak my truth strays from this regulation. Under such pressure, we can see how doggedly fear would gnaw at anybody's vocal cords.

Of course, Muslims aren't the only ones who enforce the illusion of purity by seeking to scare communal standards (or "common sense") into the individual. If I were an Australian indigenous woman, I'd still be reeling from the hubris shown by one of "my" spokespeople. In 2008, the Australian edition of a British bestseller rolled off the presses. *The Daring Book for Girls* teaches young women to do what they're told they can't. Willfully oblivious to this premise, the head of an Aboriginal educators association in Australia, Mark Rose, accused the publisher of committing "an extreme faux pas" by daring to include a chapter on playing the didgeridoo, an instrument treated as the exclusive preserve of men in many indigenous cultures.

"We know very clearly that there's a range of consequences for a female touching a didgeridoo," Rose intoned. "Infertility would be the start of it." He added, "I wouldn't let my daughter touch one." Nor, it seems, should the *book* be touched—by anyone. The educator's advice to the publisher: "Pulp it." HarperCollins Australia knuckled under. It apologized "unreservedly" and promised to replace the offending chapter in reprints of the book. So there you have it: A book about daring loses its nerve. Someday indigenous girls will win this one. At what cost, I don't know.

At best, the wages will be verbal. Randall Kennedy is a professor of law at Harvard University and an African American. "I have been called a sellout on numerous occasions," he recounts. Among the reasons? He questions whether non-white academics have "a special—racially determined—insight into race relations law, and whether, as a matter of scholarly procedure, racial-minority status should be seen as an intellectual credential." Gee, what a neutron bomb. Thanks to his questions, though, Kennedy has been blasted as "a treacherous Tonto in blackface" and his motives attributed to "securing the esteem of whites, particularly white colleagues who would assess [him] for the purposes of tenure."

None of these tactics has stopped Kennedy from investigating related taboos. In 2003, he released a book entitled *Nigger: The Strange Career of a Troublesome Word.* Whereupon, Kennedy attests, the "Council on Black Internal Affairs castigated me as a 'racial free-loader' whom they 'despise[d].' I have, they asserted, 'opportunistically used [my] status as a well-known Black public intellectual to reap profit and a perverse sort of fame."

After Kennedy testified in a court case about the fluid uses of the N-word, the profiteer found himself further besmirched as a "very cheap whore." Cheap because "I received neither a fee nor expenses for my testimony. I acted pro bono. . . . [O]ne can only imagine what would have been said about me had I been paid."

As for the brilliantly named Council on Black Internal Affairs, Kennedy observes that at the time, the pinnacle of its achievement was publishing *The American Directory of Certified Uncle Toms:*

Being a Review of the History, Antics, and Attitudes of Handkerchief Heads, Aunt Jemimas, Head Negroes in Charge, and House Negroes Against the Freedom Aims of the Black Race. Apparently, the Council thought nothing of using pejorative terms in its own titles. The ironies don't stop there. In Harriet Beecher Stowe's novel, the character of Uncle Tom chooses to die rather than let a slave master triumph. Some sellout.

But the rebukes of renegade African Americans differ from those that reform-minded Muslims must stare down. Kennedy raises the point himself: "I have not felt threatened by any ideological enemies. At no point have I felt that I was putting myself into serious jeopardy because of something I have had in mind to write." The same can't be claimed today by Muslim reformers. It's a life-and-death difference.

––––––

Muslims, we've got to have higher expectations of ourselves. We once treated thought like art, breathing a cornucopia of options into the observance of faith. In the Islam of a thousand years ago, the spirit of ijtihad—of discussion, debate and dissent—flourished. Not coincidentally, that's also when Islamic civilization led the world in ingenuity.

Under the regime that ruled al-Andalus, or Muslim Spain, students could converse with the multifaceted Qur'an. The historian George Makdisi writes that ninth-century madrassas may have been the fount of today's academic freedom. Sounds like an exorbitant claim in light of how reactionary and anachronistic madrassas have become, but back then, freedom had a prayer. An eleventh-century Andalusian skeptic, Ibn Bajjah, openly promoted "active intelligence." He also postulated that when the rational mind makes contact with the Divine, the individual finds happiness. The surly powers-that-be jailed him. But the imam of an influential mosque, La Mezquita, intervened and Ibn Bajjah went free. From about the eighth to the twelfth centuries, some 135 schools of Islamic interpretation thrived, while the more cosmopolitan cities of al-Andalus housed 70 libraries, rivaling the number of libraries in most major U.S. cities today.

Ijtihadis even bequeathed some of the West's popular culture. In my public talks I binge on examples like these: Muslims gave the world mocha coffee. (You're welcome, Starbucks.) And the guitar. (Don't mention it, Springsteen.) And possibly even the expression "Olé!"—from the Arabic "Allah!" (Our pleasure, Spain.) I get a rush just thinking about the metabolism of inquiry among our ancestral ijtihadis.

Then the sun set on the twelfth century. Muslim fanatics from Morocco crossed the Strait of Gibraltar and colonized Spain. The Islamic empire, stretching from Spain in the west to Iraq in the east, lapsed into division. Dissident denominations declared their own runaway governments. The Baghdad-based caliph, a combination of statesman and spiritual steward, cracked down and closed ranks in order to safeguard the empire's political unity.

Instead, Muslims got uniformity in the mask of unity. Within a few generations the gates of ijtihad narrowed, especially in the dominant sect of Islam, Sunnism. Out of 135 schools of Sunni thought, only four survived—each of them more or less orthodox. The demise of critical thinking legitimized rigid readings of the Qur'an. Intellectuals overturned fatwas, or legal opinions, at great personal risk. Thinking for yourself meant courting harsh punishment, including execution.

The time has come to do better. I'm not calling on Muslims to rewind the clock and exhume the corpse of an eleventh-century Islam that would be irrelevant for the twenty-first century. No need for nostalgia; you're about to see just how relevant ijtihad can still be. Nor am I calling for the jurist's job to be popularized and denuded of its intricacy. Jurists have their place—but much below God, let's not forget. I'm calling only for the *spirit* of ijtihad to be broadened beyond academics and theologians. Get rid of the elitism that cements a pattern of submissiveness among Muslims—submissiveness that stops us from speaking up about politicized and outdated dogma.

Ingrid Mattson, a scholar at Hartford Seminary and a former president of the Islamic Society of North America, has taken mainstream Muslims to task over their dogma. "Because of our very narrow vision, our legalistic vision, and our authoritarian models of decision-making, we are excluding those people who can offer us a different vision for the future," she claimed in a 2004 conversation with other scholars. Mattson went so far as to encourage ijtihad among comics, poets and musicians. Olé!

Renewing the spirit of ijtihad is about integrity, starting with Islam's. In an eloquent essay, "Innovation and Creativity in Islam," one of the world's most highly regarded Muslim thinkers characterizes ijtihad as a spiritual "duty of the first magnitude." In early Islam, writes Umar Faruq Abd-Allah, "every person performing ijtihad was ultimately right—even if technically wrong—which prompted theologians and jurists to debate whether there could be more than one correct answer for any given question."

Well, could there be? "The majority of scholars were content simply to say that every person performing ijtihad receives a reward when mistaken, not by virtue of the error but because of obedience to God in fulfilling the command to undergo the labor of ijtihad."

That's what the families of Alya, Yasmin, Phirdhoz, Elizabeth, and Sakdiyah need to know. If these young Muslims feel tremors at the thought of incensing their families with questions about Islam, I say: Put down this book. Go to my website. Type "Abd-Allah" into the search engine. Download his essay. Read it. Then share it with your parents. The fact that a traditional authority has authored the paper may lower their defenses about your need to break out of submissiveness.

I can vouch that this strategy often works because some young Muslims have deployed it when dealing with a red-hot twenty-first-century issue: interfaith marriage. As more Muslims are born in the West or migrate here, they meet people of other religions and fall in love. Muslim parents and imams regularly tell their children and young people that Islam forbids them—women especially—from marrying non-Muslims. "Is that true?" I've repeatedly been asked, panic infiltrating the voices of my questioners. "Do I really have to give up the love of my life to keep my faith?" It's the single most common question to land in my website's inbox over the past few years. Interfaith love is a spreading phenomenon, and it has awesome implications for integrating communities. In light of the stakes, I had to ensure that my reply would carry authority so that interfaith couples could present it to their families.

I pulled in Khaleel Mohammed, an imam and professor of Islam who's been educated at both Sunni and Shia schools in the Middle East. Exercising ijtihad, Imam Mohammed reinterpreted the relevant Qur'anic passages and produced a two-page Islamic blessing of interfaith marriage. In 2006, I posted the English-language blessing on my website. Within six months it became such a popular download that I had to post it in twenty more languages.

A year later, I was lecturing in Berlin. After one of my speeches, a group of German Muslim women lingered to offer thanks for the interfaith marriage blessing. Now in their twenties, they'd crossed the threshold of "marrying age." Their parents had tried to force each of them into nuptials with Muslim men they didn't know, much less love. These women placed the interfaith marriage blessing before their parents, uncles and brothers. Because an imam had written it, the families grudgingly accepted its credibility. Moreover, because the blessing could be downloaded in German, Arabic and Turkish, their parents had no linguistic excuse to plead ignorance. As one of the women explained to me, "My father doesn't like how the imam is thinking, but now he knows there is at least one Islamic authority who will marry me and my German man. Finally, I can stop being afraid of how my family will react to my choice."

Individual choices like hers can profoundly enhance an entire society's ability to get over fear of the Other. The longer I research what motivates moral courage, the more I'm taken aback by the seeming coincidence that those who risk their skins for coexistence are often married to the presumed enemy. Paul Rusesabagina saved almost 1,300 lives in the Rwandan genocide. As the manager of one of Kigali's best hotels, he gave terrorized Rwandans refuge on his premises at his own peril. A Hutu married to a Tutsi, Rusesabagina understood the Other first and foremost as human. "When Tutsi in-laws and associates turned to him for help, he responded to them as individuals, not as Tutsis," write the authors of *Courageous Resistance*, a study of ordinary people taking on corruption within their communities.

Intermarriage also lies at the heart of a stunningly improbable, albeit brief, triumph over the Nazis. It was February 1943. Anticipating Germany's final push in the Second World War, authorities detained more than 1,500 Jewish men in a community center on one of Berlin's main thoroughfares, Rosenstrasse. These Jews had non-Jewish wives, and Hitler hadn't decided what to do with them. The wives openly demanded to be reconciled with their husbands. Daily, they showed up on Rosenstrasse, despite being pelted with police harangues to "clear the streets."

Eventually, and without firing a shot, the Nazis relented. "Hitler and Goebbels wanted to avoid disturbing Berlin's female population at a time when the Propaganda Minister had just called on them to mobilize for 'total war,'" the historian Richard J. Evans concludes. The Nazis even released thirty-five intermarried Jews who'd already been hauled off to Auschwitz. While love rallied the hearts of the Rosenstrasse rebels, intermarriage itself helped stiffen their spines. For years they fought official and social harassment to divorce their husbands. Nonconformity became a habit.

The link between intermarriage and moral courage isn't ironclad, but the values that intermarriage puts into action will widen the path of Islam. "One important pre-disposition [that] many courageous resisters have is an *extensive* worldview," say the authors of *Courageous Resistance*. "They see large sectors of the population as part of their in-group (that is, 'people like me') and therefore entitled to equal treatment." In those cases, identity isn't brittle; it's constantly irrigated by a willingness to negotiate the meaning of family.

Edip Pilku had an Albanian Muslim father and a German mother. In 1942, his parents gave refuge to the Gerechters, a Jewish family from Hamburg, Germany. Whenever the Nazis would drop in on their home, the Pilkus would introduce the Gerechters as relatives— a sincere redefinition of family as much as a ruse to throw the Gestapo off course. "Naturally," Pilku acknowledges of everyone involved, "they were terrified." But like the intermarried women of Rosentrasse, his mother, Liza, rose to the occasion. One day, their street became the scene of Jew-hunting dogs dispatched by the Gestapo. "My mother came out of her house and scolded the Gestapo in German," Pilku recalls. "She told them never to come back, to remember that she was German, too." The jackboots went away.

Another Albanian Muslim, Nadire Proseku, testifies that she and her husband, Islam, sheltered Jews because "we saw [them] as brothers. As religious but liberal Muslims, we were only doing our

duty." Proseku goes further in reimagining family. "Now my grandson is an evangelical Christian," she volunteers. "This is fine with my
son and me. There is only one God."

Dževad Karahasan, a Bosnian artist married to a Serb, prompts
my optimism that the meaning of family can be negotiated even in
our more cynical times. During the ethnic cleansing campaign of
the 1990s, his mother-in-law was murdered for hiding two Muslim
families. Among the poignant stories that Karahasan narrates in
Sarajevo, Exodus of a City, one involves his neighborhood mosque:

> *The events of the previous night, which had left a huge mis-
> sile crater in my street, convinced me that any opening above
> the ground is an open invitation for death to pay us a visit. The
> bricks we had in the basement were not enough, so I decided to
> take some ashlars [square stones] from the Magribiya Mosque.
> How many missiles and shells must have hit it to raze it so
> thoroughly? . . . "May I take it?" I asked the imam of the
> Magribiya Mosque, who stood nearby.*
>
> *"Of course," answered the imam. "If these stones end up sav-
> ing someone's life, or just diminishing people's fear, they will be
> truly sacred. And this is what places of worship should do—they
> should liberate us from fear."*

Ever thought you'd hear about a mosque that liberates people
from fear? It's possible in a society of constant give-and-take, a way
of thinking that philosophers call "dialectical." Karahasan unpacks
that idea. Feel free to read this slowly, as I did, until its nuances settle in:

> *Every member of a dramatic cultural system needs the Other
> as proof of his or her own identity, because one's own particular-*

*ity is being proven and articulated in relationship to the particu-
larities of the Other. But within a dialectical system, an Other is
only seemingly the Other, while it is actually the masked I, or the
other contained in myself.*

Simply said, "opposite facts"—wife and husband, Bosnian and Ser-
bian, Muslim and not—"are actually One."

As a Muslim, I believe in Oneness. Islam, after all, derives directly
from Judaism and Christianity. The universal Creator . . . Everlasting
life after death . . . Free will . . . Prophets prone to error. Muslims owe
these cornerstone convictions to non-Muslims. Our purity can be
found in our pluralism. So whenever Muslims behave with a supremacy complex, we're waging a civil war against our composite selves. To
rein in our fears of being "impure"—or gloriously mongrel—
individual Muslims need only reconcile our identity with Islam's
hybrid integrity.

———

Identity is the sloppy scaffold that everyone else constructs to box
you in. But integrity is the indivisible, insubordinate wholeness that
you craft for yourself. Two of my readers make the point with defiant panache:

I find myself engaged to a wonderful man of character who is not Muslim. This has caused great upset to my father, and he has informed me that
my Egyptian family will never accept it. If I do this, I cannot visit them again
in the Middle East. I'm having trouble understanding why, under Islam, my
father can easily marry a French-Canadian woman, yet I have no right to
choose my own partner. I believe in accepting a person for who they are,
and I refuse to engage in the hypocrisy of converting my fiancé just to sat-
isfy someone else's religious beliefs. —Mariam

As an American married to a Pakistani, I have a close connection to both Islam and Pakistan. My husband always says the Qur'an is the true word of God because the Qur'an itself states that it will never be altered in any way. I ask: "What if THAT line was the first to be altered?" He tries hard to understand my point of view, but I don't think that we'll ever truly meet in the middle. After 35 years of searching (I was raised a Catholic), I finally understand that I don't belong to any religion, but that I firmly believe in God. For the first time, I don't care what anyone else thinks! Even if this ends my marriage, so be it. It's a freeing conclusion.   —Katherine

Good for them. Problem is, integrity requires stillness and self-reflection. You have to ask yourself what you believe and why. But identity has the roaring, revved-up engine of emotion behind it. In a crude competition between identity and integrity, guess which usually wins?

I've been dating my girlfriend for the past three years. She is an Afghan Muslim. I love her with all my heart but our relationship has not gotten any better than what it is now. Which is: lying to her parents, hiding, running from my side because she saw someone she knew. She always feels guilty. I want a life with her but she cannot let go of her fear that she is violating Islam and that her family will disown her.   —Giovanni

Eight years ago, I met the man of my dreams. We fell in love and began an incredibly honest and mature relationship that our families and friends knew about. I am Sikh, he is Muslim. I told him that I would not convert to marry him but that I respected his religion so much that I would have no problem with our children being raised Muslim. And he was ok with that too, saying he would never ask me to convert because all that mattered to him was that I believed in God.

But as we both got older his views changed to the point that he said we could not get married unless I became a true, practicing Muslim. He was afraid it would be confusing for our children and that he would be going against God. . . . We agonized over this situation. He now plans to marry a Muslim girl, simply because she is Muslim.

—DS

I am from a Muslim family but I am agnostic and in a relationship with a Muslim woman. According to her, she is committing a sin being with me and cannot marry me. We are madly in love and want to spend the rest of our lives together. But she is going to leave me because she is afraid of making Allah unhappy. We are both heart-broken.

—Ehsan

I'll tell you what breaks *my* heart: that a fear-laced Muslim identity shrivels Allah. By defining ourselves so claustrophobically, Muslims limit the possibilities of God's love. A sovereign Creator isn't threatened by our self-knowledge; only the Creator's uptight gatekeepers are. Let's depose their counterfeit god of fear, widen the gates of ijtihad and explore what happens when we put integrity first.

2

IDENTITY CAN TRAP YOU, BUT INTEGRITY WILL SET YOU FREE

Reform-minded Muslims aren't yet leaping out of the closet to proclaim themselves free-thinkers. But more and more are limping out, and they need our best efforts to shore them up. Like Kareem, a teenage boy with whom I've conversed online.

I'm half Irish and half Arab. I live in Libya and I'm currently having serious issues with my faith. The amount of hate this country inflicts against Jews and Europeans is unbelievable. In our history books, it never refers to Jews without the word "racist" beforehand, never refers to Europeans without the word "terrorist" beforehand. They teach us at one point that this is the religion of peace, and then flip to bashing various groups, including gays (which I recently discovered I am). I thank God for giving me a mother who helps me understand that love is better than religion, but my dad is blaming my access to the outside world and is trying to take away my laptop, my Internet connection, my mobile phone. Shutting myself up, like I tended to do before, just won't work anymore. I know you're very busy, but I would appreciate it so much if you give me a little support.

A little support? Hell no, bro! I'm giving you actual allies. Listen to another young Muslim whose email I received immediately after yours:

I live and work in Abu Dhabi. I belong to my thoughts and conscience more than my citizenship, which is Emirati. I am writing to you because I speak the same language as yours, defending our faith with the same enthusiasm and surrounded by those who would call us koffar. . . . I appreciate that you give it up to GOD, that He is the only one who knows the Truth and that we are only seekers. I always try to put this into words! As a matter of fact, I always say that I might be wrong in what I am doing or convinced with, but with the brain, knowledge, experience, etc., I have come up with conclusions that I cannot lie about. I will live my life with honesty and integrity no matter what. GOD knows me better than anyone, knows how I struggle to minimize the gap between what I think, say and do. That is what makes me ready for the day of judgment! —Fatema

So, Kareem, what have we learned from Fatema? We've learned that her identity as an Arab or Muslim takes a backseat to her integrity as an individual—a complex, sinuous creature that no majestic deity could possibly reject, since any God worthy of worship has to be more than a manufacturer of widgets and automatons. By putting the transcendent God at the center of her faith, she tunes out the negative noise that human beings hurl in the name of a petty god. Kareem, if your faith is hostage to the approval of others, lose it. Because it's not faith at all. It's cultural commotion and religious rust. Take strength from Fatema, who's found her conscience and her Creator under the hardened slag of theology.

Lesson two: *Identity can trap you, but integrity will set you free.*

———

Identity isn't going away. Kareem, the product of an intermarriage, immediately identifies himself as gay, half Irish and half Arab. Kareem's father ventured beyond his biological birth group to marry someone different, yet he still blames the "outside" world for his son's wavering beliefs. Networked technology will naturally be the bane of such a parent. It baffles his already flummoxed boundaries.

In *The Geopolitics of Emotion*, French analyst Dominique Moïsi says identity exercises more sway than ever, even over the Western heart:

> In the Cold War period there was never any reason to ask, "Who are we?" The answer was plainly visible on every map that depicted the two adversarial systems dividing the globe between them. But in an ever-changing world without borders, the question is intensely relevant. Identity is strongly linked with confidence, and in turn confidence, or the lack thereof, is expressed in emotions. . . .

We're all in for a rough ride—sometimes literally. In April 2008, a Muslim bus driver pulled to the side of a London street and booted the passengers off so he could conduct his afternoon prayers. When he finished, he invited the stranded passengers back aboard. "But the passengers, who noticed that he had a rucksack—similar to those carried by the 2005 London bombers—refused to get on, fearing that he might be a fanatic who would blow up the bus," reports AlArabiya.net. That news site lifted the item from London's reigning tabloid, *The Sun*, so it's sure to have been read by non-Muslims as much as Muslims. Whatever else readers took from the story, I can just hear the feral howls. I practically let out one of my own.

Only months before, AlArabiya.net posted the news that Sainsbury's, a major British supermarket chain, had decided to excuse Muslim employees from handling alcohol. That move "triggered fears other religious groups may seek similar treatment. Catholics consider selling contraceptives a violation of their doctrine, and Jews are demanding their exemption from selling pork." Excuse me while I climb the wall.

Then there's the March 2010 story of the Muslim woman from Egypt who immigrated to Quebec. A pharmacist, she chose to veil her face out of religious conviction and insisted on keeping it that way in her French-language class. The instructor adopted various solutions to accommodate her choice, including letting her make presentations with her back toward her fellow students. In the end, though, she couldn't be graded on pronunciation with a covered mouth. Expelled from the class, the woman expressed shock. She also alleged "racism."

Around the same time, a Muslim man in Sweden won several thousand dollars in compensation after complaining of discrimination. Enrolled in a worker training program, he went to a job interview at which the female CEO extended her hand in greeting. The man didn't reciprocate. Instead, he pressed his hand to his chest, explaining that Islam forbids physical contact with an unrelated woman. Later, the company declined to offer him an internship, citing his lack of qualifications. The placement agency then dropped the man from its program. He sued—and won. When that news broke, much of the online chatter wondered why he couldn't be sued for sexual discrimination.

The politics of identity are creating even more chaos, much of which is no longer considered loony enough to make headlines. Scarved Muslim girls being turned away from part-time gigs flipping burgers. Muslim boys who won't go near high school science experiments if their specimens smell of the alcohol formaldehyde. Friends in Europe constantly tip me off to such under-the-radar skirmishes. They're demoralized that knee-jerk multiculturalism might be proving the "clash of civilizations" to be true.

According to Dominique Moïsi, the so-called clash of civilizations is actually a "clash of emotions." As nations and people joust for respect in this new century, we're swept into currents of hope, fear and humiliation. Emotions, like the individuals who feel them, more than mingle with each other; often, they accost each other. Those of us who strive to be rock-solid global citizens want to feel hope. When we don't, we're plunged into guilt and embarrassment. Vexed by conflicting emotions—strained hope, serious fear and shame as a result of fear—we're disoriented. We don't know what to do.

I'm a Dutch woman living in France. I'm raised in the Christian tradition, but since long I've been humanistic, not religious. In Holland there is freedom of speech, freedom of religion, every group can establish their own schools, justice for everyone. But people are getting more and more angry towards each other, and getting afraid. What can we, not Muslims, do? How should we act toward Muslims who (just some, not all) still are keeping their women in the house, whistling to Christian women, calling them names, mistreating gay people, or people that are just looking at them? All this puts groups against each other. How to act nowadays?   —Boukje

I am an 18-year-old Sunni Muslim who lives in London. Over the past 12 months I have looked up a lot of topics concerning Islam and quite frankly I don't like a lot of the things associated with it. For example, the stoning of Homosexuals, Apostates, Adulterers. The fact that a woman can be slapped if she is disobedient. Can we reject some of the dreadful parts of Islam without angering the almighty? But I am also struggling with xenophobic attacks against Muslims. There are all sorts of groups that appear determined to smear us. I have begun to become really paranoid. How do I deal with these problems?   —Osman

I've juxtaposed Osman and Boukje for two reasons. First, they reveal the knot in which open societies find themselves. The Muslim feels affronted by non-Muslim xenophobes while the humanist feels affronted by Muslim dinosaurs. Both experiences are real and both are unfolding in tandem. The situation seems doomed since Boukje and Osman represent opposing identities. Or do they? Must people represent on the basis of labels? Can we not represent through our values? Here's a third email that kindles my own hope:

Irshad, we have seemingly nothing in common. I am a college student from Prague, a heterosexual male who does not believe in God. Still, there is something we share: our love of freedom and courage. The fact that two people with such different backgrounds share these values suggests that they truly are universal. . . . I know that you focus mainly on the Muslim world but as you surely know, even in the liberal democracies of the Western world (among which I can now count the Czech Republic), the fight for free thought is far from being won.

—Michal

Voilà. Community doesn't have to be defined by a prefabricated identity that's assigned to you; community can be improvised by different people living similar values. Hence the second reason for juxtaposing Boukje and Osman. Boukje doesn't bray that all Muslims imprison women and mistreat gays. "Just some," she reasonably points out, and they're the ones putting her society on the defensive about its egalitarian values. Osman's values mirror hers. He would agree that too many Muslims dehumanize women and gays, a denigration he doesn't want to accept. That's why he's asking a taboo question that no humanist need ever worry about: Can Muslims "reject some of the dreadful parts of Islam without angering the almighty?"

As I see it, the Osmans are allies of the Boukjes. Muslims and non-Muslims need each other if open societies are to be whole and thereby achieve integrity. Osman needs to know that humanists like Boukje will do more than invite him to her dinner table. He needs to trust that she'll stand up to anyone who assumes he can't be a capable citizen of the West because he's a Muslim. As we'll discover, it's not just xenophobes who make such spurious assumptions; so do plenty of "progressives." By the same measure, Boukje needs to know that Osman and his liberal Islam exist. She's not hearing his voice because Osman isn't yet speaking out about the need to reform Muslims. And he's not speaking out because he's still oscillating between conflicting emotions.

Osman needs to understand emotionally—not just intellectually—that God loves the individual who takes steps to wholeness. "Godly perfection is not flawlessness," Archbishop Desmond Tutu and his daughter, Mpho, write in *Made for Goodness*. "Godly perfection is wholeness." To illustrate, the Tutus tell us about Beyers Naudé, a Christian minister and the scion of a political dynasty in apartheid-era South Africa. Naudé's father helped found the Afrikaner Broederbond, a powerful brotherhood of racist Christians. After much "prayer, study and reflection," Naudé the son concluded that neither the Bible nor Christ approves of apartheid. The lullaby of denial couldn't sedate the truth: Segregation balkanizes our souls.

Naudé faced a crisis of conscience. Archbishop Tutu takes over the story, calling his friend by his first name:

> *Beyers chose obedience to conscience. One day in September 1963 he announced his decision to his congregation. "We must show greater loyalty to God than to man," he said. He hung his gown on the pulpit and walked out of the church. . . . His fellow Afrikaners ostracized him and his family. It seemed that his life*

was in ruins. . . . [But] Beyers's views were vindicated when Nelson Mandela became South Africa's first democratically elected president. Beyers spent the last five years of his life as a worshiper at Aasvoëlkop, the Johannesburg congregation that had first heard his declaration of conscience. He had dared to stand as a solitary witness against the injustice perpetrated by his people. He had traded a false perfection for godly wholeness.

As I'll illustrate, eighteen-year-old Osman can work toward wholeness, too. His integrity, like Islam's, depends on that effort.

———————

If we've fluttered into a moment of hand-holding harmony, advance apologies for the fact that I'm about to ruin it. After tuning into one of my interviews on the BBC, another eighteen-year-old emailed me:

How can you call yourself a muslim? if god wants us to be robots for him then that is what we should be. i am a muslim living in the western world, i make mistakes do not get me wrong, i smoke shitloads of cannabis and kick the fuck outta Jews and White people whenever I feel like it, with my fellow gang who are muslims, but the Whites and Jews are Unbelievers in Allah, whereas us muslims are the true believers. i dont care if you reply but i've got my point across and I certainly will in much more violent terms to any Unbelievers who cross Allah!
                                                                  —Kessar

Even though I'm a clean-living Muslim, should I hope he was high when he composed this masterpiece? Does it matter that he watches Western infidel TV (probably produced by Whites but controlled by Jews)? Where's the fatwa to help me figure it all out? Fortunately, I don't need a fatwa to realize that Kessar is a segregationist. He divides our galaxy into Unbelievers and Believers. This lad has no

interest in integrity because he's consumed with ready-made identity—and he's far from exceptional.

Ibrahim, a moderate Muslim, begins by assuring me that he's
"glad" I "take advantage of democracy and freedom of speech." However, "Islam says that if your brother is doing something wrong, then
it is your duty to correct them—but correct them within Islam, pri-
vately or out of the eyesight of the unbeliever. When kaffirs see Muslims arguing, they are going to laugh at us, and having kaffirs laugh at
us—can there be anything worse for Islam?"

Granted, Ibrahim might be a run-of-the-mill dope, unschooled,
frayed around the edges and the welter of other excuses we can sur-
mise to downplay his immoderate moderation. What, then, to make
of Fatema's experiences? She's the young woman in Abu Dhabi whom
I quoted at the top of this chapter. Fatema testifies that Muslims routinely excoriate her as a kafir. To her credit, she won't inhale their
invective. Reform-minded Muslims should be learning from Fatema,
because we're up against a gestalt that's bigger than a few potheads
and ruffians.

A widespread segregationist impulse courses through the practice
of Islam today. All religions have their segregationists, but in what religion besides Islam do *moderates* foam in this fashion? "We see it from
the time you're a child," admits Taj Hargey, head of the Muslim Education Centre in Oxford, England. We're "given this idea that *those*
people, they are kuffar, they're unbelievers. They are not equal to you."

Hargey and his wife, Jackie, battled apartheid in their native
South Africa. Now he's among the few imams anywhere who perform interfaith marriage ceremonies for Muslim women. For him, as
for me, an entire pattern of conditioning comes into focus when a
Muslim feels entitled to "kick the fuck outta Jews and Whites"
because they're "Unbelievers." Of course, most mainstream Muslims
don't pass the roach clip and converge on kosher delis (unless they're

looking to satiate their post-pot munchies). But there's a venerated us-versus-them dogma among mainstream Muslims, and it makes the wholeness of the individual subservient to groupthink.

The pioneering Moroccan sociologist Fatema Mernissi enlarges this point in *Islam and Democracy: Fear of the Modern World*. She describes a prevalent Muslim fear that "the expression of individual opinion will weaken the group and play into the hands of adversaries." Group identity is "the emotional vein" exploited by those who brandish words such as kafir—language "that is enough to make the accused the legitimate target of punishment." And because group solidarity forms at the expense of individual creativity, "the Muslim world [has] rolled towards the precipice of mediocrity, where it now vegetates—in the mediocrity that is tacked on us as the essence of our authenticity." In other words, the politics of identity dictate that to be an authentic Muslim, I must conform to segregationist thinking—or, rather, non-thinking. Being true to Islam's pluralistic nature renders me an infidel.

No wonder Mernissi smells a rat. Fixating on the group oversimplifies the individual Muslim's *identity* even as it overcomplicates the individual Muslim's *integrity*. How? By replacing God's love with man's politics. The Qur'an assures us that Allah is closer to each of us than our "jugular vein" (50:16), so that we come to our Creator by knowing ourselves. Integrity begins with accepting what makes us individuals. In *The Quran and the Life of Excellence*, Sultan Abdulhameed expands:

> *Where conformity is insisted upon, many people grow up so addicted to approval that they have little initiative in adult life. You can be so dependent on authority figures that you are unable to know your own will. You end up in a career that others choose for you, you get married to someone whom others choose for you, you live in a house that others choose for you, and you say prayers*

which others choose for you. Living for the sake of appearance is the ultimate loss. You had only one life to live, and you gave it away to please others. You did not use this opportunity to discover what makes you special and different. You did not appreciate that your uniqueness is God's gift to the world.

We fear these opportunities, he believes, because we confuse spiritual faith with the politics of identity. Group identity conscripts us into categories, but faith "is a set of beliefs that liberate you from limitations and enhance your life's possibilities." Islam, the straight path, thereby becomes the wide path to reconciling the many sides of ourselves. Individuals of all kinds, including reform-minded Osman, may walk to God honestly without fear of angering Him.

For Osman, Kareem and Fatema, the straight *and* wide path to integrity might be summed up in three equations:

- To love your uniqueness is to love that which made it, your Creator.

- To love your Creator is to love His diverse creation, whose wholeness has yet to be realized.

- To love creation is to love the persecuted by standing up for them without persecuting others in turn.

One God. Three equations. Abundant life choices.

But since the demise of ijtihad, the most vocal Muslims have taken group identity to be the same as individual integrity. Worse, they've premised integrity on three unloving equations:

+ Unity equals uniformity. In order to stay strong against the aggressor—be he Mongol, Berber, Crusader, Ottoman or American—members of the *ummah* (international Islamic tribe) must think alike. Thinking differently instigates the crumbling of empire. Thus, uniformity is the precondition of unity.

+ Debate equals division. Diversity of interpretation, once a tribute to the Creator's magnificence, is now a hammer blow to the unity that Muslims must exhibit in the face of those conniving to weaken us. Debate brings out fissures. Fissures divide. Thus, debate amounts to division (*fitna*).

+ Division equals heresy. Soon after the gates of ijtihad drew tight, the very idea of innovation became criminalized (*bid'ah*). Innovation divides Muslims by seducing us to stray from tradition. The nontraditional must, by definition, be heretical. Thus, division signals heresy.

Given such assumptions, can there be a wisp of mystery as to why Islam hasn't yet witnessed its liberal reformation? In the 1930s, Mernissi writes, Egyptian feminists built a movement that treated "respect for the individual" as "its basic article of faith." In so doing, they tried gallantly to renew ijtihad, but they failed because opponents spun the issue as a contest between division and unity. The antimodernists insisted that resuscitating ijtihad meant embracing Western ideas and cozying up to European colonizers. Their calls for Muslim solidarity—uniformity under the flag of unity—carried the day.

As they still do, and far beyond Egypt. In 2006, Judea Pearl, father of the slain *Wall Street Journal* reporter Danny Pearl, contacted me with a question. He'd approached a Muslim scholar in America about teaching my book. "The scholar told me it's divisive," Pearl lamented. "That's it. That's all. That's why he won't teach it. How can this be?"

By then I'd already grappled with being both a misfit and Ms. Fitna. My mother attends a mosque in suburban Vancouver. One night, the imam delivered a sermon in which he declared me a "bigger criminal" than Osama bin Laden. His rationale: Among Muslims, my book had allegedly caused more debate, and therefore division, than al-Qaeda's terrorism had. When Mum phoned me afterward, she gloomily implied that I'd stirred up trouble for nothing. She'd been humiliated and her identity wounded.

For the sake of integrity —hers and mine—I respectfully asked Mum to reflect rather than emote. "Have I ordered that planes be rammed into crowded buildings?" I asked her. "No? Then there goes the comparison to bin Laden. Please reflect, Mum. If Muslims are more outraged by an unarmed dissident like me than by an extravagant murderer like bin Laden, doesn't that tell you something already? And if Muslims should never debate major issues, why did God give any of us a mind and a conscience?"

In his politicized reaction, the imam exaggerated the occult powers of my book—and yet there's a sputter of sense to what he said. It's true that Muslims are more convulsed by reformist appeals than by terrorist ideologies, even in a seemingly moderate country such as Jordan. "I didn't read your book because I live in Jordan and they won't allow it," Tareq emailed me.

Thinking is forbidden. But I read an article criticizing you in the local newspaper and I did my search on the web. I never thought someone else could see in a similar way as I do. Islam needs a reform movement. . . . Learning to offer a better life for the next generation so they can live successful, healthy and happy is the best way to worship god. Social success requires a lot of work and knowledge. Many religious Muslims escape to religion to cover their failure. I don't mind being part of a group, but the group that Islam currently represents is the furthest one from me. I prefer "faith" much more than "religion."

Tareq chooses the integrity fed by faith over the identity dispensed by dogma. The identity of institutional religion prizes the in-group, but the integrity of personal faith prioritizes the individual's relationship with God. How can Muslims—or any of us— fight the voracious groupthink that gobbles up individual integrity?

———

Slavenka Drakulić, a journalist and Croat, went through the Balkan War. A similar question has seized her: "How does a person who is a product of a totalitarian society learn responsibility, individuality, initiative?" She answers, "By saying 'no.' But this begins by saying 'I,' thinking 'I,' and doing 'I'—and in public as well as in private." Drakulić stresses that the difference between "we" and "I" isn't semantic. "'We' means fear, resignation, submissiveness, a warm crowd and somebody else deciding your destiny," she writes. "'I' means giving individuality and democracy a chance." She notes that individuality "always existed under communism, it was just exiled from public and political life and exercised in private." But to this day, "it is very difficult to connect the private and public 'I'; to start believing that an individual opinion, initiative, or vote really could make a difference. There is still too big a danger that the citizen will withdraw into an anonymous safe 'us.'"

Her insight reminds me of a tangle I had with a Muslim woman who frequents my Facebook page. She emphasized to Facebookers that "Irshad doesn't represent us all." To which many Facebookers replied that I've never pretended to—quite the contrary, given my dissent with mainstream Muslims. In my view, the anxious woman was projecting her personal struggles with thinking, saying and doing "I." She assumed that anyone who speaks as a Muslim speaks for the tribal "we." The ummah-like "us." The totality.

Many more share her assumption. A couple of years ago I disgorged an entry into one of my notebooks. It reads, "To my Muslim female critics":

> The moment you reconcile yourself to your individuality, you'll feel far less threatened by what I'm saying because you'll be able to see my views as exactly that—my views. You'll be able to see that I speak on my behalf, not on behalf of all Muslims. Instead of needing to assure yourselves that "she's not a Muslim," you can sneer, "She's not my kind of Muslim." And you'd be right. Which means you don't have to fear that you're being represented badly, since you aren't being represented at all. One day, I pray, each of you will be modest enough to represent yourself only.

Looking back, I see that my catharsis contained an epiphany. When Muslims practice the modesty of thinking, saying and doing "I"—in public no less than in private—Islam's reformation will be under way. No doubt reform-minded Muslims will be accused of narcissism, a maniacal self-love that gives the finger to our families, our communities and the ultimate authority, God. But again, let's reflect on integrity to tame the emotions behind identity. If I'm overly concerned about "how I'll look to others," then I'm obsessed with my image. What's pious or humble about image worship?

I'm arguing for individuality—not individualism. Individualism damages community by declaring, "I'm out for myself and I don't care if my society benefits." But individuality declares, "I am myself, and my society grows when I express my uniqueness." There's a distinction. There's also a paradox: We expand community by daring to develop individuality.

The wide path of Islam makes room for this paradox. Khaled Abou El Fadl, who teaches Islamic law at the University of California (Los Angeles), has written *The Great Theft: Wrestling Islam from the Extremists*. In it, he highlights a message of Prophet Muhammad: Whoever knows himself or herself knows his or her God. Therefore, I grasp God's oneness by owning up to my multiple dimensions, including talents and thoughts that parents and politicians would thwart. Our duty to know God overshadows any guilt brought on by the artificial gods of family and nation.

In February 2005, during an impromptu visit to An-Najah National University in the heart of the West Bank, I found myself surrounded by students eager to talk. "Now that Arafat is gone," one of them uncorked, "it is time to accept Israel. I want the occupation to end, but I am also a human being with dreams and hopes for the future. To reach my dreams as an individual, I have to live peacefully with Jews and we all have to go into the future." He made that astonishing remark in front of other students, any of whom could have denounced him to defend the sanctity of the national liberation campaign. They didn't even nitpick his decision to identify "as an individual." That phrase—deliberate and decisive—told me he didn't wish to be lumped into an amorphous collective by his other occupiers: Arab leaders. For most of them, conformity is priority number one, as if community can't tolerate individuality. The An-Najah student confirmed that's a false choice.

Even in communal prayer, you don't need to surrender your individuality. Abdullahi Ahmed An-Na'im, a professor of human rights at Emory University, made this point to me during a public discussion about moral courage in March 2008. "When I stand in prayer as a Muslim, I stand in a huge line of people," he said. Yet "each one of us is praying as him- or herself."

"Doesn't this attitude violate the Islamic concept of the ummah—the global, unified nation?" I asked.

"That is a myth," he retorted with a sparkle in his eye. "As Muslim history would show, there has never been a unified ummah." An-Na'im added that "sometimes Muslims overemphasize solidarity to hide disunity." But "difference is not bad. I don't know why people get so nervous about difference and disagreement. . . . Each of us is an individual. What is bad is violence."

Exiled from Sudan for his reformist activities, An-Na'im looks every bit a happy traveler on the wide path of Islam. He has spearheaded a conference cheekily called A Celebration of Heresy: Critical Thinking for Islamic Reform. Some delegates balked at the word "heresy," frightened that mainstream Muslims would stigmatize them for being up-front enough to use it. An-Na'im shrugged that stigma is a given, and at the gathering itself, participants came around to his serenity. They realized that you can defuse stigma by greeting it with a smile, but as long as we're spooked into silence, the incipient movement for religious reform will be stillborn. Self-censorship is, literally, a nonstarter. "I" is the necessary prelude to achieving a fuller "we" in Islam.

———

The word "we" can be such a balm in our postcolonial age. "We" has become a hug for humanity, a kind of code that says white folks belong to a family grander than the empires of yore. Laudable, but belonging isn't a blemish-free notion. Belonging may mean "choosing to identify with" or it may mean "being owned by." Fatema, our friend in Abu Dhabi, informs us that "I belong to my thoughts and conscience more than my citizenship." Hurrah! That's as it should be, for it's a choice made by her. She decides her "we."

However, other young Muslims have their "we" orchestrated for them, even when living in the West. They often face the assumption that, as the children of Muslim immigrants, they're owned by the ethnic communities of their fathers. Papa's culture must be the children's culture too. With "belonging" so defined, the individuality of a new generation, a *European* generation, gets concealed in someone else's "we." In the next chapter I'll introduce an anthropologist who documents how this injustice happens at the hands of humanitarians. Right now, it's enough to convey that non-Muslims play a part in either eclipsing the individuality of Muslims, or letting it shine.

Which is why non-Muslims could use a crash course in the West's own history of group identity. According to Aristotle, for example, the individual has no agency—not really. You are what you were born to be. In a virtuous system, at least, even the slave will know his place and have a place, making his existence meaningful. He will belong. Some two thousand years later, Thomas Hobbes posited the opposite. The individual has gobs of agency and, for the sake of social stability, a ruler will have to suppress every man's ambition. Hence the need for "Leviathan," the politically sovereign über-agent of the people. From dramatically different perspectives, Aristotle and Hobbes reached a comparable conclusion: Orderly progress demands a system that submerges the individual.

The Nazis took such conclusions to a devastating apotheosis, abetted by the nineteenth-century idea of *Volkgeist*. A baby of the German Romantics, Volkgeist refers to the galvanizing essence of a people, the collective character that cements their nationhood and imbues them with honor above all else. In his fire-breathing 1923 beer hall speech (among many others), Hitler appealed to the shredded honor of Germans. Convalescing from the First World War and made malleable by daily misery, Hitler's listeners rocked the roof with approval. Alain Finkielkraut, the French philosopher, traces the epidemic of the tribal "we"—identity politics—directly back to the scourge of Volkgeist.

Here's the upshot. Yes, individuality runs counter to centuries of Islamic practice, but it also collides with much of Western tradition. *"Non, madame, non!"* the European identity purist might want to finger-wag. "Do not deign to liken Islamic tribalism with Western behavior. Who was it that married a nine-year-old?" That would be Prophet Muhammad. Case closed? *Non.* A leading scientist at the time of the European Enlightenment, Antoine Lavoisier, wed a girl of thirteen. Lavoisier's child-bride became his lab assistant—but not for long. In a tactic worthy of the most seasoned Arab despots, Rottweilers of the French Revolution chopped off Lavoisier's head. Next on the block: his father-in-law. Whether in the name of God or godlessness, dogmatists can commit barking mad atrocities. When I visited the official English-language website of North Korea in February 2006, I read a statement that's since been removed. The dictatorship peddled itself as one "that embraces science and rationalism." Atheists can't be thrilled.

Look, I have no interest in a cage match among atheist, humanist and religious orthodoxies. A cage necessarily restricts space and recirculates stale air; it doesn't exactly give rise to free-thinking. Outside the cage, we can discover values that allow any of us to migrate and integrate without having to coagulate. That's the virtue of individuality. Thanks to its boundary-busting implications, individuality is universal. It's also universally feared by identity purists, which makes individuality central to exercising moral courage—the willingness to pierce groupthink, in Islam and beyond.

––––––––––

Prophet Muhammad taught that what I desire for myself, I ought to desire for another. Immanuel Kant, a prophet of the European

Enlightenment, reiterated Muhammad: I should act only according to principles that can be applied universally. When filtered through the funnel of malice, this message becomes deadly. A universal Islamic caliphate, for example, is the last thing I desire. But some Muslims do, and they can mangle the anti-tribal words of Muhammad to suit their totalitarian ends just as international socialists, à la Trotsky, have done with Kant. Mind you, such "universalists" are abject hypocrites. Polarization—the believer versus the kafir, the capitalist versus the proletariat—saturates their worldview.

Another aspect of their hypocrisy, however, elates me. The purity preachers prove that we all borrow from foreigners. Immigrant imams in the West who plead for violent jihad against the infidel owe some of their freedoms to the heretic Voltaire. Many of those imams scurry for places to hang their shingles after being kicked out of their homelands; Voltaire "also had to skip across frontiers to escape persecution and keep dissenting," writes Jacques Barzun in his monumental study of the modern West, *From Dawn to Decadence.* He goes on, "Even the terrorist who drives a car filled with dynamite toward a building in some hated nation is part of what he would destroy: his weapon is the work of Alfred Nobel and the inventors of the internal combustion engine."

Chauvinists of the European Enlightenment should heed the same lesson: We all borrow. Ibn Rushd, the twelfth-century Muslim polymath, stimulated thinking among Jewish and Latin scholars well into the 1600s. Enthrallment with Ibn Rushd in Italian universities "had a direct impact on the emergence of modern science," notes the philosopher Paul Kurtz. "Out of this context Galileo emerged." So did Galileo's rudimentary telescope, which opened up God's infinite galaxy for the English poet John Milton. As Dick Teresi, a founder of *Omni* magazine, delights,

Milton alludes to Galileo in Paradise Lost, calling him the "Tuscan Artist" and writing about the moon seen through the artist's "Optic Glass." . . . The previously accepted Aristotelian universe, with all the stars contained neatly in a finite sphere, was now gone, replaced by a grander vision of stars scattered throughout all of space. Much as Star Wars and Star Trek took their cues from modern cosmology, poetry in the seventeenth century was transformed by Copernicus and Galileo.

And therefore by Ibn Rushd, the buoyant Muslim believer who welded rationality and faith by engaging in inquiry—as distinct from doubt.

Wonder also filled the man behind America's Statue of Liberty, who birthed his colossal idea in the Middle East. Around the mid-1800s, French sculptor Frédéric-Auguste Bartholdi visited Luxor, Egypt, where he got jelly-kneed at ancient architecture that telegraphed to him a "limitless future." Later, at the opening of the Suez Canal, a vision engulfed Bartholdi. He would "carve the likeness of an Egyptian peasant woman holding aloft a torch of freedom. The monument, twice as high as the Sphinx, would guard the waterway's entrance," writes the historian Michael Oren. "Its name would be *Egypt (or Progress) Bringing Light to Asia.*" But before the work could be completed, Bartholdi's Arab benefactor went bankrupt.

Bartholdi licked his wounds on a cruise to the United States. Upon entering New York harbor, wonder struck him again and he reimagined the torchbearer. Through years of fund-raising, negotiating and constructing the project, he remained connected to the Middle East: The Statue of Liberty's American engineer, Charles Pomeroy Stone, served as a military general in Egypt's revolt against the British. Decorated with the Star of Egypt medal, Stone left only when, in his words, "all hope had vanished as to the building up of an independent state."

Since learning of these relationships, I've sometimes referred to Lady Liberty as Leila Liberty—for my late grandmother, Leila Nasser, who could have been the model for Bartholdi's "Egyptian peasant woman" and who found "Amrika" endlessly fascinating.

Embodying Lady Liberty's promise, America's antislavery icons borrowed too. W. E. B. Du Bois crossed the color line for literature that spoke to his values rather than his labels. "I move arm in arm with Balzac and Dumas, where smiling men and welcoming women glide in gilded halls," he effused. "I summon Aristotle and Aurelius and what soul I will, and they come all graciously with no scorn nor condescension. So, wed with Truth, I dwell above the veil."

Another of America's abolitionist titans was Frederick Douglass, a runaway slave. He attested that magnetic British orators "gave tongue to interesting thoughts of my own soul, which had frequently flashed through my mind, and died away for want of utterance. . . . What I got from Sheridan was a bold denunciation of slavery and a powerful vindication of human rights. The reading of these documents enabled me to utter my thoughts."

Borrowing is the name of the civilization game. If human rights are a strictly Western concept, how to explain Cyrus the Great? Father of the Persian Empire, Cyrus made freedom of religion a principle before anybody else understood it as such. His foresight lent spine to the United Nations commission that drafted the *Universal Declaration of Human Rights* after the Second World War. Led by Eleanor Roosevelt, the commission's vice chair was Ghasseme Ghani of Iran. India, Lebanon, China, the Soviet Union, the Philippines, Chile, Egypt—delegates from each sat side by side with Westerners to produce a document that would move their societies to higher expectations. Sometimes it reads more like a mash-up of clashing cultural priorities than a seamless articulation of human rights, but the charter's contradictions reinforce my point: Nobody can legitimately depict its drafters as shadowy figures in an Anglo-Saxon conspiracy. They borrowed from each other big-time.

Dietrich Bonhoeffer also borrowed. A German Lutheran pastor who famously opposed the Nazi regime, Bonhoeffer lifted insights about Christian discipleship from African Americans in 1930. He studied at Union Theological Seminary in upper Manhattan, but it was in Harlem that his faith became vascular. While "the German church is unwittingly selling its soul," observes the Methodist pastor John Hay, Jr.,

> *Bonhoeffer is yearning for, discovering and exploring what his native church never offered him—a Biblical sense of community. . . . While his church is coolly making governmental alliances, Bonhoeffer's heart is being warmed by the witness of the Abyssinian Baptist Church. . . . While his church is aligning its future with Hitler, Bonhoeffer is discovering the way of creative nonviolence.*

Mahatma Gandhi borrowed, if only for affirmation. Born in India, he campaigned against the racist structure of the country to which he'd immigrated as a young law clerk: South Africa. When he faced apathy from Indians there, Gandhi's spirit sometimes flagged. In such moments, Western sources supplied at least as much comfort as Eastern texts. For instance, Britain's suffragettes accepted imprisonment as a step in the struggle for women's voting rights. Their example roused Gandhi to challenge his constituency: "If even women display such courage, will the Transvaal Indians fail in their duty and be afraid of jail?" Behind bars, he also sank his teeth into Henry David Thoreau's essay, "On the Duty of Civil Disobedience." A classic contribution to American individuality, Thoreau's defense of conscientious dissent furnished Gandhi with "arguments in favor of our fight."

Where did Thoreau turn for much of his own inspiration? The East. He penned another staple of American literature, *Walden*, a meditation on his experiments in living simply. Thoreau included the tale of a man who intends to carve the perfect staff and loses friends in his single-minded focus on fulfillment. This passage presses my universalist buttons:

> *And now he saw by the heap of shavings still fresh at his feet, that, for him and his work, the former lapse of time had been an illusion, and that no more time had elapsed than is required for a single scintillation from the brain of Brahma to fall on and inflame the tinder of a mortal brain. The material was pure, and his art was pure; how could the result be other than wonderful?*

The brain of Brahma prefigured what positive psychology calls "flow," a state of immersion in doing what you love. Flow facilitates the pursuit of happiness. How very American—yet how very Asian.

Martin Luther King, Jr., borrowed from Gandhi's creed of nonviolence as much as from Christ's parables of love, from the Hindu Gita as much as from the U.S. Constitution. The fluidity of it all enraptures me. The Gita influenced Thoreau. Thoreau influenced Gandhi. Gandhi influenced King. And of late, they've all influenced Iranians rallying for their freedoms. Ramin Jahanbegloo, a human rights scholar at the University of Toronto and a former prisoner in Iran, has referred to "the Gandhian Moment" of his compatriots in the Islamic republic.

Years ago, an Iranian friend named Ali ignited my personal "King Moment" by urging me to read the civil rights leader so I could effectively push back against today's identity purists. King found himself squeezed between white racists and their supremacist counterparts, black nationalists. On top of which, he had to deal with the "force of complacency." That's the term King used to capture the mind-set of "Negroes who, as a result of long years of oppression, have been so completely drained of self-respect and a sense of 'somebodiness' that they have adjusted to segregation." My friend compared them to Muslims who settle for justice only in the hereafter. Their "somebodiness" must wait for another life, or so they've been defrauded into believing.

King would have presented a corrective to the complacent. "There is the more excellent way of love and nonviolent protest," he proposed in his "Letter from Birmingham Jail." To King, the hereafter was God's business; the here and now is ours. For my friend, as for so many Iranians, the universality of this "more excellent way" sustains dignity—right here, right now.

———

Traveling from East to West and back again, we've assembled a set of human values: individual liberty, freedom of conscience, and pluralism of nonviolent ideas. Human values transgress the borders that segregationists, imperialists, isolationists and other fearmongers concoct. Human values make it possible for individuals to practice moral courage, and if enough of us do, we vanquish spasms of supremacy.

I'm grateful for Mona Eltahawy. A syndicated newspaper columnist based in New York, she raises eyebrows for not letting her Muslim identity dwarf her integrity as a morally courageous individual. In March 2008, Eltahawy voiced what few will: "*The main target of Muslim violence is fellow Muslims in the Muslim world* [her italics]."

The frequent demonstrations held across the Muslim world don't call for an end to the slaughter of Muslims by Muslims, but demand petulantly that the "world" stop offending Muslims. For this Muslim, no number of Danish cartoons or Dutch films will ever be more offensive than the seven suicide attacks that have killed at least 100 in Pakistan in the past three weeks alone.

In 2009, a major research study validated Eltahawy's argument, confirming that over the past several years a staggering majority of al-Qaeda's victims have been innocent Muslims.

I'm grateful for Akbar Ladak, who lives in India and proclaims "I"—publicly. Well before the Bombay terrorist assaults of November 2008, Ladak composed a manifesto for fellow Muslims living in open societies. After the bombings, I featured it on my website:

I will not shrink from the fight against Islamic fanaticism.

I live in a secular, democratic country, where I have the freedom to practice my faith, Islam. I value being a Muslim because it gives me the moral framework by which to live my life. While I find the framework given by my religion to be the most appropriate one for me, I know that my fellow citizens and fellow human beings find other religions or philosophies more appropriate frameworks for their lives.

I am indebted to my country's democracy, however imperfect it may be, for letting me choose the faith that I practice. I also value the opportunity afforded in my society to disagree, debate and befriend people whose views are different from mine. I would be a poorer person had I not been born in such a country.

To whom much is given, much is expected.

Today, our relatively free, increasingly multicultural societies are under threat, first and foremost by Muslim extremists who have declared their intent to bring about a global caliphate. Theirs is a hateful and misogynist philosophy, financed by oil-rich dicta-

tors. That it twists my beloved faith to justify a simplistic ideology gives it a powerful allure for Muslims who haven't had the exposure to varied ideas and strains within Islam.

We, Muslims living in free societies, need to be in the forefront of this fight. We fight not only for the security and integrity of the societies we live in, but also for the soul of our faith. Only we can present an alternative interpretation of Islam which promotes the vision of peace, progress and equality.

So let us make our faith, our countries and ourselves a promise today. We will not sit silent when someone uses our religion to legitimize bigotry, misogyny, or violence. We will counter it loudly. We will not be bullied by the self-appointed guardians of faith who say the Islam they know is more pure than the Islam we know. Muslims define Islam, and we are all its guardians.

We must defend our democratic societies despite some people in them who suspect and doubt our motives because of our faith. Our faith and our countries need us today. We cannot, we dare not, shrink from the fight.

Ladak begins with "I" yet ends with "we." Just as Islam borrows from Judaism and Christianity, Ladak enriches his manifesto with a sentiment from the Bible: "To whom much is given, much is expected" (Luke 12:48). And he notes that simply because he follows Islam, he'll be instantly deemed dubious by some. But Ladak moves forward anyway. His low defenses and high expectations make him an example for Osman, the eighteen-year-old in London who's torn between taking ownership of reform and giving in to defensiveness. Ladak not only has made his choice; more radically, he recognizes that he has choices.

All of us have choices. Muslims remind me of this when they advise me to sculpt my message to fit the conventions of their identity so I won't get as much flak. But mainstream Muslim identity quarantines the individual and extinguishes the flame of conscience, so adapting to those conventions would defeat the purpose of reform. My question for Muslims has consequently been, "What's more important—your popularity with each other or your integrity before Allah?" I'd like to hope that some have huffed away thinking about that choice. Maybe they'd go so far as to change their minds if they knew the story I'm about to share.

————

When Prophet Muhammad first received the revelations about one God, he knew that he'd be in for a vicious time from fellow Arabs. The early Muslim historian al-Tabari reports that the prophet wanted to commit suicide by flinging himself off a mountain rather than spread a message that would make him sound unglued. Khadija, the prophet's wife, calmed her husband and convinced him to accept his new status as a divinely chosen, albeit profoundly human, messenger.

At the same time her uncle, Waraqa, pulled no punches about the challenge ahead. Waraqa told the prophet, "They will call you a liar, molest you, drive you out, and fight you." The Arabs of Mecca didn't disappoint. They demeaned the prophet as "jinn-possessed." However tenuous his confidence, the prophet stood his ground. The longer he did, the more intense the threats against him became.

After all, his message of one God jeopardized a hopping tourist trade. People from all over Arabia made pilgrimages to Mecca to worship three local deities, al-Lat, al-Uzza and Manat. Not only did the worshippers bring money to splurge, but they gave the pagan Meccans pride in their culture. By contrast, the prophet shamed his society. He denounced false gods, later opposing oppressive customs such as slavery and female infanticide. A turncoat extraordinaire, Muhammad tarnished the reputation of his own noble tribe, the Quraysh.

Feeling the heat of few initial converts and rising resentment, the prophet made a strategic decision: He diluted his message to curry favor with Meccans. For starters, Muhammad massaged the name of God. What he'd earlier referred to as "Lord" became "Allah"—the "familiar Allah of the pagan Quraysh," writes Subhash C. Inabdar in *Muhammad and the Rise of Islam*. Still, anger at his proselytizing only picked up speed.

Enter the "satanic verses." These are Qur'anic passages that the prophet, in his fallible human judgment, approved as divine revelations. He had them chronicled by his companions, only later learning that these verses deified heathen idols. Muhammad then withdrew the verses, blaming his mistake on a trick by Satan. It's a textbook case of "the devil made me do it." But if God's unswerving love guided the prophet, why did Satan succeed in the first place? When we ask that question, the story becomes more than interesting; it becomes enlightening.

Apparently, the devil capitalized on the prophet's eagerness to remain trusted by his tribe. We all need legitimacy to sell a message, so what's the harm in packaging it for maximum marketability by catering to group identity? Indeed, when the Quraysh heard their goddesses being exalted, "they were delighted," al-Tabari tells us. For the first time, the whole gathering prostrated, "saying Muhammad has spoken of our gods in splendid fashion." The prophet's street cred shot up. Both the sincere and the insincere listened, with sincere believers "not suspecting a vain desire or slip" on the part of Allah's messenger.

Trouble is, prostration made for obfuscation. The prophet hadn't told the truth. What he offered to the pagan Arabs was a culturally correct bastardization of Islam; a version that watered down, even wiped out, the challenge of personal reform. Instead of emphasizing that the worship of idols is a commercial ploy to seduce travelers to Mecca, and that these idols should be replaced by one God who treats all His creatures with compassion, the prophet satisfied himself with the superficiality of ritual. Desperate to be heard, he drained his mission of its meaning.

Ibn Ishaq, a Muslim historian, narrates the legend of what happened next, courtesy of a loving God:

> [The Angel] Gabriel came to the Apostle and said, "What have you done, Muhammad? You have read to these people something I did not bring you from God and you have said what He did not say to you." The Apostle was bitterly grieved and was greatly in fear of God. So God sent down (a revelation) for He was merciful to him, comforting him and making light of the affair and telling him that every prophet and apostle before him desired as he desired and wanted what he wanted and Satan interjected something into his desires. . . . God annulled what Satan had suggested.

In this story, fear of being stigmatized by his community led the prophet to compromise primary principles. Isn't there a lesson here for more Muslims? We're told to emulate Muhammad, but we're never educated to do that by refusing to be held ransom to identity politics. An Arab reader of mine crystallized the lesson for me: "It's better to speak the truth, no matter how much it may hurt, than to remain silent about it. That is the tradition of Prophet Muhammad. Muslims have to understand that every issue must be debated. Every last one." To me, that's what the parable of the satanic verses teaches: Tribal identity is no reason to suffocate criticism of one's family, community or country.

Until now, though, I haven't used this parable to illustrate the error of identity politics. Why? I'm embarrassed to say it's because of my own fear that I'll be accused of preening as a latter-day messenger of God. Check out this email:

What the heck is wrong with you, Irshad? What in the world are you trying to do? Can one person like you change this world? There are so many
Muslims who suffer from exactly the same feeling you do. But I don't see a
lot of people campaigning like you. Allah created this religion. It's His religion. If something bad happens to His religion, wouldn't He send someone
to save it? Is that you? Are you the chosen one? As a human, thanks, but
STOP it!   —Syed

How the heck am I supposed to answer that one? If I remind
Syed that the prophet was "one person" too, I'm playing right into
his suspicion that I regard myself as a prophetess. Not helpful.
Jihadis, of course, don't hesitate to harbor delusions of grandeur,
commonly citing Muhammad as their avatar. Meanwhile, reform-
minded Muslims wilt. By evoking the example of Muhammad, I'm
embroiling myself in "the same game as the jihadis," a Muslim ally
chastises me. But holding up the nonviolent side of a highly human
prophet hardly mimics the jihadi playbook.

Still, lots of us feel inadequate to the task because liberal interpretations of the prophet, as of anything Islamic, are so much harder
to come by than conservative ones. That's exactly why we have to
step forward and tell stories like these. If we don't, we're allowing
conservatives to dominate more of the field, further undermining
any chance to widen the path of Islam.

After healthy introspection about whether I'm mired in some
Muhammad complex, I responded to Syed:

You acknowledge that many Muslims know there's a problem with mainstream Islam today, but because most aren't doing anything about it, you
don't want me to, either. You've taken conformity to new highs—or, should I
say, new lows. Read the story of how the prophet almost changed God's
message to suit pagan culture. God had to restrain Muhammad's conformity.

I interpret this as a Divine command: Don't adjust to the culture's ignorance and injustice. Following that command doesn't make me "chosen," Syed. It makes me aware of my choices.

The episode of the satanic verses shows that whatever our cultures absolve as "normal" behavior, cultures themselves don't make choices. Individuals do. Cultures don't take decisions. Individuals do. And if certain customs lead to oppression, as did the rituals of economically stratified and morally bankrupt Mecca, then they should be exposed no matter who curses our father and our father's mother and our future children.

Muslims often pay lip service to this principle, insisting that there's no trouble with Islam; rather, it's culture that degrades the practice of Islam. Why, then, don't more of us rise up against the cultural crimes that disfigure our faith?

In the next chapter I'll argue that Muslims have to stop posturing as if culture were sacrosanct. When we end that charade, we'll become "countercultural" Muslims—a new identity that serves integrity by countering the culture that loots Islam of God's love. I'll also explain that non-Muslims need to become countercultural in their own right, by resisting orthodox multiculturalism. Whether on religious or on humanist grounds, there's nothing sacred about culture.

3

CULTURE IS NOT SACRED

On Christmas Day 2009, twenty-three-year-old Umar Farouk Abdulmutallab landed in Detroit with a grilled groin and a lot of explaining to do. He'd botched his mission to blow up a flight from Amsterdam. The explosives, stuffed into his crotch, didn't detonate.

At least he retained his all-important honor: In one of its videos, al-Qaeda christened the underwear bomber a hero. Damage control? Of course it was. But this wouldn't be the first time that the Arab cultural custom of honor made its way from the Middle East to Detroit. I have personal experience with the impact of honor on young Muslim Americans.

Shortly before *Faith Without Fear* aired, Mum and I went to Detroit for a screening. My mother, Mumtaz, stars in my documentary. The tension between her traditionalism and my liberalism crackles throughout, so PBS figured it would be fun to have us plumb our differences in front of a morose Muslim audience. Somebody at the Detroit Public Library had second thoughts about what a hoot this would be. The library, our original venue, inexplicably canceled at the last minute. Relocated, the show did go on.

It's estimated that more Arabs live in suburban Detroit than in any metropolitan area outside of the Middle East. Not all are Muslims— in some neighborhoods, Arab Christians outnumber Muslims—but it was Muslims who attended in droves that night. After the film credits faded to black, Mum sat onstage with me, flanked by a hijab-wearing student, a male Muslim professor and a non-Muslim moderator who couldn't have appeared more nervous if he'd choreographed his twitches. The panelists, gracious to my mother, remained grudgingly polite toward me.

The anger of the audience, though, shook Mum to her solar plexus. (Later, she told me that she finally understood why I'm too depleted to phone her more often. A mother-daughter rapprochement: yet another reason I'm so grateful to my critics.) After the screening, Mum and I attended a public reception where we heard again from audience members, did media interviews and signed copies of my book—freely provided by PBS. Noting the length of the lineup, Mum wondered, "Do you really think all of them will read it?"

It occurred to me that somewhere in Detroit a bonfire beckoned, but I didn't say that. "Do you think most of them will even read the Qur'an?" I asked her. She sighed. "Let's just hope they leave my book lying around for relatives to see," I quipped. "That's how conversations get started." Mum sighed again, this time prompted by the word "conversations." What I took as an opportunity for more Muslims to think, she took as a chance for more Muslims to bad-mouth her child.

Over the course of the evening, my hawk-eyed mother twigged to something else. She noticed young Muslims huddled in a corner of the reception hall, peering at us every so often. After the last of the journalists disappeared, they walked up to Mum and me. "*Asalaamu Alaikum*," several of them shyly said in bumper-to-bumper chorus.

"*Wa Alaikum Salaam*," we replied, Mum's body language betting that I was in for another shellacking.

"Well," one of the girls hesitantly started. "We just want to thank you for supporting Irshad. We support her too. The other guests tonight should have showed more respect for her ideas."

"And for you as her mother," chided a boy.

"That's nice," Mum told them. "Very nice, actually. Thank you." A fraught silence ensued, then my mother cut to the chase. "I'm curious, okay? Just curious. Why didn't you say any of this during the question time? Everything we heard has been quite harsh."

The gang began to shuffle. "Or," I gently suggested, "could you have talked to us before all the cameras left? If the media had been able to air what you're telling my mother, then other young Muslims who think like you might learn that they're not alone."

One of the girls locked eyes with Mum. "You and Irshad can walk away from this community in the next few hours. We can't. Our families are here. We would be accused of dishonoring them."

Under the Arab code of honor, Muslims are taught to abdicate our individuality and accept our fate as the property of our families. Our lives don't belong to us; our lives belong to our tribes—usually blood relations. If you cross their moral boundaries, you "dishonor" many more besides yourself. Consider the pressure on you to quash your questions when the honor of your entire family rests on your self-censorship.

Is that why the underwear bomber severed ties with his biological family rather than come clean about his subterranean questions? Questions about his urges toward girls? Questions about the fear that his being consummately human would violate his parents' reputation? Questions that he developed as a university student in the open society of Britain?

Through elders who conflate culture with religion, tribal honor gets exported well beyond the Middle East to ensnare young Muslims in the West. The Detroit students couldn't bear to "dishonor" family by using their freedom to speak their truths out loud. "Why should these kids feel trapped by a custom that isn't even theirs?" I vented to Mum. "They're Americans, for God's sake!" Once I recovered from my meltdown, calmer words crawled out of my clenched jaw. "The custom of honor existed before Islam. If we hang on to culture in the name of Islam, then we're worshipping what man, not God, has created. Isn't that idolatry?"

Mum sighed, "It's stupidity."

Lesson three: *Culture is not sacred.*

————

Brian Whitaker, former Middle East editor of *The Guardian* newspaper, did an experiment when researching his book, *What's Really Wrong with the Middle East.* He presented his Arab interviewees with ten critical statements about the Middle East and asked them to choose which they wanted to discuss. One statement beat out the rest as a matter of urgency—so much so, Whitaker reveals, that "towards the end I was saying to people: 'Please, let's not talk about that one, I've heard enough already.'" That statement? "The family is a major obstacle to reform in the Arab world."

Whitaker's interviews bore out that in Arab society the family is "the primary mechanism for social control"—the first clamp on individuality and the mold for many more constraints. Political leaders, he quotes a Syrian sociologist, "are cast in the image of the father, while citizens are cast in the image of children. God, the father, and the ruler thus have many characteristics in common. They are the shepherds, and the people are the sheep: Citizens of Arab countries are often referred to as *ra'iyyah* (the flock)."

Mona, a thirty-seven-year-old Egyptian, echoes this analysis almost verbatim. "I read *The Trouble with Islam Today*," she emailed,

and I can't tell you how much of an eye-opener it was for me, the muslim woman, raised with fear of the dad, the teacher and God. For the first time, the things I was brought up not questioning became questionable. I started thinking and reasoning. . . . There's turmoil now in my brain, and I'm glad there is. I still can't help relating every small bad thing that happened to me to God's wrath for something I've done, though I'm very innocent. ☺ I've always lived by the book and did the right thing. I guess fear is so embedded in my soul and hopefully one day, I'll get rid of it.

Culture, anthropologists say, is the "sum of learned or acquired knowledge and experience among a collectivity of people." A sum, by definition, includes redeeming qualities. So I understand why the famed Iraqi blogger Salam Pax defends the Arab family structure. "I know very well that if anything goes wrong I can always fall back on something," he told Whitaker.

> *I've got that safety net under me all the time. That's the plus. But again, because I'm depending on the family so much, I need to constantly make sure that they approve of all my decisions. . . . Most governments in the Arab world function like that, too. There is the person who is the head of the family, the head of the tribe, the head of the state, who has final call on every single decision, and you will do what he says, otherwise there is always the fear of being cast outside the family, which is shameful. To be thrown out of the family is something that from a young age you should be worried about.*

Individuals as exiles-in-waiting. Citizens as sheep to be herded. Autonomy as a threat to social order. Such cultural paradigms reflect "the underlying problem," which, according to Whitaker, is "a fear of independent thought." Time will tell whether the 2011 Egyptian revolution has dislodged that fear once and for all.

But growing out of cultural insularity isn't purely an Arab challenge, it's a challenge for most Muslims because tribal culture has merged with Islamic practice. The Turkish commentator and faithful Muslim Mustafa Akyol names this merger "Islamo-tribal-ism." His phrase fits an insight offered to me by Eyad Serraj, the world-renowned Palestinian psychologist whose candor drove Yasser Arafat to arrest him more than once. "Islam was introduced to move Arabs beyond tribalism," Dr. Serraj said. "But Islam has not conquered Arab culture; Arab culture has conquered Islam."

Observers can be forgiven for not realizing there's supposed to be a difference between Islamic faith and Arab culture. More than 80 percent of the world's Muslims are non-Arab; still, Arab Islam is assumed to be authentic Islam. This wouldn't pose such an issue if Islam's spokesmen used religion to sanctify the best aspects of daily Arab life. Hospitality would be a wonderful custom to favor with fierce fatwas. However, it's the worst aspects of tribalism that get blessed by the blandishments of Muslim authorities.

My Jordanian friend Imad can testify. He spent time in Zarqa, the Jordanian town where terrorist superstar Abu Musab al-Zarqawi came of age. Imad then emailed me:

Just back from the burial of a guy's brother [who] works for my dad. Bearded sheikh in rags stood up amongst the 80 or so who were gathered around the fresh grave and started preaching. Everyone listened. Sound bites:

—"Do all that is needed on this earth to avoid the burning hell that God has prepared for those who disobey Him."

—"Be wary of the kuffar. Christians, Jews, Buddhists, Hindus, all are infidels."

—"God has given you Islam as a way of life and manual to follow for everything in life. Forget your brain, forget philosophizing, it's all in Islam, the ready answer. It's not hard to follow."

Emphasizing his disgust, Imad reiterated to me that the sheikh "actually said: 'Forget your brain.' I'm not shitting you. That's exactly what he said, and in clear context too. . . . This stuff is common here, not hidden."

Sophisticated Muslims can snicker at a scruffy cleric in the industrial hub of Jordan as if he's nothing more than a harmless hick, but Imad wrote me to make a sobering point: For unsuspecting Muslims, God's voice booms through the sheikh. Whatever he does thanks to culture will be accepted as a requirement of religion. The loser isn't the sheikh; it's Islam, a faith whose scripture, I must repeat, contains three times the number of passages urging mindful awareness over mere submission. And whom do we have as its modern mouthpieces? Not just dumpy, semiliterate evangelists but also learned enforcers of intellectual suppression at Cairo's Al-Azhar University, the Harvard of Sunni Islam.

But why leave it there? The real Harvard, a citadel of individual freedoms, recently saw the effect of tribalism on educated young Muslims. In April 2009, the university's newspaper, *The Harvard Crimson*, reported that the Muslim chaplain on campus had justified death for apostates. Later denying that he personally holds this view, the Ivy League sheikh nonetheless emailed a student to say that "even if it makes some uncomfortable," we "should not dismiss it [capital punishment] out of hand."

To my mind, Harvard's newspaper missed the bigger story:

Muslim student reactions. The article named a couple of students who questioned the chaplain's stance, yet more of those who opposed him refused to be identified—out of fear. *The Crimson* quoted a Muslim student saying that the chaplain's comments "are the first step towards inciting intolerance and inciting people towards violence." But the same student "requested that he not be named for fear of harming his relationship with the Islamic community." A student at the Massachusetts Institute of Technology (MIT) chimed in that "it is very shocking and not something that I would expect or want coming out of a chaplain at any major American university." This person "also asked to remain anonymous to preserve his relationship with the Islamic community."

In the strongest denunciation of all, a third Muslim student made clear that the sheikh "doesn't belong as the official chaplain. If the Christian ministers said that people who converted from Christianity should be killed, don't you think the University [would] do something?" Good news: The student behind that admirable statement was identified in the print version of the story. Bad news: The online edition expunged his name. He'd been "granted anonymity when he revealed that his words could bring him into serious conflict with Muslim religious authorities."

Detect a theme? Fear, yes, but also low expectations and high defenses. Low expectations of fellow Muslims and high defenses against possible retaliation.

The exasperating thing is, it would be retaliation against Muslims who embrace God's mercy—and therefore the Qur'an's versatility. Here's what I mean by versatility: A year before Harvard's Muslim chaplain made headlines, a stunning decision about apostasy and choice came down in the Sunni Muslim world. Egypt's grand mufti, Sheikh Ali Gomaa, concluded that a Muslim may adopt another religion and that no power in this earthly realm has the right to punish an ex-Muslim for bailing on Islam. God might hold it against the defector, but you and I can't. Sheikh Gomaa pointed to several Qur'anic verses affirming freedom of conscience: First, "Unto you your religion, unto me my religion" (109:6); second, "Whosoever will, let him believe and whosoever will, let him disbelieve" (18:29); third, "Let there be no compulsion in religion" (2:256). His verdict scandalized Muslims in Egypt and elsewhere. Cultural conditioning dies hard. So, then, does Islamo-tribalism.

The ultimate travesty is this: Islamo-tribalism is a form of Islamophobia, or fear of Islam. Today, there are two types of Islamophobe. There are those who fear Islam because they're convinced that any interpretation vibrates with violence. These Islamophobes equate all of Islam with the narrow path. Then there are those who fear the wide path of Islam—the path that leads to freedom of conscience, thought and expression. These Islamophobes are Muslims who genuflect before tribal culture, fearing Islam as a faith of personal transformation. Our university students fell in line with those Islamophobes by refusing to dissent *on the record*, abdicating their own freedom of conscience, thought and expression.

Islamo-tribalism will be whittled away when Muslims stop being slaves to the fear of dishonoring our communities—our tribes—and begin speaking truth to power visibly. Only then will Muslims transform ourselves into people who walk our talk. Put another way, Muslims must reform ourselves for the irksome phrase "Islamo-tribalism" to be displaced by "Islam" proper. After all, Islam in theory doesn't much matter to the fulfillment of peace; it's Islam in practice that does.

Moderate Muslims can ardently assure non-Muslims that Islam goes hand in glove with freedom, but until moderates behave as if it does—by going public with their individuality—should we hold it against anyone for scoffing? Didn't Muslims spin the globe with a collective eye-roll when President George W. Bush announced that America doesn't torture? Ideally it doesn't, but experience tells another tale. Likewise, Muslims can theorize from the tallest ivory tower that Islam itself doesn't incite fear. And I sincerely believe it doesn't have to. The reality remains, though, that Islam is implicated in our fear as long as Muslims scramble behind anonymity when a challenge arises that involves religion in any way.

If I could, I'd ask those Muslim students at Harvard and MIT a few questions. You don't want to be named because you wish to maintain good relations with "religious authorities," correct? Here's what trips me up. Why be fazed by the egos of "religious authorities" if the problem is cultural and not religious? Why reward their ignorance if they're wrongly equating culture with religion? You wouldn't reward the ignorance of non-Muslims, would you? Why expect less of Muslims? Are non-Muslims the only mixed-up bunch? Or are you too?

As Sheikh Gomaa shows us, the Qur'an features verses that support individual liberty. Those verses can be cited simply. What, then, is preventing Muslims—even in a liberal democracy—from defying tribal culture in our midst? What more is messing with the hearts and minds of Muslims who find themselves poised to create positive, life-affirming change?

———

Hawa, one of my readers, scratches her head about this. "As a Muslim, I am very aware of the need for reform in Islam, but even in the United States, my Muslim relatives and friends are hesitant to criticize traditional Muslim orthodoxy. . . . It used to be that the liberals were more critical, but now they are complacent. These are very confusing times." She's bang on. We live in an era of moral bewilderment. Many people assume that just because human beings are born equal, cultures are too. But cultures aren't born; they're constructed. Cultures aren't God-given; they're man-made. Since humans are an eminently imperfect lot, our cultures will be as well.

These basic points are washing away in our capitulation to "cultural rights." In only fifty years, the myth of cultural rights has leapfrogged from arcane anthropological circles to the world's institutions of higher learning. Since 1947, anthropologists have been debating among themselves whether cultures deserve the protections that individuals do. With the rubble of the Second World War practically still smoldering, and memories of the Holocaust still scorching, the American Anthropological Association sent its Statement on Human Rights to the United Nations. It began by asserting the need to respect "the cultures of differing human groups." The Nazis eviscerated groups such as Jews and gays, and American anthropologists wanted to ensure that "Never Again" would apply to identifiable communities everywhere.

Their statement, though, begged a crucial question: How do we deal with abuses of power *within* collectivities? If groups and their cultures are to be tolerated as much as individuals, what do we say to individuals who find themselves oppressed by traditions inside those groups and cultures? In short, are human rights truly universal or are they reserved for those fortunate enough to be born in families and societies that already defend individual freedoms? For questions like these, the 1947 statement had no ready response.

Over the decades, anthropologists have shuddered at the statement. "Indeed, the term *embarrassment* continually is used," notes the human rights scholar Karen Engle. Still, the Holocaust-heavy premise—that tolerance of groups is a moral imperative—has only gained gravitas. One result: relativism, the now-rampant belief that no cultural norm is better than another. Exonerating his country's willingness to stone women to death, the head of Iran's human rights commission recently declared on CNN that "cruelty is a notion which is very much culturally relative."

Translation: You can't criticize another's culture because your culture has crap of its own. Unless you're a person of color, in which case you can criticize white people's cultures because you're only speaking truth to power. Unless you're speaking truth to the powers-that-be *inside* your culture, in which case you're a self-loather. Well, maybe you're not—maybe you're a true human rights advocate—but white people can't say so because that would amount to judging another's culture and one can't comment if one doesn't "represent." Unless you're a brown woman or a black man, in which case you can judge white people's cultures even though you don't "represent," but white people can't tell you that you don't "represent" because they'd be colonizing your ass-of-color yet again. But if the actual colonization is coming from your own, then speaking up is selling out. That's right; you're selling out the group that won't tolerate you but demands tolerance from everyone else. You call this a contradiction? Yeah, well, you're so inauthentic.

I call this the rabbit hole of relativism. It's reminiscent of the madness captured by Lewis Carroll's story in *Alice in Wonderland*: Alice tumbles into a rabbit hole and upon landing, opens the door to an alternate universe. But relativism is no fairy tale. Just ask Polly Toynbee, a columnist with the most pro-Muslim mainstream newspaper I know, *The Guardian*. Toynbee campaigns for the equality of women everywhere. Her writings have won awards—among them "Islamophobe of the Year," as bestowed by a clutch of activists anointing themselves the Islamic Human Rights Commission.

They parachuted Toynbee into the same company as Nick Griffin, the leader of the British National Party and an unadorned racist. "I was really shocked," Toynbee admitted. "But that's what happens to you if you speak out at all. . . . And of course, I got an avalanche of emails from all over the world as a result of this. I was getting thousands a day, profoundly abusive, really seriously abusive, and very threatening—you know, 'Watch out for your children; we know where you live.'"

Massoud Shadjareh, one of the men who crowned Toynbee "Islamophobe of the Year," acknowledged that "we need to engage and discuss." But, he sternly added, "there is a limit to that." And of course, he'll unilaterally define the limit. Shadjareh went on to compare the feminist Toynbee to Nazi anti-Semites. Strange, since elsewhere he endorses vigorous conversation about human rights: "Every time we exclude someone from this discourse on the basis of their (perceived) particular interest, we create yet another victim of human rights abuse—that is, someone who has been denied the opportunity to express their agency as rational beings."

By the by, the Islamic Human Rights Commission has been a frequent consultant to the UN, so Shadjareh would know how to exclude the culturally incorrect Toynbee from a full and fair hearing. He could simply take cover in the American anthropologists' 1947 statement to the UN, or in one of the illustrious UN bodies whose politics parrot that statement. In June 2008, David Littman of the Association for World Education came before the UN Human Rights Council. There, he proposed that the Grand Sheikh of Al-Azhar University issue a fatwa against the crime of stoning women to death. Whereupon the Egyptian delegate, Amr Roshdy Hassan, interjected, "Islam will not be crucified in this Council!" Crucified? By resorting to a religious—Islamic—solution? The rabbit hole deepens and darkens.

I can't blame anybody for feeling dazed by the kookiness that has infected multiculturalism. Hang tight—in a moment I'll help you find your way out of the rabbit hole. First, though, we need to get real about the politics that foment group grievances today.

The Organization of the Islamic Conference (OIC) is a union of fifty-seven Muslim-majority countries. For the past several years the OIC has pushed an honor-soaked resolution through the UN. Termed "Combating the Defamation of Religions," this resolution reflects tribal honor's perverse logic. Tribal honor turns victims into criminals by holding them responsible for sullying the reputation of their families and, by extension, their communities. (Remember the Detroit kids?) Using the same cultural "reasoning," the UN Human Rights Council has censored interventions about the stoning of women. It has also nixed discussions about girls as young as nine being married off. All because Muslim diplomats have fulminated that revelations of marriage by force and of murder by rocks defame Islam.

Never mind that the crimes themselves defame Allah by cloaking man-made culture as divine edict. Never mind that the actual Islamophobes—Muslims who debase the Creator's love and the Qu'ran's mercy—present themselves as victims of Islamophobia. Never mind that an inhumane power play is being humored by a human rights council. Never mind that its Godforsaken game offends plenty of Muslims who won't have our say inside the UN's culturally circumspect corridors. Offense only rates when felt by those with the authority to define respect for culture, and thus define culture itself.

In its defense, the OIC has objected that "new trends" are "threatening the multicultural fabric of many of our societies." Trends plotted by Danish editors, Dutch filmmakers and British teachers armed with teddy bears named Muhammad. But "new trends" don't explain why Pakistan presented the first antidefamation measure to the UN in 1999—before 9/11, before the cartoon crisis and before the presidency of George W. Bush. What explains it is the refrain on which the OIC falls back: that "fundamental rights and freedoms" should be enjoyed not just by individuals but also by "groups of individuals and communities."

Increasingly, the cultural rights choir can be heard outside of Islam. In July 2009, Ireland "updated" its blasphemy laws. The justice minister singled out immigration as the reason for adapting his country's constitution, which protected the beliefs of Christians only. But why not scrap the blasphemy clause altogether? That way, no religious community would have a constitutional condom with which to shield itself from the views of others. Every community could proudly expound what it believes because liberal democracy itself protects freely made choices, including the choice to disbelieve. The Almighty doesn't need a political prophylactic; it's His self-nominated ambassadors who do. Irish legislators, like the OIC, slander a Creator that can take the pinprick of human skepticism.

More sleazy is how the Catholic Church robes power politics as cultural sensitivity. For much of July 2008, the Vatican exercised the "right" not to be offended. Police in Sydney, Australia, wielded unprecedented powers to arrest anybody who annoyed participants of the Vatican-sponsored World Youth Day. How might one inflict annoyance? By approaching the festival grounds in a T-shirt that defends abortion, condoms or sex-abuse survivors. No need for a high-voltage protest when cotton-blend T-yranny will do. For such a felony against the Body of Christ, the penalty could have been a partial strip search, suggesting that nudity has its nonreproductive place. Go figure. Late that month, Australia's federal court struck down the law that immunized the Vatican against offense—a minor setback in the bigger picture.

The pope's phalanx has also left its fingerprints on a case involving "Sikh rights"—again, the rights of a group (as defined by power brokers) over the rights of an individual within that group. A few years ago, Gurpreet Kaur Bhatti, a countercultural Sikh, planned to stage a play in Birmingham, England. Entitled *Behzti* (Dishonor), the play punctured communal secrets by depicting sexual abuse inside a temple. Sikh spokespeople, invited to attend a rehearsal, took full advantage of their access to carp about "negative portrayal." Negotiations with them went nowhere, but the Birmingham Repertory pushed ahead—until some religious Sikhs stormed the venue. When police threw in the towel, *Behzti* folded and Bhatti had to live in hiding.

Meanwhile, the pope's man in Birmingham effectively told the playwright to kiss his ring. Archbishop Vincent Nichols said that "such a deliberate, even if fictional, violation of the sacred place of the Sikh religion demeans the sacred places of every religion." He'd know how sexual violations demean sacred places, given the molten lava of molestation charges against the Church. Had Birmingham's archbishop supported Bhatti's moral courage, he would have faced calls to come clean about some of the clergy's own behzti-like behavior. It's safer to fan the myth of cultural rights so that culture acquires the emotional radioactivity of race, making it hazardous to question.

This strategy hit its peak—or its valley, as I prefer to think of it—during Easter week in 2010. As accumulated sex abuse scandals gripped the Vatican, the pope's personal preacher tipped his culture-as-race hand. The Reverend Raniero Cantalamessa announced that a Jewish friend had sent him a letter comparing accusations against the Church to anti-Semitism. His friend stated that Jews "are quick to recognize the recurring symptoms," among them, "the use of stereotypes." Cantalamessa's calculation? With culture as the new race, those who reveal a tradition's ugly underbelly can be dismissed as bigots.

If the tradition being questioned is "non-Western," the power politics intensify. The label "non-Western" should mean little in light of the fact that civilization is universal, a hodgepodge of influences imported from every direction. But our identity-coveting hearts tussle with that truth, so we empower identity purists to grab us by more than the heart. That's how otherwise intelligent people can plummet into the rabbit hole of relativism.

In Frankfurt, Germany, a Moroccan-born woman beaten by her husband petitioned for a speedy divorce. The judge denied it to her because "in Moroccan culture it is not unusual that the husband uses physical punishment against his wife." The judge—a woman—was yanked from the file, but not before journalists exposed the case. Did German authorities remove Madame Justice as a public relations gesture? Or did they genuinely appreciate that culture means nothing without individuals acting on its behalf? I have an inkling it's not the latter.

So let me elaborate on why cultures, even when posing as sacred religions, don't deserve rights. Cultures aren't sentient beings with free will and a conscience; individuals are. Cultures don't speak for themselves; people speak for them. To accord rights to something that lives only through the judgments, perceptions and actions of humans is beyond gratuitous—it's downright dangerous because it boosts the power of the already powerful.

Unni Wikan is an anthropologist with moral courage. A former UN researcher whose fieldwork has taken her to Egypt, she specializes in child development. For the past fifteen years Wikan has analyzed how her country of Norway strips immigrant Muslim children of their human rights by putting the culture of their parents on a pedestal. Policy makers, social workers and teachers have assumed that Muslim children are owned by the culture from which their mothers and fathers hail, an assumption that steals from these children any meaningful sense of belonging to their de facto home, Norway.

Muslim immigrants aren't the sole culprits here. This bedeviled process thrives on the sycophancy of native Europeans. Despite their eighteenth-century Enlightenment, many Europeans fawn over culture as if it's a fourteenth-century holy man who can't be questioned. Writes Wikan,

> Culture is often portrayed as if it possessed uncontested and uncontestable authority, whereas authority actually rests with those who hold power. Some people have the right—or seize the right—to define what is to count for what, and the result, the authoritative "truth," is often called culture. Culture and power go hand in hand, in every society, at all times.

Attempting to make a similar point, I once engaged in a volley of views with a Syrian scholar. We met at a conference on global security in Washington, D.C. After I spoke about reviving ijtihad, Islam's spirit of critical thinking, the scholar took hold of a roaming microphone. He endorsed my message with one qualifier: There's already an "Islamic consensus" about important issues. I told him that until many more Muslims get over the fear of expressing themselves, any "consensus" is illusory because it's only the privileged few who feel safe enough to speak. I described it as the consensus of the confident. The scholar shook his head testily—not surprising, since he's part of an elite that wants to seal its vise grip on voice. It's the culture-power relationship on full display.

By pretending that culture has a legitimacy all its own, we guarantee that the most self-assured members of any group can continue to lord it over the weakest. Sensitivity to difference, taken to thoughtless extremes, ends up producing the opposite of sensitivity: tolerance for abuses of power. In a tribal context, that's lethal. This email comes from Ann, a reader of mine in the United States:

A close neighbor has just retired as the chief trauma nurse for a major hospital in New York. She held that position for over 20 years and told me that she never saw so much violence toward women as she has in the last 5 years, mostly among Muslim women, generally from Pakistan. She is still upset by the savage beatings at the hands of their husbands and other male relatives.

It was her responsibility to inform these women of their legal rights and counsel them to press charges to pull themselves out of the cycle of violence. Time and again, this help was refused, often accompanied with the words, "You don't understand, this is part of our culture. Our men have this right." She was also told by many young women that their brothers began helping their father beat them shortly after turning 15 or 16.

This issue must be taken out of the shadows. The level of political correctness that pervades any discussion about Islam only assists in keeping the religion and its followers in the dark ages.

Muslims, don't be distracted by Ann's reference to "Islam" instead of "culture"; we haven't yet proven to her that tribalism can be purged from the practice of Islam. For now, it behooves us to take Ann's concern as a recognition that Muslim women are human above all else. Therefore, they're entitled to the same human dignities as anyone else. Better to have Ann's elevated expectations than a brooding suspicion that all Muslims cleave to brutal customs, so why bother saying anything? Happily, Ann does bother. Something in her says, "It doesn't have to be like this. By writing about it, maybe I can do my part."

That's a cue, fellow Muslims, to do our part. Become countercultural Muslims. Speak up. Assert your radiant individuality. And understand that cultural rights shouldn't apply to Islamo-tribalism—not if we want a reason to drop "tribalism" from that noxious phrase.

Non-Muslims, you can do even more than Ann. Whether you're a school counselor, a corporate manager, a college educator or a local legislator, you should tell Muslims that you expect us to be individuals rather than products of a cultural assembly line. This means believing that we're capable of individuality, which may demand of you some introspection about what good people take for granted in our multicultural age. On a ferryboat one evening, another anthropologist, Anne Knudsen, met a Danish Turkish woman fleeing her husband. He'd assaulted her one too many times and the woman now needed help from family in Istanbul. Knudsen asked her why Danish social workers couldn't intervene. "Those!" the woman replied. "They just think it's culture!" But her relatives in Turkey "are modern human beings."

I understand non-Muslims who throw their hands up and blurt, "Huh? How do I figure out if a Muslim woman could use my help?! Irshad, you've just told us about Pakistani women who claim that their culture justifies wife abuse. Now you tell us about a Danish Turkish woman who hates hearing that culture justifies wife abuse. What's the deal, sisters? Sort it out and send us the memo." Duly noted. These two stories shed light on a dilemma that can, in some cases, be resolved.

————

The answer has to do with how we see the potential of others. Kenan Malik, a British critic of multicultural dogma and a veteran antiracism activist, lays it out like so: Think of the words "attachment" and "capacity." In Malik's analysis, attachment implies rigidity. Capacity, on the other hand, implies fluidity. We have to choose which of these frames we'll wear when we view others. If we perceive them through the frame of attachments, then we're choosing to see them as tethered and unable to grow. But if we perceive others through the frame of their capacities, then we give them room to blossom into their own.

Take the Pakistani women. They told Ann's neighbor, the head nurse at a New York hospital, that they can't accept intervention because their culture sanctions the battering of women by men. Ann could have interpreted their claim to mean, "We're attached to this version of our culture, so back off." Yet suppose they were saying, "We can't conceive of another life for ourselves, and until we can, our only compass is culture as we know it." Then what? Then capacity would enter the frame. If these women are capable of dreaming that life can be free of welts and bruises, then with more choices they'll possibly make new decisions. Possibly.

I realize that for those of us who rejoice in our individuality, "attachment" is an affirmative act. Apologies to any Buddhist who believes that all suffering comes from attachment, but you might love being attached to your spouse. Or to your children. Or to your hobby. Or, like me, to your life's purpose. When born of free will, these can be positive attachments. But Malik is asking us to slip into the shoes of those who don't yet have the freedom to know themselves as individuals, those for whom tribal identity poses as personal integrity.

Evangelical Christians and ultra-Orthodox Jews routinely contact me about this conundrum. For many, their place in the social order depends on whether they follow the rules dictated to them. They want breathing space but don't know how to get it because, so far, their denominations' cultures have determined their human worth, and congregational culture is the only compass they've got. Naturally, they feel attached to it. After reading this book, they'll have a different compass—one that reveals new choices. I wouldn't impose new choices on them, but I can explain that dogma isn't the rock it appears to be: Dogma is insecure and compels us to cling.

Faith, on the other hand, is confident and frees us to explore. I have faith in their potential to grow, so I adopt the lens of capacity, not attachment.

Ann, too, viewed the Pakistani women through the lens of capacity rather than attachment. She dignified them with a dynamic humanity. Instead of being static and bloodless relics of a culture fossilized in somebody else's past, she saw that these women deserved to be individuals with a shot at shaping their own future. At least a few social workers in Denmark can learn from Ann. Those assigned to help the woman on the Turkey-bound boat framed her as a hapless victim of attachment. Notice, though, that she didn't feel married to her husband's culture of origin. In fact she invoked the word "modern" to describe her Turkish relatives, in sharp contrast to the communalist crowd at the Danish social service agency.

By "modern," the Muslim woman meant "respectful of my individuality." Far from being arbitrary, this definition comes directly out of the European Enlightenment, a project that sought to replace Europe's feudal, hierarchical mind-set with an ethos of achievement, ennobling the individual with a right to surpass her inherited social status. But an unexamined submission to tribal culture has poisoned the aquifers of the Enlightenment, as it has the aquifers of Islam. Both Islam and the Enlightenment are being betrayed by their heedless beneficiaries.

The "clash," then, isn't necessarily between Islam and the Enlightenment. It's between practitioners within each tradition who asphyxiate individuality, and thus capacity. Muslims who see this happening among themselves need to call their fellow Muslims on the carpet. Ditto for non-Muslims. Yet imagine that we all venture an extra step. What if we speak up when the other is misusing his or her tradition? The Danish Turkish woman took this step in describing the antimodern proclivities of the social workers she had to wrangle with. It didn't alleviate her immediate problems, I know, but if more Muslims expose how obliviously tribal "enlightened" Europeans can be these days, might the message penetrate? After all, it's coming from Muslims—it must have credibility! (Bad joke.) At the very least, we'd be planting seeds of introspection in people who assume they're helping when they're not.

Now imagine that non-Muslims tell Islamo-tribalists something similar. In the previous chapter I mentioned an Egyptian immigrant to Quebec who enrolled in French-language classes. Repeatedly, the instructor found ways to accommodate her needs, but she refused to remove her veil. This, despite the fact that a fair assessment of pronunciation required the instructor to watch each student's mouth move. Ultimately, she was expelled from the course. Three weeks later, Quebec announced its intention to ban veils from all government premises—and to deny tax-paying, veil-wearing women essential public services. A bloated reaction, I'd say, to the ignorance of Islamo-tribalists.

Rather than let it spiral that far, the instructor could have told his student this: "You're demanding that I make concessions for tribalism, not Islam. Sorry, but tribalism is not a recognized religion—Islam is. And if you aren't already aware, the Qur'an clearly states that there's no compulsion in religion. As a Muslim, you have flexibility when needed. As your instructor, I'm informing you that it's needed now." The woman might very well have blown a gasket upon hearing those words. *Quel dommage.* Rest assured that she'd have reflected on the instructor's words later. So would the Swedish Muslim man who wouldn't shake hands with a female CEO because of Islam. "No," he could stand to hear, "it's not because of Islam. It's because of tribal culture. Islam itself is capable of more versatility than you're showing. As a Muslim, you're capable of it too."

Daniel Bacquelaine, a Belgian parliamentarian, lunged in that direction during his country's debate about the veil in April 2010. He told journalists, "Nothing in Islam, in the Qur'an, or in the Sunnah imposes this form of dress. It seems to me it's more a political or ideological sign." Bravo Bacquelaine! He busted Islamo-tribalists with inconvenient facts. Trouble is, he made these vital points as the sponsor of a bill to criminalize the veil—a context that Islamo-tribalists can pounce upon to proclaim that it's secular democrats who do the imposing. Thus, the truth of Bacquelaine's analysis is lost on the very Muslims who need to be deprogrammed from tribalism.

We shouldn't wait for these issues to become legislative red meat. It's in daily interaction that Muslims and non-Muslims must press one another to live the most positive aspects of our traditions. At first, nobody will take kindly to the effort. Your Hallmark thank-you card is decidedly not in the mail. Still, shared wisdom is on your side. While the Qur'an teaches that "God does not change the condition of a people until they change what is inside themselves," the Enlightenment thinker Jean-Jacques Rousseau affirmed that a "distinguishing characteristic of man" is "the faculty of self-improvement." I can't conceive of a more humane navigation tool than the compass that points to capacity.

For good measure, let me give you a final example of how to use the compass of capacity in dicey situations. I'm about to demonstrate, yet again, the ease with which Europeans often swallow tribal culture while presuming to practice enlightened politics. Unni Wikan remembers a public debate in which she and another guest queried political party leaders on the quality of life for immigrants in Oslo. The co-questioner, born in Bosnia, had lived in Norway for twenty years and "presented himself emphatically as Norwegian, not Bosnian." He arrived with a specific question for the candidates: "Why is it that if a Norwegian won't let his daughter marry an immigrant, it's called racism, but if an immigrant won't let his daughter marry a

Norwegian, it's called culture?" Recalls Wikan, "The politicians were speechless, at a loss for a response, so he turned to me afterward and asked, 'Do you think they didn't understand my question?'"

Oh, they got the question, but it's worth wondering why the question got them. My hunch? All of these leaders viewed "authentic" Norwegians—native-born whites—through a different frame than the one they used to view immigrants. The authentic Norwegians had capacity on their side. "You're capable of moving past the outdated prejudices of our Nordic culture," I can hear the politicians assuring a brother, colleague or friend. "It's because I know you're capable of better that I have to say you're being a penny-ante racist. There's no excuse to stop your daughter from marrying a decent man like Haneef. Go to the fjords and chill out."

But what of the reverse scenario, in which Haneef's parents douse their daughter's burning hope to marry Lars? "That's not racism against us," the progressive European would protest. "That's their culture." His unspoken assumption: Haneef's Muslim parents feel tethered to a certain way of doing things. Really? Would the politicians challenge Haneef's parents to do otherwise, the way a Norwegian could expect to be challenged? If not, why not? Why tacit faith in the one and a pat on the head for the other?

Kenan Malik tantalizes me with an insight about his country, Britain. In 1955, the Colonial Office concluded that a "large coloured community as a noticeable feature of our social life would weaken ... the concept of England or Britain to which people of British stock throughout the Commonwealth are attached." Blimey. Their attachment didn't have much stick, did it? It turns out the government underestimated the people. While some folks of "British stock" do feel unsettled (or repelled) by the heterogeneity around them, most Brits have evolved. Would you say that their willingness to grow makes people of British stock less authentically British?

These questions should help Muslims and non-Muslims think clearly about how to reform ourselves for the greater good. Muslims need to tap our capacity—let's never lose sight of that word—to blaze the wide path of Islam. We do so by resisting tribal tendencies and speaking as individuals. Out loud. Don't worry about the spittle-flecked furor of religious authorities. Our beef is with their culture, not their Creator. Equipping ourselves with this reminder, and reminding our families of it, will blunt the bite of the elders and become part of our emotional armor.

At the same time, to revive the promise of the Enlightenment, all of us need to modernize our perception of an authentic Islam. If we rely on Islamo-tribalists to "represent" Islam, then enlightenment is doomed. The spirit of inquiry, permitted by the Qur'an and promoted by the *philosophes*, will be displaced by ever more inquisitions against "racist" Westerners and "self-hating" Muslims. We need to authenticate countercultural Muslims as worthy of Allah, whether in daily conversation between ourselves, among scholars or with the media.

Undoubtedly, you'll hear Islamo-tribalists accuse countercultural Muslims of cherry-picking from the Qur'an. Inform them that by deviating from the Qur'an's freedom-friendly passages, they're being no less selective. The difference is, countercultural Muslims expand choices for all because we accept that God and nothing else owns the full truth. Our monotheism recognizes the Creator as final judge and jury. Tribal bullies, however, perform the role of God. If that's the only authentic Islam to speak of, Islamo-tribalists can tell it to the final judge.

Some might respond that you got this argument from that "lesbian kafir" Irshad Manji. If so, you have a sterling opportunity to ask: *Is it the lesbian kafir who wrote chapter 3, verse 7, of the Qur'an?*

Educate them about what this passage transparently says—that some verses are precise and others are ambiguous, but it's men and women with disbelief in their hearts who prey on the ambiguities so they can decree particular interpretations. The verse ends by cautioning us that God alone knows the meaning of His words. *Did Irshad Manji smuggle this passage in? If not, then why do you violate the Qur'an by insisting that your interpretation is the only possibility? Are you one of those with disbelief in their hearts?*

More than a few Islamo-tribalists, I predict, will try to divert your attention by thundering about "Manji's gay agenda" and trumpeting that the Qur'an decries homosexuality. If I may offer further thoughts, continue to invoke 3:7. *There you go again, breaking faith with the simple Qur'anic passage that urges you not to get excited about ambiguous verses. The Sodom and Gomorrah story—Islam's parable of Lut—is ambiguous. You're certain it's about homosexuals, but it could be about the rape of straight men by other straight men as a display of power and control. God punished Lut's tribe for cutting off trade routes, hoarding wealth and dissing outsiders. Male-on-male rape might have been the sin of choice to instill fear in travelers. I don't know that I'm right. According to the Qur'an, though, you can't be sure that you're right either. Now, if you're still obsessed with cursing homosexuals, aren't you the one who has a gay agenda? And while we're at it, you didn't answer my earlier question: What's with the disbelief in your heart?*

All you need to hold your own with Islamo-tribalists is a laser-like focus on Islam's prime directive—that God and none other possesses ultimate truth. The rest of us, however gruff our tones or exalted our titles, can only ever be pursuers of truth. Muslims, once you're at peace with that humble approach to faith, you have what it takes to be countercultural. But—and this is a point for all of us, including non-Muslims—we can't be humble about validating countercultural Muslims. Lives are on the line.

Three years after I visited Detroit and met the young Muslim Americans who lived a double existence, Samia emailed me from that city. She's a college student. "I wish I could follow you on Twitter or become a fan of yours on Facebook," she wrote, "but I feel that my safety and sanity would be at risk if my parents or anyone else found out. I know that this is something you must hear a lot so I am completely sorry if it disheartens you that I can't publicly proclaim my support for you." Samia contacted me for help with publishing her story, which indicates that she's capable of declaring her individuality.

By her own admission, she needs encouragement. Sexually violated by a family friend years earlier and "devoured by guilt" ever since, Samia hints that she doesn't differ much from the average American teenage girl—save for the crushing fist of family honor:

I know that in American society, it would be supported by the public to tell someone of this incident. . . . The conflict is I cannot do it. It is not because I [her emphasis] don't want to but because if I do, my family will hate me for it. The family's honor will be tarnished, all because of something that was not my fault.

Shame, Samia divulges, "is revered so highly and prevented so greatly that our hearts have become sterile of sympathy."

She recounts a particularly stinging outburst from her mother, who "placed the family's name and honor ahead of my own safety." The night of the sexual assault, Samia got home late. She wanted her mom "to hate me because she worried about ME and not about THEM"—that is, other Muslims. Instead, Samia's mother flew into a rage over the prospect that the family's Muslim neighbors, peeking through curtains, would blab about Samia's tardy return.

"I wanted love, not fear, to appear in my home. For once, I wanted my mother and my father to look at the world through their eyes and not those of our neighbors." To do that, her parents would have to appreciate the virtue of saying, doing and thinking "I." I don't know if it's too late for them, but I know it's not too late for Samia, who's striving with every corpuscle of her being to amalgamate "the values of my home and the ones that I believe silently in my mind."

Samia's parents, although South Asian, practice the Islam of an Arab culture that exports two types of honor. In traditional Arab society, *sharaf* refers to the honor of the family or society, while *'ird* refers exclusively to the honor of women. In reality, *'ird* determines sharaf. When a woman "dishonors," she disgraces the family. All members are sullied until they take drastic measures against her. Trad Fayez, a tribal leader in Jordan, favors this analogy: "A woman is like an olive tree. When its branch catches woodworm, it has to be chopped off so that the society stays clean and pure."

Bushra, another young Muslim woman, doesn't share the Jordanian leader's attachment to custom. But does she realize her capacity? Not without our help. The eighteen-year-old New Yorker emailed me despondently:

I'm a lesbian. I've always hated myself for it and asked forgiveness from Allah. I punished myself by cutting. I've also thought about committing suicide but I know I would go straight to Jahannam [hell]. I even tried to force myself to like boys but that didn't work. So it seems I can't change who I am, but I wish I could. You are so fortunate. You have a mother that accepts who you are and at the same time is a devoted Muslim. My parents are very close-minded people and religious and strict. I want to tell them but they would probably do an honor killing on me or force me to marry someone that I barely know. You would think I have a little freedom because I live in New York. But no.

In subsequent conversations with Bushra, I learned that for years now her parents have been pressuring her to marry a man in their home country.

Muslims, who among you will join me in assuring Bushra that the Almighty made her as He chose to? Who will explain to her that by countering the culture of saving face, we contribute to a culture of saving faith? And because I ain't queer enough to show up alone, who will go with me to speak with Bushra's family about the wide path of Islam?

The longer we wait to reform ourselves, the more this path will be littered with corpses like that of Aqsa Parvez. In December 2007, the sixteen-year-old Muslim Canadian died at the hands of her family. Aqsa long feared what her father would do if she stood by her decision to reject hijab. That's not the "Islamic" headscarf for women; it's the headscarf mandated by *pre-Islamic* tribal honor, taken as a punctilious religious requirement by Islamo-tribalists such as her dad. Aqsa confided to adults and friends at school that she felt safer in a shelter than at home. A couple of educators listened, but Aqsa's peers downplayed the danger even though she explained that her Pakistan-born dad swore on the Qur'an that he'd kill her if she fled again from their Toronto-area house. Her friends assured her that he "could not be serious." Thirty-six minutes after Aqsa returned home from a second runaway attempt, Mr. Parvez phoned 911 to say he'd done away with his daughter. Cause of death: "neck compressions."

More than two years later, Aqsa's brother, Waqas, joined the family patriarch in formally confessing to the murder. According to the agreed statement of facts, Waqas felt as constricted as Aqsa; he was prohibited, for example, from marrying the woman of his choice. When police asked Aqsa's mother about her views of the murder, Mrs. Parvez replied, "I cannot say anything. Whatever he thinks . . ." *He* is Mr. Parvez, and he didn't regard strangling his daughter as a shameful act. Quite the inverse: Under the code of tribal honor, a woman is the vessel of shame. When she crosses the moral parameters set by men (custom, as it's typically known), she unleashes disrepute on her father's household. "She is making me naked," Mr. Parvez hyperventilated about Aqsa. "My community will say you have not been able to control your daughter." From the Islamo-tribal perspective, a father has no choice but to cleanse his family's reputation before the prying eyes of fellow Muslims—even in the cosmopolitan suburbs of Toronto.

As soon as the story became news, Islamo-tribalists in Canada went through their minuets of denial, for who knows what stresses plagued Aqsa's family? In media interviews I responded that killing can never, ever be an acceptable approach to relieving family stresses. Later, I received blistering emails saying that I need to learn basic morality because the Qur'an obliges faithful women to wear hijab — something that the "twin kafirs Irshad and Aqsa" hadn't yet fathomed.

Lord have mercy. Yet another instance of Islamo-tribalists blending culture with religion into a tall, stiff drink called the moral negligence martini (virgin, of course) and getting wasted on the stuff.

I educated my email buddies that hijab comes from a culture prior to Islam. The Qur'an, on the other hand, asks both women and men to dress modestly. Why can't this mean wearing long sleeves? And if a woman must cover her hair, why not with a baseball cap should she choose? Then again, why "must" she cover her hair? If you as a Muslim man worry about being aroused, why not do as the Qur'an recommends and glance down for as long as your hormones necessitate? Why does compensation have to be the exclusive cargo of women and girls?

Oddly, I didn't hear back from any of the Muslim men whose objections I took the time to address.

Odder still is politics among non-Muslims who should be allies of Aqsa, Bushra and Samia. In the United States, for example, liberals rarely call out illiberal Muslims as the cultural right-wingers that they are. More frequently, liberals enable the Muslim Right. After 9/11, the Interfaith Center of New York circulated a postcard. It showcased Muslim women of varied ages, sizes and skin colors praying side by side in the middle of a Manhattan thoroughfare. A fully veiled woman sat at the end of the prayer line. The picture became less conservative with each passing supplicant, but not to the point of including a Muslim woman who prays *without* a head-scarf. Every last one of the women is marked as a Muslim by her pre-Islamic mode of dress. Adding to the incoherence, the blurb on the back of the postcard celebrates "the diversity of Muslim communities in the city." Diversity? In the all-hijabi homage to Islam? Terminally stereotypical.

But maybe stereotypes matter only when they emanate from institutions trusted by neoconservatives. The FBI has buckled to demands by Muslim lobbyists that the phrase "honor killing" be excised from "Wanted" posters of men who allegedly murdered their daughters or wives for the sake of family honor. The take-no-prisoners FBI seems itself imprisoned by the fallacy of cultural rights. Moreover, the U.S. Army wouldn't allow its first Muslim woman corporal to serve as a chaplain. The reason: She can't lead men in prayer. It's not that she's unable; it's not that she's unwilling; it's that she's prohibited by the cultural norms of the Islamo-tribalists, male and female, whom the army consulted. The U.S. military can presume to fight for the equality of Muslim women, but not in America itself. Lady Liberty weeps.

This bias toward conservative Islam reaches beyond America too. When President George W. Bush authorized the invasion of Iraq, I made a brazenly naive assumption: that his administration would forge ties with Iraq's most consistent tribunes of democracy—secularists. Any committed alliance with them would have ensured that the new Iraqi constitution gave civil law more prominence than religious law. Muslim fanatics would then have been on notice that they couldn't get away with human rights violations by using Islam as cover.

But the opposite transpired. Newly "liberated," Iraq and Afghanistan have adopted Sharia supremacy clauses in their constitutions. Article Two of the Iraqi constitution makes clear that "no law that contradicts the established provisions of Islam may be passed." Any bets that Islamo-tribalists are the deciders, so to speak, of what's "established" in Islam? Article Three of Afghanistan's constitution states that "no law can be contrary to the beliefs and provisions of the sacred religion of Islam." The word "sacred" guarantees that the rulers of the day may do as they wish while assuming providential permission. Under George W. Bush, the United States sanctified these linguistic sleights of hand, caving to the logic of relativism—namely, that's the way those people do things and who are we to tell them otherwise?

Set aside the guilt-fueling phrase "Who are we?" I'll address that question in a moment. First, let's home in on the phrase "the way those people do things." Culture is how people do things. Or, more passively, how things are done. So culture is an intrinsically conservative concept. Muslim conservatives don't need the help of any liberal to keep the world as it is; they can handle the job all by themselves. It's countercultural Muslims—Aqsa, Bushra and Samia—who need all of us.

Thus my response to the question, "That's the way those people do things and who are we to tell them otherwise?" If you value moral courage—speaking truth to power within your community for a greater good—then you're someone who ought to prioritize individuality over groupthink. Which means you must consider what impact your action, or inaction, has on the individual who's striving to bring a fresh perspective to his or her community. When it involves life-and-death matters, your responsibility only heightens.

Martin Luther King, Jr., preached the same. Learning from Reinhold Niebuhr, the Christian theologian and lover of liberal democracy, King voiced an idea that would make multiculturalists squirm. He wrote, "Groups tend to be more immoral than individuals." Grasping this simple point loosens the grip of cultural correctness. Having spent her life studying the unintended consequences of cultural correctness, Unni Wikan brings us back to the reality of power politics within groups. Membership in any community has its price, "but the price is unevenly distributed. Those with the power to decide what is to count, and for what, will usually define custom or culture in such a way that its serves their own interests." In that case, "respect for 'the culture' is a flawed moral principle."

The remedy for cultural correctness comprises three tiny actions that any of us can take as individuals. One: Keep in mind that culture is a human construct, imperfect and therefore open to reform. Two: Ask a particular question. Three: Ask it habitually. The question: *When I respect custom, what does that do to the weaker members of the group?* Wikan's research confirms that such a question is "necessary to prevent sacrifices on the altar of culture." She's talking about sacrifices foisted on the vulnerable—women and children, for example—when we fail to discuss power plays within cultures.

Martin Luther King, Jr., alerted his tepid white allies, the liberals of their day, to the same unconscious impulse in them. With their respect for law and order—how things are done—they were requiring of blacks an unjust sacrifice, unjust in the first instance because even liberals wouldn't tolerate making such a sacrifice themselves. In his "Letter from Birmingham Jail," King argued, "An unjust law is a code that a numerical or power majority group inflicts on a minority group but does not make binding on itself." He offered this explanation to Alabama clergymen who, although in favor of civil rights, felt squeamish about moving too fast.

Do you see the parallel between their attitude and ours? Their desire for change, but not too much and not too soon, was fundamentally selfish. It kept the burden of pain on the most vulnerable, those who had no say in the system.

Today, many of us replicate that mistake by making the dignity of Islam's most vulnerable someone else's problem. Even more selfishly, we impose sacrifices on the vulnerable so we can feel good about ourselves. And we feel good about ourselves by looking good to the people we truly esteem: the powers-that-be within certain cultural communities. Without thinking twice, or even once, we empower illiberal Muslims as if that's the liberal thing to do. We thereby corrode the soul of liberalism: individual liberty.

Here's the culminating paradox. It's not just Muslims who labor under a code of tribal honor; in matters Islamic, non-Muslims have come to do so too. Group honor demands a singular focus on one's public image, despite the prodding of personal conscience. But if we're going to expand liberty, we have to think about how steeped we all are in the culture of group honor. Then we have to rethink the very meaning of honor. Should it be about your reputation, or should it be about your integrity?

4

YOU DEFINE YOUR HONOR

Ms. Manji, my name is Haroun and I am from the UK. I think you should know that I am in fact one of your cousins. However, while most of my family have a very negative view of you and your opinions, I do not. I believe that your intentions and ambitions are admirable, and though I have only read extracts of your book, I can see your viewpoint and in most cases even agree with it. The reason I have not purchased it is because I am not allowed to do so—for the reason that the people within my family refuse to even listen. I am deeply enraged by this.

While as a child I was forced to agree with my parents, as well as my madressa teachers, I am now 15 years old and have come to terms with the fact that not everything I hear is true. These people find it hard to even consider the idea that perhaps not all of what we are told by the [clerics] is true, and because of this, they believe that you are sending out negative views of Islam. Most of these people haven't even read your book, but every time I try to argue this point over (that they cannot make a rational decision without at least consulting the book first), they argue back with family history (which I also believe is biased) or claim me to be unreligious and unpatriotic to my faith.

Just like you, I am sick of the culture that Muslims have embraced today. I see some Muslims living normal lives and embracing the cultures of East and West, but there are others (my family in particular) who are still stuck in one culture. I see them forcing religious ideas into the minds of their children and not allowing them to question it. They are just producing what I refer to as "machines," people who do not know what they are practicing or why they are doing it.

I agree with you that people are treated unfairly in culture. Though I am not homosexual myself, I am sorry that they are constantly harassed and subjected to hate. People are people, regardless of sexual preference, race, religion, or personal belief. This is why I am angered when I see others mocking what I believe is an admirable action by yourself.

I can see that while you have not dismissed your heritage, you have adopted a style of Islam that allows you to connect to both Eastern and Western cultures. I will get a copy of your book, even if that means I have to buy it in secret!

Lesson four: *You define your honor.*

────────

While many Muslims contend with a culture of honor that lionizes the family's name above all else, non-Muslims may speak their minds—in theory. In fact, too many non-Muslims remain paralyzed by the fear of being dishonored as bigots if they talk about the putrid abuses of power within contemporary Muslim cultures. Eileen, a reader in Belfast, wrote me a message that echoes others I've received:

It is time we had the moral courage to admit the truths that you tell in public. But it is difficult for non-Muslim women to criticize the treatment of women in Islam without being wrongly accused of racism. I work with women who have been raped and abused. I have no doubts about how the Christian religion has also been used to subjugate women. However, the honor killings, female genital mutilation and forced marriages taking place in Western societies have been ignored for too long under the guise of respecting other cultures. It is time that all decent people, regardless of race, religion, or gender, stood up against violence and tyranny.

To Eileen, I replied, "Right on!" I also observed that Westerners today often want it both ways, touting the universality of human rights alongside the equality of all cultures. "But that's not sustainable," I explained. "Because if you believe that all human beings are entitled to basic dignities, then cultural practices that violate those dignities can't be defended." Those with the most power in any group, community or society have the swagger to stipulate what "respect" is. There's no escaping their hubris. What *can* change is our submission to their hubris. Our consciences murmur what our heads already know: that mistreating a community's least powerful members is manifestly unconscionable. To give our consciences the upper hand, we need to ask straightforward questions. I've already suggested some and I'll put more on the table.

Preparing ourselves to ask questions means confronting personal insecurities. Non-Muslims sheepishly tell me that "if I support your efforts to reconcile Islam with freedom, I'll be called an imperialist for shoving my nose in other people's business." Yes, you will be called an imperialist for giving a damn about human dignity. Get used to it. But you don't have to believe it. In a world where your country's safety is bound up in village politics far away, where your investments rise and fall with the fortunes of nations you might never go to, where the evaporation of glaciers will dent the sunbelt in another hemisphere, and where the concept of "interdependence" has spread well beyond college seminars, is there really such a thing as "other" people's business?

Not to Martin Luther King, Jr. Recall the eight Alabama clergymen whom I mentioned in the previous chapter. They reprimanded King as an "outsider" because he didn't live in Birmingham and couldn't know the local culture; therefore, he had no business transporting the fight for equality beyond the formal courtroom to the hurly-burly of Birmingham's streets. King responded with the reality of interdependence: "We are caught in an inescapable network of mutuality, tied in a single garment of destiny. Whatever affects one directly, affects all indirectly. Never again can we afford to live with the narrow, provincial 'outside agitator' idea." It's one of King's most famous statements, but its significance for the twenty-first century has yet to sink in.

Vehement emotions underlie our deference to group honor. Just look at non-Muslims who, hell-bent on being approved by Muslims, immediately deprecate themselves. "I'm the overweight, nosy American who eavesdropped on your interviews in Oxford last week," Karl wrote me from (of all places) Birmingham, Alabama. He was referring to the days after the July 2005 London transit bombings when, by coincidence, I'd been scheduled to speak at a conference on the grounds of Oxford University. Journalists turned up in full force and Karl listened in.

Between interviews, I had a casual conversation with him. Given the ease with which we talked, he didn't have to put himself down in a follow-up email to me. Karl felt less sure of that. He continued: "You politely answered my simpleton question about Islam without denigrating it, me, or my motivation. Thanks!" He told me of his past attempts to converse with Muslims. Every time, "I've gotten nearly the same reply, which is more or less along the lines of 'who are you to question . . .'" Not wanting to be misunderstood again, Karl audited himself to come off as exceedingly sincere, even to a Muslim who already saw him as such. It's as if the only choice was between eggshells and bombshells.

"I really don't hate you," congenial non-Muslims want Muslims to know. "And I'll go the extra mile not to hurt your feelings. I'll fib if I have to." The popular American situation comedy *Will & Grace* lifted the lid on this willingness to lie as part of multiculturalism's intricate poker game. Grace, an interior designer, is a straight, white, Jewish woman who lives in New York with Will, a lawyer and gay white man. Their differences, accentuated by her neuroses, mean Grace is always ready for a duel of the divas. Except when she hires an Iranian woman as her assistant. Neurotic herself, the new assistant destroys one of Grace's designs, tosses her chewing gum in and crams it all into the garbage can. A flabbergasted Grace objects, "It took two years to come up with that design!"

"It took me eighteen years to raise the money for my plane ticket to America," the assistant strikes back. "You don't see me yelling at you!" Grace apologizes. Moments later, the assistant mentions her bat mitzvah, the ceremony that inaugurates a Jewish girl into womanhood.

"You're Jewish?" Grace gasps. "This is great! I'm Jewish too! I don't have to be tolerant of my own kind. I don't owe you anything. You're fired. See you at temple!"

Can honesty and honor be reconciled? Abraham Lincoln, whose presidential leadership helped save America's union, recorded this as his deepest ambition: "Being truly esteemed by my fellow men, by rendering myself worthy of esteem." But Lincoln openly sympathized with slaves, some of the least powerful in his society. If Lincoln craved adulation, why didn't he simply conform? Because Lincoln wanted "to be 'truly' esteemed, not merely esteemed," writes the historian Robert Faulkner. Honest Abe sought approval "not by mere public opinion, but rather by the opinion of a discriminating public." A public, that is, whose members rein in their passions long enough to think.

It's an arresting hint for today. Why would you care to be held in high regard by any Muslim who won't have a rational discussion with you about your questions of Islam? If he or she won't make the effort to hear your views in the spirit in which you intend them, then what renders that person's judgment of you worth *your* while? Arthur Schopenhauer, the philosopher, raised a similar question: "Would a musician feel flattered by the loud applause of his audience if it were known to him that, with the exception of one or two, it consisted entirely of deaf people?" Holy harmonica. All these years I've been channeling my inner Schopenhauer. I've often had to break it to my detractors that "you assume I seek your approval. I don't. The only approval that matters to me comes from my conscience and my Creator." With that clarification out of the way, the choice facing my critics is to take their leave or to engage with my questions.

On second thought, maybe I'm channeling my inner Oprah. Early in her megawatt media career, Oprah Winfrey attracted sniping from academics who likened her to the "mammy" in U.S. slave history. As the female house Negro tasked with caring for her master's children, the mammy paid more attention to white babies than to her own flesh and blood. Oprah, went the charge, showed more interest in cultivating a white audience than in sustaining the black sisterhood. "That was the hardest thing for me in the beginning," the queen of talk TV later unloaded to an African American women's magazine. "I used to get criticism all the time." Then the poet Maya Angelou told her, "You alone are enough. You don't have to explain anything else." For Oprah, the waters parted to reveal a sense of honor that's self-determined: "I finally got it. Just because you're part of my culture doesn't mean you can decide for me. . . . Once I got that, I was free." I feel her freedom. How sweet it is.

In *Status Anxiety*, Alain de Botton shows that, through the ages, those with something to accomplish in life have felt stalked by how they're perceived in the process. But to achieve anything at all, we have to subject our critics to the test of reason. As one example, he turns to Marcus Aurelius, the Roman emperor. Aurelius asked his fellow Romans, "Does what is praised become *better*? Does an emerald become *worse* if it isn't praised? And what of gold, ivory, a flower or a little plant?" Behold the power of questioning—out loud!

On third thought, did Aurelius forget how tender egos are? What most of us fret about isn't the intrinsic beauty of the emerald. We know jewels don't become better just because they're praised, but this knowledge is so spectacularly beside the point. It's public perception of the gem that needles us, because that undoubtedly does alter the value it's presumed to have. Doesn't the same go for public perception of us?

Salman Rushdie appreciates a thing or two about being judged. His novel *The Satanic Verses* contains 5 pages (out of 550) that shocked a puny hive of British Muslims. They in turn torched his effigy and called for his assassination. The controversy flared at an opportune time for the Ayatollah Khomeini, who needed to divert Iranians from their country's mounting casualties in the Iran-Iraq War. The Ayatollah announced a multimillion-dollar bounty on the head of the author-cum-kafir. Little did it matter that in his novel Rushdie ushers us into the self-made prisons of people who take the perceptions of others too literally. In a prescient stroke, he brings the protagonist, Saladin Chamcha, to a holding tank for illegal immigrants. Saladin can't help but notice that the incarcerated humans have morphed into animals. Some are scaly reptiles; others, hairy buffaloes. Saladin himself becomes a goat and wonders to an inmate how all this has happened. The inmate mutters dryly, "They describe us. That's all. They have the power of description and we succumb to the pictures they construct."

Isn't this part of what's tormenting good people today? The wardens of cultural sensitivity describe any critic of Muslims as an Islamophobe. Soon enough, those of us with uncomfortable questions start to believe that's what we are. So we gag ourselves instead of asking more questions like, *How does wishing for dialogue make me an Islamophobe? Wouldn't I be keeping my distance—out of fear—if I were phobic?* But asking questions takes emotional excavation. It jeopardizes your standing among those who feel queasy and feel, further, that you should too. Much easier to let it go.

Easier, but not terribly useful. During a trip to Egypt in May 2006 for the World Economic Forum, I moderated a roundtable discussion of Middle Eastern and North African youth. The Palestinian delegates grumbled that their politicians treat them as "suspect" and "deviant." Innovative ideas are tarred as "dangerous" by "inaccessible" elders. Then this: "We cannot keep blaming the Israelis for our problems. We all know that opinions in our Arab societies are determined by family loyalties instead of reason. My brother and I against my cousin; my cousin, brother and I against an external threat." Nobody disputed that claim. Trust me, these students knew how to argue. You should have seen the Saudi girls rip into the guys. Whatever their grievances with each other, everyone concluded that liberation means succeeding on your own terms—as individuals, not as mascots of family or clan honor. Like the students I'd met at An-Najah National University in February 2005, these young Palestinians proclaimed a fantasy fatwa against the occupations of both Israeli soldiers and Arab oligarchs.

Their voices followed me into the next memorable event of my visit, which revolved around the *Arab World Competitiveness Report.* Having digested all the expert chatter about increasing access to education, technology and the arts, I took a deep breath. Then I took the floor. "The tribal code of honor prevents women and men from pursuing their dreams for fear of bringing shame on their families," I ventured. "What role does defying honor play in the Arab renaissance we're talking about here?" The shifting in seats reverberated in my pounding heart. "Be bold," I encouraged with what I hoped was a disarming smile. I was speaking to myself as much as to the panelists, but the responses skirted the issue. Afterward, a Syrian woman approached me to affirm that I'd asked "the great unspoken" question. "Why does it have to be unspoken?" I persisted. It shouldn't be, she replied. But "accusations of racism" carry a fatwa-like stigma of their own.

How many ways can one be disappointed when the very experts in innovation—innovation!—pander to failed formulas? When they do an end run around a new generation of potential visionaries? Above all, when they muzzle themselves despite having created the cushion of glorifying past Arab achievements in their report? And so the hamster wheel of honor rotates round and round, low expectations reinforcing each other.

I can't lay it on the business interests that run the World Economic Forum because honor-induced silence spans the gamut of ideologies. Sara Mohammad ought to enjoy the vocal support of Western feminists. A Kurdish-born woman living in Sweden, she arranges refuge for immigrant Arab girls being threatened with murder in the name of family honor. The crime that vaulted her into action involved a young woman, Fadime, who successfully sued her father and brother for their death threats against her and her Swedish boyfriend, Patrik. Shortly after the court case—on the day he and Fadime were to move in together—Patrik died in a car accident. Planning to leave Sweden, Fadime made a farewell stop to her mother and sisters. The farewell proved permanent. Fadime's mother tipped off her husband, who shot their daughter in the head.

"When Fadime was alive," writes journalist Rana Husseini, "she provoked sympathy among Swedes but there was little willingness to get involved in what was seen as a family matter. It was only once she was murdered that this young victim of an 'honor killing' drew a lot of attention to the cultural double standards she had battled for so long." Those double standards haven't been buried with Fadime, says Sara Mohammad, the rescuer of girls endangered by honor crimes in Sweden. More often than not, Swedish feminists reproach her because they're afraid of appearing intolerant toward Muslims.

That's emotion at work, and it's mind-boggling. Muslims who would brand Sara "intolerant" don't believe in saving those girls' lives. Should the opinions of moral troglodytes trump those of Muslims who defend human dignity? "It's insane," raves a member of my Facebook community, "that we have arrived at the point where we worry about offending people who not only care so little for life but who seem to find joy in grotesquely violating it."

Feminists argue that patriarchy is global. Has our handbook been completely rewritten? If so, where's my revised copy? And if not, then why should Muslim men be exempt from accountability? Do I have to remind my Swedish feminist friends that they're not exactly being inclusive by excluding Muslims from the club of adults?

These contradictions became even more transparent after Tiger Woods, then the world's top golfer, got busted for having multiple extramarital affairs. Elin Nordegren, his Stockholm-born wife, allegedly swung a golf club at his head. (He denied getting thwacked.) "Swing it again, Elin!" erupted Jan Helin, editor in chief of the prestigious Swedish newspaper *Aftonbladet*. "Next time, I hope she uses a bigger club," snorted one of his star reporters, Ann Söderlund.

Britta Svensson, a columnist for *Expressen*, professed that "our Swedish hearts are overwhelmed with pride, because our very own Elin didn't take any s***. Just like a tough Swedish girl shouldn't. Elin is our heroine."

Why wouldn't more Swedish feminists want for immigrant Arab girls the independence of mind, heart and soul that they admire in Elin? Is it that Elin is "our very own" and Arab migrants aren't? Is it that Swedish feminists have faith in Elin's ability to fight but not in an Arab girl's ability to do so? Have we come back to the all-important distinction between capacity and attachment?

Personally, I have faith in the capacity of more Swedish women—indeed, more people everywhere—to grow beyond multicultural orthodoxy. In the wake of Fadime's murder, *Aftonbladet* monitored public debate. The overriding divide, it found, had less to do with natives versus immigrants than with human values versus patriarchal traditions. That's the *right* divide. But it's not the only reason I stand by my higher expectations of Swedes. After touring Stockholm in 2009, I received an email from "just an 'ordinary' girl in Sweden," as she described herself. She urged me to stay strong. Then she wrote, "This is very strange for me, but I can't stop thinking, you sound like the next Olof Palme." Prime Minister Palme led Sweden's Social Democratic Party and was gunned down on a Stockholm street in 1986. Millions of Swedes cherish Palme's "revolutionary reformist" spirit, as it's been characterized. One of them is the "ordinary" girl who relates to me, a Muslim, through the prism of a Swedish hero. (I would have pegged myself more as Pippi Longstocking than as Olof Palme, but either one exhilarates!) Since she can hear my challenge, there's every reason to expect that her compatriots can also unblock their hearts to it.

A thoroughgoing Swede, our girl flirted with the fear of being perceived as a racist. "I am not against islam or the koran," she assured early in her email, adding that Islam "is nothing that affects my life so far." But it does. This is what non-Muslims must finally realize in order to appreciate why the business of Muslims is their business too. When the culture of honor becomes enmeshed with the practice of Islam, it's a problem for the whole world.

I'll now synthesize the moving parts. According to Islamo-tribalists, shame resides in the woman. Much more so than her brothers, sons or uncles, a woman bears the freight of her entire family's reputation. In effect, men are off the hook. They're assumed to be morally weak, so they can be exonerated for their choices. Since men have all the self-restraint of children, it's up to women to curtail their choices. Which is why women must cover their hair and sometimes their entire bodies. They're compensating for the inherent deficiency of men who neglect the Qur'an's guidance that they lower their gaze in front of women. It's also why a woman may not lead congregational prayers; men wouldn't be able to hold themselves together at the sight of a woman's rear. After all, we're told, they're not capable of following the Qur'an to begin with.

To say that this cultural assumption about men demeans both sexes is to understate understatement. Because Arab norms set infantile expectations of men, something else emerges: a victim mentality that allows Muslim men to commit assorted abuses of power, including rampages against anybody who seemingly humiliates their frail and fragmented sense of self. Whether real or imagined, their trauma imperils the security of more people, from their own families to citizens of the West.

If I'm crackers, then so is sociologist Fatema Mernissi. The "modesty of the Arab woman is the linchpin" of the system, she writes. In current Islamic practice, which confuses culture with faith, women find themselves "suppressed by the law of the group. Condemned for so long to silence, their song rhymes 'liberty' with 'individuality.'" Where the Muslim woman has the psychic space to rise up—in open societies such as Europe, North America and Australia—notions of Muslim manhood can also mature. But not if she's forced into burqa-style modesty, for "how, please tell me, can the masculine be distinguished if the feminine is banned from sight, if femaleness is a black hole, a silent gap, an absent face?"

Mernissi's question leads us to why this is everybody's fight. What she refers to as "the crippling effects of segregation" only start with women. They add up to a far-reaching fear of the Other, with Islamo-tribalists dividing humanity between two politicized categories: the foreign and the authentic. "Identifying democracy as a Western malady, decking it out in the chador of foreignness, is a strategic operation worth millions of petrodollars."

As we know, that strategy has global repercussions. In an interdependent world, what's internal to Islam can have seismic implications for what's external to Islam. It's in everyone's interest to reform cultural norms that undermine everyone's dignity, be they men or women, Muslim or non-Muslim.

"You want to talk cultural norms that undermine everyone's dignity?" I can imagine the conversation heating up. "Try the wretched code of honor in the U.S. South. It stoked the arrogance of white masters who enslaved not only 'their' women but black folk as well. Put that in your hookah pipe and smoke it!" Pipe down. I'm with you. America's original sin, slavery, drew sustenance from a homegrown culture of honor whose entire apparatus of oppression revolved around maintaining the reputations of white men. Laws prohibited literacy for blacks in order to "close off external sources of contamination," as Kenneth S. Greenberg documents in *Honor & Slavery*. In court, the testimonies of blacks held next to no worth—if entered at all. And slave rape, among other forms of violence against blacks, didn't register with the government as actual felonies.

Unni Wikan's warning that culture is shot through with power clangs loud and clear here. One story told by Greenberg stands in for countless more:

> *Harriet Jacobs well understood the relation between honor and power when she tried to maintain the mask of respectability as she fought off the sexual advances of her master. When she turned fifteen, her fifty-year-old owner, Dr. James Norcom, "began to whisper foul words" in her ear. "He told me I was his property," Jacobs later recalled, "that I must be subject to his will in all things." He followed her everywhere trying to get her to submit to his advances—even as she walked outside after a day of work, or knelt by the side of her mother's grave. Sometimes he held a razor to her throat.*

Today, most Americans take pride in the fact that the cruelest elements of their Southern culture got whupped. "We defeated those ideas and the individuals, leaders and institutions that propagated them, and we did it with such ferocity that five generations later some of their offspring still have not forgiven the North." So wrote Tom Friedman, the *New York Times* foreign affairs columnist, in a commentary about the need for a root-and-branch routing of violent jihadists. It's urgent not only from a counterterrorism perspective, but also from a human rights one.

After all, the honor culture that propped up master-slave relationships in America has striking similarities to honor culture in

Arab (and Arabized) communities. Illiteracy among women and girls, though lower now than twenty years ago, is widely cited as holding back Arab economic development. Moreover, honor-based crimes against women often don't get catalogued as crimes at all since the testimonies of women carry little legitimacy. Even when Muslim men commit honor crimes in the West, it's not unusual to hear them demand that they deal solely with male police officers. All women are beneath them.

Finally, like the commodified Harriet Jacobs, women who live under the tribal code of honor are owned by their masters. A husband-to-be, notes Rana Husseini, considers virginity as "evidence of exclusive possession." The blood of his bride's broken hymen proves that "the 'merchandise' is brand new and his wife will not be able to compare his performance unfavorably to that of another man." When rumors circulate that the merchandise has been spotted with an unrelated man, her owner may act with a draconian version of buyer's remorse. He can murder her.

In Jordan, Husseini has interviewed young men who excuse their subhuman treatment of women as a cultural command. "No, I do not regret killing Kifaya," Khalid admitted about his sister. In retrospect, though, he'd make another choice for how to deal with his property: "I would tie her up like a sheep in the house until she either died or someone married her." On a different occasion, Husseini spoke with Sarhan, who pumped bullets into his sister after a brother-in-law raped her. No longer a virgin, Yasmin became damaged goods. Only sacrificing her would restore the household's name, a skewed definition of honor that turns the victim into vermin.

Adding insult to injury is the infantilizing of the perpetrators. Like Khalid, Sarhan pleaded helplessness. "No one wants to be the one to kill his sister," he told Husseini, "but traditions and society inflict things on us." Would he do it again? "I would kill my sister and any other sister who goes through the same thing. This is our society, this is how we are brought up and it will never change."

Never? Husseini has higher expectations of, and more faith in, her fellow Jordanians. She and a handful of friends struck a committee to demand that Jordan's penal code be reformed. In their opening petition they described themselves as "free individuals" mobilized by "one unifying issue": a society that "abides by the Constitution that assures equality to all in front of the law in rights and duties." Martin Luther King, Jr., would have beamed. Husseini's committee heard from male teachers who wanted to know if their students could also sign the petition. She bounced from customer to customer in restaurants—"a captive audience!"—who often "gladly signed." So did "waiters, waitresses, cooks, cleaners and managers." Even a garbage collector got in on the action. "Of course I will sign," she remembers him saying, because honor-based crime is "against our religion." A far cry from the Jordanian cabinet minister who once moaned to Husseini, "What can we do? The concept of (family) honor is socially imbedded in our society."

When politicians finally touched the issue, they voted so fast that Husseini "almost missed it." She ruefully reports, "The bill was rejected without even the dignity of a count of hands." But never say never. Two days later, despite a former royal adviser assuring Husseini that Jordan's monarchy won't provoke the traditionalists who dominate its power base, Prince Ali called for a march to Parliament in "protest against honor killings." Husseini's committee once again issued a press release insisting that "each one of us has individual rights."

Jordan's penal code remains unchanged, although the committee's efforts have scored two new laws. One of them relaxes the rules for Jordanian women seeking divorce, a minor miracle given that no female member of Parliament attended the rally for this proposal. According to Husseini, "They all entered the Parliament building via the back door that day." As revealing—for the better—is another evolution: Judicial prejudices appear to be dissolving in Jordan. Sarhan, who killed his already-raped sister Yasmin, had a judge who went easy on him. Erasing the individual who premeditated a course of action, the judge told Husseini that "this murder was a product of our culture." Now, she writes with a patina of relief, "judges and criminal prosecutors are keen to call to my attention harsh verdicts they have seen. . . . [In] many instances, the judiciary has rejected the fit of fury argument."

While mounds of credit must go to the moral courage of Husseini's campaign, she reserves some applause for a British-funded program that trained judges, prosecutors, police, investigators, doctors, social workers and even religious scholars to care more about crimes against women. Those efforts, she believes, paid off in a "landmark case" involving two sisters hacked by their ax-toting brothers. The women couldn't be spared. The perps, however, got longer sentences than any Jordanian would have expected even a decade earlier.

As in Jordan, tribal honor in the U.S. South didn't erode instantly, but neither was it left to crumble on its own. Foreign interference— the snarky term that some would use today—accelerated domestic efforts. In 1788, for example, a British potter and antislavery activist, Josiah Wedgwood, sent Benjamin Franklin medallions that featured a kneeling African, hands and feet in manacles, asking his fellow human beings, "Am I Not a Man and a Brother?" That message from Britain would electrify America's antislavery movement. Whether we're talking abolitionists across the pond or individuals in Canada and the northern United States who helped slaves break free through the Underground Railroad, these sons and daughters not-of-the-South chipped away at an edifice that looked as if it could never collapse.

A century later, as slavery's segregationist residue had to be tackled, civil rights marchers clasped arms with Christians, Jews, agnostics and atheists of varied hues. Rosa Parks, the black seamstress who wouldn't give up her bus seat to a white man, couldn't have made that December 1955 trip—and made it such a milestone for human dignity—without first being trained in social activism by both whites and blacks.

For all the laws that passed before and after her celebrated act, enforcement of the law lagged. So Northerners and Southerners had to collaborate again. In May 1961, seven black and six white volunteers sat side by side on the Freedom Ride, a bus voyage through the segregated holdouts of the Deep South. The riders included a Michigan union member, a Tennessee theology student, a navy captain and a Wall Street broker. Soon enough, a mob besieged their bus, slashing the tires, firebombing it, then holding the doors shut, the faster to incinerate every passenger. Barely escaping, the first team of Freedom Riders was replaced by a second—this one whaled on by Ku Klux Klan members. With impunity granted by police, Klansmen singled out whites for especially ruthless thrashings. Among them: a justice department official dispatched by Attorney General Robert F. Kennedy to join the Freedom Riders.

Abandoned by ambulances, the bloodied got whisked to hospitals by local blacks, themselves showing the moral courage to interfere. Without "interference"—the activism of individuals where they weren't wanted—there could be no reconciliation. Indeed, the Freedom Rides germinated out of a 1947 bus trip led by civil rights titan Bayard Rustin and known as the Journey of Reconciliation.

All along the uphill path to reconciliation, whites gave serious financial support. An elderly Jewish man told me of his meeting with Rustin, then the chief organizer of the 1963 March on Washington at which Martin Luther King, Jr., would enunciate his dream. Rustin had come to the man for funds, explaining that Jews could always be counted on to donate more than anybody, even when they had less to part with. The Jews' own enslavement in ancient times remains, for many, the reason for empathy and action.

Today, women in Iran fight for their equality using lessons from the American and British antislavery movements. An Iranian activist wonders just "how moral is a society that treats one sex as a kind of master race and the other as a collection of servants with few or no rights?" Her question leaps off the page of a book about the Iranian Women's One Million Signatures Campaign for Equality, which educates women as it collects their signatures. If petitions sound like an anemic approach to changing laws, remember abolitionist history. "What really worked" to end Britain's role in the transatlantic slave trade "was the national campaign of petitions to Parliament," notes Kwame Anthony Appiah in *The Honor Code: How Moral Revolutions Happen*. In America, signatures took on a significance that bullheaded politicians didn't bargain for. At one point Congress banned antislavery petitions. That move trampled on freedom of speech for white people, which propelled more and more petitions over the years. In time, slavery came to be seen as an enemy of everybody's liberties. The Iranian Women's One Million Signatures Campaign has this universalizing pedigree.

From the Americas to the Arab world, from Iran to India, reforming honor culture needs all hands on deck. Rana Husseini explicitly advocates "individual rights" as the goad. Even in the West, individual rights have to be taken more seriously. British police are reopening murder cases in the belated understanding that they may have been honor killings. Police, God bless them, have a strange burden in our multicultural age. They must uphold order, but in precincts such as the mosque, upholding order can be a mammoth vote for the further empowerment of Islamo-tribalists. Public security suffers when the police remain neutral.

They ought to listen to countercultural Muslims such as Asra Nomani. In February 2010, Nomani wrote about an uprising against gender segregation at the Islamic Center of Washington, D.C. In "a moment akin to Rosa Parks' refusal to give up her seat," four Muslim women prayed in the men's section of the mosque. D.C. police, contacted by mosque officials, confronted the demonstrators:

> *Police officer Barry Goodwin soon arrived and awkwardly walked over to the line of women. . . . "I'm not a Muslim. I'm just here to do my job," he said politely. "Ladies, this is how it works. You have to obey the rules of the church here. . . . I'm sorry. The church or temple. However you want to call it. You have to obey the rules. . . . If they ask you to leave, you have to leave." Failure to leave, he pointed out, would be grounds for arrest for unlawful entry."*

Nomani tried to help Officer Goodwin, an African American, understand the stakes:

> *"Think sit-ins, 1960s," I said. If he appreciated my history lesson, he didn't acknowledge it. He walked outside for backup. The conflict escalated when Police Officer R. S. Lowery threatened to arrest the women if they refused to leave.*

Lest anybody dismiss the relationship between an obscure sit-in at a Washington mosque and the future security of their children,

Nomani painted the mural for us—no doubt with her own little boy in mind. Whether a mosque segregates women from men "is an indicator of whether the interpretation of Islam being practiced is puritanical and dogmatic, or open and inclusive. This one choice is a harbinger ..." A harbinger of practices that enable "honor killings, suicide bombings [and] violence" in general. Not coincidentally, Nomani added, "this week, a hard-line Saudi cleric issued a fatwa on his Arabic-language website calling for the killing of Muslims who don't enforce strict gender segregation."

None of this is to portray non-Muslim America as squeaky-clean. Shades of patriarchal honor blight the U.S. Christian landscape too. Shortly after Nomani's report, I read in the news about a Bible-based pamphlet floating around Bristol, Virginia, and arguing that women, dressed just so, "make men want to be sinful." It turns out that Christian males can't rein in their lusts either. When raped, the pamphlet asks, can such women "really say they were innocent victims?"

I reflected on why these age-old calumnies about the lasciviousness of women and the childishness of men would be considered news. The article, I think, answered my question. It accurately described the pamphlet as an "exceptionally extreme" Christian example of those canards. Yet my own inbox bulges with messages from moderate Muslim men (and some women) who swear by the pamphlet's views. When the women-make-men-do-it defense becomes "exceptionally extreme" among Muslims, honor will have been rethought.

Arabs such as Rana Husseini, Americans such as Asra Nomani, Indians such as Akbar Ladak and Europeans such as Sara Moham-mad offer hope that honor can be founded on one's personal con-science rather than on opaque group consensus. As agents of moral courage, these individuals stand atop the shoulders of Frederick

Douglass, the nineteenth-century fugitive slave and master of self. For him, "a patriot is a lover of his country who rebukes and does not excuse its sins." I live for the day when more Muslims will declare—with unflappable confidence—that "a true believer is a lover of his God who rebukes and does not excuse the sins of custom."

Until then, we'll have young Muslims in Detroit who quake at the thought of expressing their Douglass-like spiritual patriotism. We'll have Muslim students at Harvard and MIT who forfeit their names when opposing a man with a penchant for seeing ex-Muslims put to death. We'll have a rising number of Muslim women in the West fleeing home, their pain compounded by supposedly benign social welfare workers. These Muslims appear to be living in freedom, but tribal honor too often represses what's real about them. As it does to non-Muslims who would ask questions out loud were it not for the dishonor of being thought "anti-Islam." A fatal symbiosis.

Individuality is the essence of a redefined honor, one that impels each of us to do what's right despite how we're judged by those who confuse feeling with thinking. My mind turns to my cousin, Haroun. Living in Britain, he could easily finger the catchall specter of racism as the source of his humiliation. Instead, he's "enraged" at his family, who force-feed him convictions. Haroun hungers for autonomy. Subversive acts—buying a book in secret—serve as a statement that his honor is precisely that: his. To keep going, self-aware Haroun will need the support of a wider community. Who steps up to the plate, and how, matters. It's time for a concrete example of how more of us can stand by young Muslims in the quest to reconcile faith and freedom.

———

Since the 2005 London bombings, I've spoken with a number of Muslim men who knew the twenty-nine-year-old ringleader,

Mohammad Sidique Khan. Independently of each other, they've emphasized to me that Khan left his family's moderate mosque for a Saudi-financed surrogate down the road. There, he could examine theology and upend mainstream imams whose feudal traditions ooze the warning: *Do as you're told.*

It must have been galling for Khan to experience such condescension at his family's mosque. Being treated like an infant didn't quite square with the fact that Khan and his mates had already taken the initiative to combat drug addiction and crime in their neighborhood. They baptized themselves the Mullah Boys. These mullahs detested their parents' out-of-touch clerics, whose tribal bent shunned Khan's brain and almost shattered his heart.

He passionately wanted to marry an Indian Muslim from outside his clannish Pakistani community, only to be forbidden by his parents and their *pir*, the traditional religious authority they brought in to dissuade their son. Islamists—Muslims who treat Islam as a political ideology—grabbed hold of Khan's grief. They assured him that his family deformed Islam by preventing his nuptials merely because the bride-to-be was culturally unsavory. On this one, the Islamists spoke truth. Luring the lovesick Khan to their mosque, they plied him with more reasons to feel humiliated: Iraq, Afghanistan, Chechnya, Palestine, Kashmir.

Shiv Malik, an investigative journalist, dissected Khan's radicalization. Malik concluded:

> *Khan may have felt indignant about western foreign policy, as many anti-war campaigners do, but that wasn't the reason he led a cell of young men to kill themselves and 52 London commuters. At the heart of this tragedy is a conflict between the first and subsequent generations of British Pakistanis—with many young people using Islamism as a kind of liberation theology to assert*

their right to choose how to live. It is a conflict between tradition and individuality, culture and religion, tribalism and universalism, passivity and action.

Before hooking up with Islamists, suppose Mohammad Sidique Khan had met Abdul Ghaffar Khan. "Abdul who?" you might ask. Abdul. Ghaffar. Khan. He's sometimes known as Badshah—"the King"—except that he donned no regalia. What Ghaffar Khan did was to build an army of God that performed community service and fought imperialism with the arsenal of nonviolence. Mahatma Gandhi considered it a precedent for humanity. Those who despair that you can't define honor for yourself need to hear the story of a tall, strapping and faithful Muslim man who deserves to be heralded in his own right, but for our purposes is the answer to the long-standing question "Where is Islam's Gandhi?"

Abdul Ghaffar Khan was a twentieth-century Muslim reformer. The son of a middling landowner, he lived in the region we refer to today as the North West Frontier Province of Pakistan, an area now teeming with the Taliban. Life there could have taken a much different turn. And for a while, it did. In the years leading up to India's independence in 1947, thousands of Khan's people, the Pathans, reinterpreted honor and Islam. They showed that freedom comes from disciplining the self, not conquering the Other. Root out the fear within ourselves and our communities, these Pathans believed, and you'll seed a type of honor that ennobles every individual, including the female.

Ghaffar Khan's movement marched up to—and into—the volcano of segregationist tradition. "One of his first concerns was the role of women," observes the biographer and peace educator Eknath Easwaran. Ghaffar Khan "encouraged them to come out from behind the veil, as the women in his own family had done." His sister often toured the Frontier with him, addressing crowds herself as well as listening to the fiery orations of her brother. He knew his Qur'an, choosing to publicize those rarely recited passages that give women and men equal responsibilities. "My sisters," Ghaffar Khan announced to a large gathering,

> *God makes no distinction between men and women. If someone can surpass another, it is only through good deeds and morals. If you study history, you will see that there were many scholars and poets amongst women. It is a grave mistake we have made in degrading women. . . . Today we are the followers of custom and we oppress you. But thank God that we have realized that our gain and loss, progress and downfall, are common.*

Ghaffar Khan didn't limit his empowerment efforts to speeches. He established a school for girls and published a journal, *Pushtun*, that questioned honor-drenched practices. In one issue, a contributor named Nagiria tells it as she sees it. "Except for the Pathan," she asserts, "the women have no enemy. He is clever but is ardent in suppressing women. . . . O Pathan, when you demand your freedom, why do you deny it to women?"

Both women and men demanded freedom from the British. As part of northern India, the Frontier was as colonized as the rest of the subcontinent, and maybe more so: Britain used the Pathan province as a rampart to keep imperial Russia's influence at bay. When the Indian freedom struggle picked up speed, Ghaffar Khan's alliance with Gandhi dovetailed with his countercultural Islam to ensure that Muslim women would be central players. Notes the Gandhi scholar Joan V. Bondurant, "Pathan women participating in nonviolent action campaigns would frequently take their stand facing the police or would lie down in orderly lines holding copies of the Quran."

What did the proud Pathan men do? Some 100,000 became the Khudai Khidmatgars, or Servants of God. Ghaffar Khan recruited them as uniformed soldiers who would replace blood feuds with peaceful means to advance home rule for India. While "intensely Islamic," in the words of Bondurant, the Servants of God promoted Muslim-Hindu unity with moral courage. "He who forgives and is reconciled, his reward is with God," the soldiers learned. Gandhi came to view them as such dedicated exemplars of his nonviolent vision that he prayed the "Frontier Pathans may not make only India free, but teach the world." All this, despite being vilified by fellow Muslims who pressed for a separate homeland—Pakistan—and despite being brutalized by the British, who perceived the Pathans as incapable of rising above their vendettas with each other. Ghaffar Khan had higher expectations and deeper faith, which allowed him to glimpse possibilities that others waved off as hallucinations.

To be sure, his self-described "experiment" would be strewn with outbursts and near-mutinies. "Any animal can find a place to live, find a mate, rear its young," he lit into the locals at one meeting. "Can we call ourselves the crown of creation if we do just that and nothing more?" However mercenary the British could be, Ghaffar Khan charged, Pathan culture displayed worse "defects." He singled out the code of honor for pitting family against family, clan against clan, sowing fear in every generation for past humiliations yet to be avenged. Yet precisely because of their warring ways, Khan detected in the Pathans a certain steeliness. If redirected, that virtue could put them on the path to their liberty and Allah's love.

Ghaffar Khan dove headfirst into the experiment by getting to know himself, and thus the God that created him. Having engaged in introspection—fasting for days in mosques, harvesting fields in the Swat Valley, grinding corn in colonial prisons—he spent stretches of time learning to accept a mission whose origins he couldn't quite explain. Even before he knew of Gandhi, the young Pathan knew his own task: "to educate, to enlighten, to lift up, to inspire." Self-awareness also prevented the contortion of his spirit as he dealt with adversaries across the board. The British could harness every resource of empire to incite the already volatile Pathan nation, thereby justifying further beatings, jailings and hangings. The mullahs frothed at the mouth over foreign incursion—always good for almsgiving—and then colluded with the British Raj. Rich landlords banished the thought of a peasantry awakened. Nobody of consequence wanted ordinary Pathans to be chasing social reform, much less self-reform.

Only later did the gust of Gandhi become wind behind Ghaffar Khan's back. With the Mahatma's ideas animating India and vindicating his own, he sensed that the hour for collective introspection had arrived on the Frontier. Easwaran lets us in on Ghaffar Khan's thinking: "A nation that was unfit to fight, he had said, could not prove the virtue of not fighting. Well, Pathans were ahead there! All they needed was the understanding" —the understanding, that is, of each individual's capacity to reimagine his or her honor. "What could possibly take more bravado than facing an enemy in a righteous cause without weapons, neither retreating nor retaliating? It was the loftiest kind of honor."

And it all made exquisite sense until Ghaffar Khan and Mahatma Gandhi witnessed their dreams of Muslim-Hindu unity unravel. Pakistan, a state for Muslims, would be carved out of India, a Hindu-majority country. The August 1947 partition presaged yet more communal slaughter—and the worst news of all: In January 1948, Gandhi was killed. Ghaffar Khan lost his kindred spirit to a Hindu nationalist who accused the Mahatma of being too pro-Muslim. In turn, Ghaffar Khan incurred Muslim wrath for being too pro-Hindu. Pakistan banned the Servants of God, gutted their headquarters, imprisoned a thousand members and arrested and incarcerated Ghaffar Khan for sedition. Over the next four decades his life amounted to a series of penal sentences. At the age of ninety-five, he protested martial law in Pakistan, only to be rearrested.

Ghaffar Khan died in January 1988 in Peshawar, but not before announcing one last fast to stop Muslim-Hindu violence. "I have considered myself a part of you and you a part of me," he told the citizens of his birth country, India. "I have come to see for myself if I can be of some use."

I hope Ghaffar Khan knew how useful he'd one day be to liberty-loving Muslims and non-Muslims. His granite devotion to Allah confirms that Islam, shorn of tribal honor, can be reconciled with freedom and human rights.

For me, Ghaffar Khan's aborted legacy is something of a gauntlet. More of us will have to pick it up—and we can do that by becoming part of his proverbial village. His life attests to the fact that behind every agent of moral courage is another whom we don't know about yet. Gandhi's ability to defend Muslim-Hindu harmony would have been bolstered by his tight bond with Ghaffar Khan, who helped feed the Mahatma's moral courage.

Likewise, Ghaffar Khan's moral courage took nourishment from a nucleus of other individuals. There were his siblings, including his older brother, who openly backed his campaign for cultural reform. There were the Hindu, Christian and Muslim leaders of Indian independence who, jailed with Ghaffar Khan, interpreted each other's holy texts for an evolving, pluralistic nation. There was Annie Besant, a British woman living in India, who stood up to the savagery of her government and spoke up for the humanity of Pathans. There was Reverend Wigram, Ghaffar Khan's schoolmaster, who impressed the boy as being more invested in the excellence of Pathan children than many of their own parents were.

Above all, there was his father, Behram Khan, who sent his sons away for a British-run education in Peshawar despite the mullahs' mantra that "those who learn in schools are none but money's tools. In heaven they will never dwell; they will surely go to hell." It's not as if Behram Khan invited *them* to go to hell. Instead, writes Easwaran, he "was known throughout the district for a most un-Pathan-like quality: forgiveness." Over and over, he "chose to forgive rather than seek revenge—a decision that must have deeply influenced the character and career of his youngest son."

Sir John Maffey, a British official, once summoned Behram Khan to his office. "I have noticed," he intoned, "that your son is touring the villages and opening schools. . . . Would you kindly ask your boy to give up these activities? Tell him to stay at home like other people."

Behram Khan went to his son. "Father," Ghaffar Khan responded, "if everybody else stopped doing *lemundz* [daily prayer], would you advise me to follow their example?"

"God forbid!" the old man winced. "Lemundz is a sacred duty."

So is educating the people, Ghaffar Khan insisted, a subtle salute to his own father's bravery in sending his children to nontraditional schools.

Whether intimate or distant, these connections suggest that moral courage doesn't have to be the herculean act of one person toiling in isolation. Counterintuitive as it sounds, individuality takes a village. For the individual to leave a legacy that a new generation can build on, a network of people needs to get involved—before, during and after.

We come full circle to the ringleader of the London bombings. What if a teacher, employer or fellow congregant had told an increasingly agitated Mohammad Sidique Khan about Abdul Ghaffar Khan? That Ghaffar Khan had battled British policy, but did so by mobilizing the best in his fellow Muslims? That he helped his father develop more backbone, demolishing the feudal fable that youth have nothing to teach elders? That he would have even welcomed Mohammad Sidique Khan's intercultural marriage? Ghaffar Khan's own brother wed an Englishwoman. When asked by Gandhi whether his sister-in-law had converted to Islam, Ghaffar Khan replied, "Why should marriage alter one's faith?" No wonder the Mahatma lauded him as a "universalist."

Would this story have persuaded Mohammad Sidique Khan to educate his immigrant parents and dodge the Islamists? We can only know that it would have been worth the try. Ed Husain, an ex-jihadi who cofounded a counterterrorism center in London, says that he became radicalized, in part, by British society's low expectations of him as a young Muslim. "Nobody ever said you're equal to us, you're one of us, and we'll hold you to the same standards," Husain explains. "Nobody had the courage to stand up for liberal democracy without qualms. When people like us [at school] were holding events against women and against gay people, where were our college principals and teachers, challenging us?"

See why it takes a village? The principals and teachers wouldn't have to get all "secular is supreme" on students. They could simply challenge junior jihadis to hear the story of a valiant Muslim man who prayed diligently, recited the Qur'an, opposed imperialism and got the glamour of going to the slammer. Yet he also preached nonviolence to defeat the colonizers and encouraged women to jettison their veils. With that, don't bank on turning around jihadis-in-training; our audience is the swing vote whom they're seeking to influence.

Hence the value of *attempting* to talk about Ghaffar Khan at, say, a campus event. If the jihadi-types drown out the attempt, they'll expose their hypocrisy, and if they do let others listen, Ghaffar Khan's example will reach more ears and hearts, giving the assembled a reason to distill their anger in a different direction. As a mentor to young Muslims, Mohammad Sidique Khan might have found transcendent purpose in crusading peacefully for Islam's Gandhi to become a part of Britain's school curriculum.

There's an idea for the rest of us. Muslims and non-Muslims, parents, teachers and students, can grip this gauntlet by making Abdul Ghaffar Khan a lesson in local schools. I've incorporated him into my New York University course about moral courage; each of you can take it further by speaking to one educator. One librarian. One principal. One school board member. One city councilor. En route, wave goodbye to the complaint about not knowing what you can do.

All of which reinforces the larger point about what *we* can do. We have to legitimize countercultural Muslims as credible Muslims, not watered-down believers or Western wannabes. Abdul Ghaffar Khan never set foot in Europe or America, yet he epitomized universal values that Muslims, including the tens of millions of us who live in the West, can identify with through and through. Countercultural Muslims are his heirs. We're waging the next stage of a struggle to interpret Islam in ways that are bound to offend tribalists everywhere—just as Ghaffar Khan elicited shrieks from the mullahs, the woman-bashers and the Hindu-haters. Giving offense goes with the territory of fighting for diversity.

Many of us in democracies believe otherwise, emotionally browbeaten into accepting the illiberal notion that diversity is all about appearances. The embellished costumes. The rehashed scripts. The clichéd roles. The predictable performances. Another term for this confection? Acting. Truer diversity drills down to reach minorities within communities—the individuals with the unorthodox views. Individuality will always rattle assumptions and jar feelings. That's the nature of nonconformity. Offense, then, isn't a problem to duck at all costs. It *is* the cost of meaningful diversity.

Frederick Douglass, whose example taught Martin Luther King, Jr., adds perspective. "Those who profess to favor freedom and yet depreciate agitation are people who want crops without ploughing the ground," he observed. "They want rain without the thunder and lightning. They want the ocean without the roar of its many waters." His wisdom applies to more than the struggle with external oppressors. For four decades Douglass had a black wife. Two years after she passed away, he married again—only to confront race-baiters among African Americans themselves. A column in one newspaper, black-owned, bitterly declared that "Fred Douglass has married a red-head white girl. . . . We have no further use for him. His picture (hung) in our parlor, we will (now) hang it in the stable." Countercultural Muslims have been there. We're still there.

Martin Luther King, Jr., told Americans about two kinds of peace: "Negative peace" is the absence of tension, while "positive peace" is the presence of justice. As the price of realizing a diverse nation, King accepted tension—the oceanic roar that arose from offending white and black segregationists. In the twenty-first century, such backlash is the price of inhabiting a diverse globe.

5

OFFENSE IS THE PRICE OF DIVERSITY

very so often, avowedly moderate Muslims dub me a "fascist." I
find their use of free speech juvenile and offensive, but I don't
tell them to shut up. Nor do I threaten to sue. My right to speak
survives when theirs does too. I had to keep that principle top of
mind during a trip to Madison, New Jersey, in December 2004.
Some local Muslims objected to my impending appearance at Drew
University. Rather than pull my invitation, which has happened
elsewhere, organizers allowed the disgruntled to circulate a bro-
chure at the event. My detractors also got pride of place during the
question-and-answer session. Both solutions preserved everybody's
freedom of expression.

After my lecture, a religious studies professor who facilitated the
event emailed some Muslims, Jews and Christians to congratulate
them for maintaining their cool. The professor wrote:

It would be hard for me to think of a more controversial speaker for Muslims than Irshad Manji. Yet . . . members of our community witnessed the
reality that Muslims are perfectly capable of engaging in an honest, rational,
polite and civil debate, in mixed company, with other Muslims with whom

they profoundly disagree. . . . There were forces at the Drew campus who argued actively against Ms. Manji's appearance on campus right up to the last minute. What mainly lay behind their hesitance, I believe, was an unspoken assumption that Muslims just "can't handle" serious conversation about their faith. I rejected that line of thought . . .

The professor had raised the bar. Higher expectations cut through the rancor, helping to transform a private dustup into a constructive public exchange. The beauty of it is, the professor "mollified" nobody. Appeasement lost out to achievement.

A Cinderella ending, however, didn't quite materialize. Behind closed doors, one of the grumbling Muslims slid a list to me across the table at which we both sat. Printed on the letterhead of an interfaith dialogue group, the following words jumped out at me: "Suspend last paragraph . . . Entire paragraph is false . . . Historically untrue and unnecessarily provocative . . . Entire page has no relevance to main text . . . Entire page is untrue and redundant . . . Also, alter the title to . . ."

Sweet Jesus. Oy vey. And, as Prophet Muhammad might ask, what the fig? I was staring at a catalogue of sentences to censor from the next edition of my book, starting with a passage on page 2: "Entire paragraph offends sentimentally."

"You want my publishers to edit out these thoughts?"

"Oh yes," the dialogue dude confirmed. "Otherwise, you're like a fascist."

But wait, I thought. It's fascists who censor. It's fascists who suppress. It's fascists who ban. That's what you're badgering me to do so I'm no longer "like a fascist"? Falling into a speechless stupor, I blinked at the list, registering only the masthead on every page: "The Voice of Modernist Islam, Judaism & Christianity." Modernist! My next thought: "Brother Censor, your chutzpah eats mine for breakfast." Anxious to leave a room heaving with weirdness, I made no further comment, and later I berated myself for saying nothing more.

My personal honor has since recovered. Whenever I get thanks from Muslims who live in places where they can't dissent as readily as in America, I'm reassured that Brother Censor doesn't speak for all believers. "People like you serve as a source of energy for ones like me, living in Muslim states, who cannot afford to speak out loud," writes Muhammad from Pakistan. "I tried to, but was made to realize that I would offend many and win almost none, with harassment being the cherry on top. May Allah always bless you with the best, and bless me with the courage to stand up like you have chosen to do." Muhammad holds out hope that he'll one day defy the commissars of religious and cultural propriety. His capacity to be an individual may yet prevail.

Some believers are already harnessing offense for personal growth. "I am a young professional from Pakistan," begins Awais.

A few months back, one of my friends mailed me the Urdu translation of *The Trouble with Islam Today*. It was a pleasant surprise mainly because I had already read the book and never mentioned it to anybody. . . . My friend's moral courage provoked me to find some part of it in myself. I forwarded your online translation to a couple of friends [because] I believe it will create a positive change in their lives. Perhaps this is how grassroots movements work.

During those days, an Islamist at my workplace mailed the whole office a speech from a Taliban representative. It was so outrageous that it forced me to re-think my strategy of remaining silent. I have been blogging since that day to promote free thought and rationalism. Also, me and my friends spend time having useful discussions with the rest of our friends, which may push them to raise questions and think freely.

An "outrageous" Islamist perspective motivated Awais to the nonviolent action of counterarguing through a blog. At the same time, reading my book with friends—a book that rankles some Muslims more than the Taliban does—helped Awais openly promote reason within Islam. A Pakistani with less freedom than an American created ways to expand his choices rather than constraining the choices of others. My would-be censor in New Jersey could learn something.

Lesson five: *Offense is the price of diversity.*

————

The Danish cartoon affair sprouted diversity. Many of us remember only the fracas that boiled over in early 2006, once a handful of journalists, politicians, diplomats and mullahs in Denmark had sufficiently manipulated their audiences to magnify misunderstandings into a cosmic crisis. Months after publishing images that came off as mocking Muhammad, the Danish newspaper *Jyllands-Posten* apologized. Still, the controversy metastasized. Throngs of Muslims torched Scandinavian missions in Syria, Lebanon and Iran. Bomb threats hit the offices of more than one European paper. Thousands of Palestinians shouted, "Death to Denmark!" Some Muslims in India and Indonesia desecrated Danish flags—which feature the cross, perhaps the holiest of Christian symbols. Chechnya expelled Danish humanitarian workers. Copenhagen evacuated Danish citizens from the Gaza Strip. Ordinary Muslims were crushed underfoot in riots, and wanton murder marked the whole flipping firestorm.

But it also triggered a tidal wave of emails to my website, mostly from young Muslims. "I'm even more offended by the riots than by the cartoons!" exclaimed Mahmood, a student whose reaction typified the others. He then asked, "Can Islam and free expression live together?" At the height of the cartoon wars, that question cascaded into my inbox. Fed up with one upheaval after another, the Muslims who contacted me turned their offense at violence into a desire for diversity of interpretation.

They got it. In my replies, I wrote that the Qur'an itself points out there will always be nonbelievers, and that it's for God, not us Muslims, to deal with them. Moreover, the Qur'an bluntly opposes compulsion in religion. Nobody should be forced to treat traditions as untouchable, including traditions that result in the messed-up Muslim practice of equating our human prophet with some inviolable idol. Monotheists are to revere one God, not one of God's emissaries, which is why humility requires people of faith to lampoon themselves—and each other—once in a while.

So when a caricature satirizes Islam's beloved messenger in a turban-turned-time-bomb, should we sit there and take it? Not exactly. Take it, but no need to sit there. The Qur'an recommends that we get up and cordially walk away from those who distort our faith. In retrospect, just as I did from the Muslim in New Jersey whose censorious spirit offends the Qur'an's generous spirit. Generous enough that the Qur'an also advises we remain open toward the offenders. Pack up in peace, it suggests, then pick up the conversation when the dust settles. It's not Socrates's approach to dialogue—remorseless, relentless cross-examination—but neither does it have to be the unctuous exchange of platitudes that so often passes for interfaith dialogue.

During the cartoon crisis, diversity of interpretation had a new lease on life precisely because of offense. Mehdi, one of my readers, made the case jubilantly:

Considering the number of people from all sides standing up and giving their opinions, and the values-based discussions that are happening within the Islamic world and various western communities, I feel the cartoons accomplished what they set out to do: break the deadlock in conversation and get people talking again. Say something, anything, but don't stop talking. So hooray for the Danes!

In my own tribute to free speech, I posted (and responded to) emails from Muslims who caught my TV interviews about the cartoons:

As a convert to Islam and an ethnic Dane, I have been so sad and shocked to watch my brothers and sisters behave in the most undignified way. Can't they see that they portray Islam as a violent and unforgiving religion? Personally, I can't see why non-Muslims should ever submit to an Islamic taboo. Actually, I found the drawings to be hilarious. I know they were harsh, but that is Danish humour. And I think that Mohammad, peace be upon him, had a sense of humour.   —Østen

He must have had a great sense of humor to put up with the ignorance and threats from his fellow Arabs. Speaking of ignorance and threats . . .

i hear ur interview . . . u said that why r there huge protests in the muslim world. my answer is why not. print the cartoon of jesus and see what the christians will do. remember me because by gods promise u n ur partner that bastard rushdie will die with lot of pain n u both will pray for death but death will not come so easily inshallah. n u will die soon inshallah. n ur soul will rot in hell. read this n remember every day.   —handsome_guy

I challenge u 2 read the next letter every day n learn the difference between thuggery n disagreement. . . .

I'm a girl who grew up in Denmark, but I'm originally from Bahrain. You say that the Muslim world should be more tolerant when it comes to freedom of speech. I agree. However, freedom of speech doesn't mean that you have to use it to hurt, offend, or humiliate people. To represent the Prophet as a terrorist is like saying all the Muslims are terrorists. I know I'm not. You don't see me making cartoons of Christianity in the shape of a Nazi symbol. It's wrong! All I ask as a Muslim is to be respected. I do not consider myself a "religious" person, but one thing I do know is that Islam means a lot to me.   —Fatima

Islam means a lot to me too, yet I also understand that nobody can humiliate me without my permission. Consider the next correspondent . . .

Caught your interview on CNN. Where did you get your ideas from? I know you like white cocks in your wide and stinky pussy but keep in your limits you dumb fuckin bitch ass gang banged hoe.   —Anonymous

I don't know where YOU get your ideas from because I've never had such, uh, penetrating sex. Ever. But that, my friend, is the kind of pleasure you may need, at least according to the next Muslim . . .

I saw you discussing the hysteria over the Danish Muhammad cartoons. I also read your book when it came out and at that time I joined with other Muslims in condemning it. I'm a white boy who converted to Islam when I was 17 out of a combination of seeking meaning in my life and rebelling against society. I am also gay, and only came to terms with that about a year or so ago. And now, while I still believe in Allah and Muhammad as His messenger, I get the feeling that God gives us plenty of room to be human.

I guess while I love Allah, I dislike Muslims. Most, if not all, annoy me to the core of my being. Sometimes I feel that Muslims deserve to be offended by such trivial things as the Danish cartoons. I thought they were kind of funny, actually! I especially liked the quote by one of the editors of a Jordanian paper who reprinted the cartoons: "What is more insulting to Islam, someone drawing a cartoon or someone blowing up a wedding party in Amman?"

Muslims need to wake up. They also need to start drinking wine, embrace any and all homoerotic tendencies, write some poetry and for the most part free themselves from the fundamentalist chains they have created (for themselves and everyone else!). The Muslim world will only be free when bars fill the streets and women show off their natural, feminine beauty. Muslims need to grow up and stop expecting everyone to be mindless sheep before a 1,400-year-old oral tradition. Nakedness will free Dar-el-Islam!

—Jamal

Getting plastered and shaking booty as the ideal of freedom? Too hedonistic for me, Jamal. My soul would starve for meaning. But if your revolution comes before mine, count on me to shave my legs.

In the end, I posted links to all the cartoons, including those portraying the prophet as a pedophile and a pig—caricatures fabricated by radical Danish imams and falsely attributed to *Jyllands-Posten*. By publicizing this debate, I wanted my Muslim foes to see that they too rely on freedom of expression. The more vile their commentary, the more they reveal a dependence on the very liberties they would confiscate from others.

The contradiction resurfaced for me five months later. A Muslim woman roamed outside the Vancouver Public Library, demonstrating against a lecture I'd be giving that day. She carried a stack of flyers urging "brainy intelligent young Muslims" to "keep away from this lunatic deceiver." In front of my documentary crew and their rolling cameras, the woman accused me of "demonizing" Muslims. Not wanting to squander our brief time together by contesting her impression of my work, I instead proposed that she was demonizing me.

"No," came the brisk denial.

I motioned to the words emblazoned on her flyer: "The Devil in Disguise."

"Not you," she said.

"Irshad Manji," I recited off the flyer. "The Devil in Disguise."

"Okay," she conceded. "So what? Freedom of speech."

Sing it from the mountaintop, sister. It's a lip-smackingly democratic moment when both parties can agree that despite their heartfelt differences, the answer to perceived hate speech is more speech. As in, a better argument by the irritated and a response from the irritant, who may in turn be irritated by what she perceives as the deliberate distortion of her arguments. And so I invited the demonstrator to come inside the library, distribute her flyers, listen to my lecture and pose an inconvenient question. She declined, but agreed to let the footage of our encounter appear in my documentary as a way of giving her message a bigger bullhorn.

Far from being a divisive threat, free expression is a unifying thread—a crucial part of the social contract—for any place that pulsates with diversity. What, except such a social contract, would let the demonstrator communicate her displeasure? What else would let me and others hear her? What else would disrupt our certitudes and nudge us to think? What else would challenge her to do likewise? The demonstrator's right to argue can't be segregated from mine. If diversity is to mean more than circling holidays on a calendar, we have to accept the connection between being offended and being educated.

I'd like to return to my journey through the Danish cartoon tempest. It shows that in the muddled diversity department, clarity needs to displace delicacy. Clarity, in this case, about how Muslims and non-Muslims can uphold diversity of thought—together.

During the cartoon free-for-all, Caroline Fourest, a French scholar, followed the dialogues on my website and noticed that I argued for freedom of expression based on the Qur'an itself. An atheist, she asked me to join her, Salman Rushdie, Ayaan Hirsi Ali, Bernard-Henri Lévy and seven others in signing what came to be the Manifesto of 12. It reads:

> *After overcoming fascism, Nazism and Stalinism, the world now faces a new global totalitarian threat: Islamism. We— writers, journalists and public intellectuals—call for resistance to religious totalitarianism. Instead, we call for the promotion of freedom, equal opportunity and secular values worldwide.*
>
> *The necessity of these universal values has been revealed by events since the publication of the Muhammad drawings in European newspapers. This struggle will not be won by arms, but in the arena of ideas. What we are witnessing is not a clash of civilizations, nor an antagonism of East versus West, but a global struggle between democrats and theocrats.*
>
> *Like all totalitarianisms, Islamism is nurtured by fears and frustrations. The preachers of hate bet on these feelings in order to form battalions destined to impose a world of inequality. But we clearly and firmly state: nothing, not even despair, justifies the choice of obscurantism, totalitarianism and hatred.*
>
> *Islamism is a reactionary ideology which kills equality, freedom and secularism wherever it is present. Its success can only lead to a world of greater power imbalances: man's domination of woman, the Islamists' domination of all others.*
>
> *To counter this, we must assure universal human rights to oppressed people. For that reason, we reject "cultural relativism," which consists of accepting that Muslim men and women should*

be deprived of their right to equality and freedom in the name of their cultural traditions.

We refuse to renounce our critical spirit out of fear of being accused of "Islamophobia," an unfortunate concept that confuses criticism of Islamic practices with the stigmatization of Muslims themselves.

We plead for the universality of free expression, so that a critical spirit may be exercised on every continent, against every abuse and dogma. We appeal to democrats and free spirits of all countries that our century should be one of enlightenment, not obscurantism.

I loved that the manifesto appealed to the "free spirits of all countries," rejecting the "clash of civilizations" for battle lines that made far more sense: those between democrats and theocrats. I didn't love that most of the signatories were confirmed atheists. Was I their token confirmed believer? The word "token" gored me emotionally—for about five resentful minutes. Then I laughed at myself. A gift had just landed in my lap. As a faithful Muslim, I could show that "a critical spirit," "equal opportunity" and "secular values" don't have to be the exclusive domain of atheists.

I could use the manifesto to educate skeptics, from Muslims to journalists, about why secularism and faith can be defended at the same time. Only in a secular society can diversity of belief thrive. Secular values open up space for all of us to worship, or not, as our personal consciences require. Theocracies—including supposedly rationalist ones such as Nazi Germany and North Korea—marginalize personal conscience, making for insincerity. Secularism creates opportunities to explore multiple perspectives, sparking a competition of consciences. It tests my sincerity, as a person of faith, about leaving the last word to God. At its best, then, secularism is good for faith and bad for dogma.

But when practitioners of "faith" become dogmatic, as Islamo-tribalists tend to, secularists have reason to spring into action with legislative restraints. That's because secular values are meant to ensure that no religion can take over the public square and bulldoze the freedoms of those who choose not to believe, or who choose interpretations that religious community leaders would want to censor. On the wide path of Islam, there's no showdown between faith and secular values because these values have a home in the Qur'an's transparent teaching against compulsion. Wherever diversity lives, the spirit of secularism is an indispensable feature of the social contract.

The Manifesto of 12 went viral. Ummah.com, an Islamist website administered in Britain, then posted an unvarnished death threat against the signatories: "Excellent—makes killing the kuffar all that bit easier. . . . now we have drawn out a hit list of a 'Who's Who' guide to slam into. Take you time but make sure their gone soon—oh and don't hold out for a fatwah it isn't really required here." Because this post slithered from a source that attracts more than a few radicals, Fourest and I had to regroup. Our fight now needed a show of solidarity from people around the world who would openly declare that death threats won't chill their consciences.

We crafted a petition stating, "I wish to express my unequivocal support for the twelve signatories and my outrage at the Islamist movement's attack on them. I stand firm with the 12 against this reactionary movement. I join in their call to resist religious totalitarianism and to promote freedom, equal opportunity, human rights and secular values for all." We asked the public not only to sign their names but also to specify their towns, cities or countries. Fourest and I understood that this extra request might limit the number of signatures. A fair trade, since the exercise was intended to bump up expectations of people who wished to take a stand. Now they'd know how, but they'd also be mindful that standing for progress means risking more than the scribble of a pen. If some couldn't go that far, freedom granted them that choice—an irony, we hoped, that the hesitant would reflect upon.

To ensure that *Muslims* heard our appeal for secular values, we hosted the petition on my website. So far, the thousands of signatories include Muslims in Saudi Arabia, China, Iran, France, Afghanistan, New Zealand, Turkey, India, the West Bank, the Netherlands, Malaysia, Australia, Syria, South Africa, Algeria, the United States, Nigeria, Canada and Pakistan. The Manifesto of 12 got it right: Free spirits clearly do wander within Islam. Democrats everywhere can't let ourselves be cowed by theocrats anywhere. Civilization is, has always been, and must continue to be a shared enterprise.

I've learned that wisdom can be wrung from white-hot episodes such as the Danish drama. To make our way toward wisdom, we can't get sucked into the scheming and screaming of community representatives. Being serious about diversity demands that we stop investing so much clout in the usual suspects. Let's give choices, as the petition does, to the *unusual* suspects. The un-approved. The un-official. The un-established. They're the ones who will take Muslims as well as multiculturalists beyond a contrived diversity of appearance and toward an infinitely more necessary diversity of thought.

———

Dear Irshad,

Finally, my concern proved to be correct. The publishing house was gutless. The board of the publishing house was intimidated and fooled by their "very well established professor" . . . The so-called scholar condemned and insulted the work as "unscholarly," "fringe," "controversial," and "hateful," without providing any argument on the substance. He (most likely he) insulted me by falsely accusing me of being a cult member. Those who know my person and my work know well that I am a free spirit . . .

Edip Yuksel, a Turkish American Muslim, fired off that email in December 2006. His publisher, Palgrave Macmillan, had just quit on his project, *Quran: A Reformist Translation*. Since signing the publisher's contract in 2004, Yuksel and his coauthors had worked on a translation that they described as "God's message to those who prefer reason over blind faith." As an academic imprint, Palgrave Macmillan had to shepherd the manuscript through a review process involving scholars. It appears that on the basis of one negative review—the only one cited by a senior editor in private correspondence with Yuksel—this book died on the corporate vine.

Other scholars had endorsed Yuksel's experiment. Reza Aslan, author of *No god but God*, called it a "bold and beautiful translation that serves as a timely reminder to all believers that the Qur'an is not a static scripture, but a living, breathing, ever-evolving text." Feminist professors offered qualified encouragement. I too backed the effort without claiming the interpretation to be "correct." But the sole scholar who mattered made my support a strike against the project. "It was like a medieval publishing house turning down Martin Luther's book after consulting a Catholic Bishop," Yuksel chafed. One has to wonder if Palgrave Macmillan ran scared after the conflagration over the Muhammad cartoons. Regardless, the publisher showed that non-Muslims play a pivotal role in Muslim reform—or the lack of it.

Its decision deprived the book-reading public of exposure to liberal Qur'anic interpretations. For example, to violent jihadis, the question of beheading isn't a question at all, but a divinely determined right. Not, however, according to *Quran: A Reformist Translation*, which suggests two ways of treating captives: Set them free, and if that's politically pie-in-the-sky, then release them after securing a fee for their aggression against you. That might sound like extortion, yet it's a vivid improvement over the butchery in most war zones today.

Speaking of securing fees, should Muslim governments levy a tax on non-Muslims? Even at the zenith of tolerance in Islamic civilization, religious minorities had to pay a special surcharge, or *jizya*, to their Muslim overlords. But the translation by Yuksel and his colleagues treats *jizya* as "reparations"—that which ought to be restored to its prewar condition, not exploited for ongoing taxation. And that's only if Muslims suffered attack first. Does feeling offended amount to being attacked? No. "We are not permitted to kill or punish people for their mockery of God's revelations or signs," goes a recurring commentary in the translation. "Any aggressive behavior against those people is against God's law that recognizes freedom of choice, opinion, and expression." What a shock that in his review the traditional Muslim academic recoiled.

Eager to release their work at a time of deepening distrust between Muslims and non-Muslims, Yuksel and his coauthors self-published in the United States. Their translation can also be downloaded, free of charge, from my homepage. Julie, an American Muslim, did just that. "I converted 7 years ago and the basic faith principles were appealing," she emailed to me, "but I quickly learned that my views were NOT accepted by mainstream Muslims. I wondered if I really was Muslim? . . . Now I have some material to read and help me interpret the Qur'an."

Julie's excitement about thinking for herself—with guidance that she can understand—is the stuff of democratizing ijtihad. She shows Muslim leaders that Islam isn't a pact between them and the believer; it's a covenant between God and the believer. When Muslims take that relationship to heart, we'll care less about offending community authorities.

And we'll give non-Muslims the incentive to expect better of those who presume to speak for all of Islam. In June 2006, Canadian police arrested young Muslims for plotting to blow up Parliament and behead the prime minister. The Toronto 17 (soon to number 18) called their campaign Operation Badr, an homage to the Battle of Badr, the first decisive military victory by Prophet Muhammad. Police knew that religious symbolism helped motivate the Toronto 17's intention to commit terror.

Still, at their initial press conference about the arrests, police didn't mention "Islam" or "Muslims." At their second press conference, where a covey of Muslim leaders joined them, cops actually boasted about avoiding the words "Islam" and "Muslims." It turns out that police lawyers wouldn't let the law enforcers utter these words in public, so they had to characterize their omission as sensitivity—sensitivity, that is, to Islam as "represented" by a cadre of men and women who'd be offended and likely litigious if the truth came out.

Ready to be reminded of a truth that should come out over and over again? Neither religions nor cultures speak for themselves. People speak for religions. People speak for cultures. And people are fallible. Therefore, people ought to be questioned about what happens on their watch—even more when we're discussing public safety.

Understanding is served by analyzing, not sanitizing. Bringing Islam into the analysis should be entirely legitimate to religious people because it's not the Divine that's being interrogated, it's mortal interpretation and human judgment that's being questioned. From that standpoint, when Muslims tolerate their feelings of offense, they're leaving the final analysis to Allah, as the Qur'an requires.

———

I'm not arguing that the fight against discrimination should be left up to God. I'm asserting that being offended isn't synonymous with being discriminated against. One can be offended by having to accept the same standards as everyone else. At the World Economic Forum in January 2006—just before the Danish cartoon crisis—I attended a session about the U.S. religious right. A cartoonist satirized one of America's most influential Christian ministers, Pat Robertson. In the audience, chuckling with the rest of us, was the head of the Muslim Council of Britain, Iqbal Sacranie. But his smirk folded into a pout at the first glimpse of a cartoon that ridiculed Muslim clerics. Equal treatment may cause offense, but it needn't signify oppression, let alone Islamophobia.

Yasmin Alibhai-Brown, an impeccable advocate of Palestinian rights, a vociferous critic of the Iraq war and the chair of British Muslims for Secular Democracy, talks tougher than I do about the uses and abuses of Islamophobia. She told the documentary program *Are Muslims Hated?* that in Britain, "I would never deny that Muslims have had a hard time and are still having a hard time."

> *But I think it would be dishonest of me if I didn't say that all too often, Islamophobia is used as an excuse in a way to kind of blackmail society. . . . The lowest achieving community in this country, whether we're talking about schools, universities, occupations, professions and so on . . . the majority are Muslims. When you talk to people about why this is happening, the one reason they give you, the only reason, is Islamophobia.*
>
> *Uh uh. It is not Islamophobia that makes parents take 14-year-old bright girls out of school to marry illiterate men, and the girl has again to bring up the next generation who will again be denied not just education, but the value of education. What Islamophobia does is it just becomes a convenient label, a fig leaf, a reason that is so comfortable for Muslims whenever they have to look at why they aren't in the places that they have to be.*

Does Alibhai-Brown's honesty offend some mainstream Muslims? Apoplectically so. Does it oppress them? Absolutely not. Countercultural Muslims such as she help defeat Islamophobia by puncturing the myth that Islam is a monolith. Countercultural voices unmask the faces of moral courage within Islam: Muslims who own their community's dysfunction rather than reflexively blaming the United States, Israel, Christianity, materialism, MTV, KFC and those perpetually kosher piñatas, "the Jews." Countercultural Muslims torpedo the assumption made by Lise, a woman from Quebec City who contacted me during the cartoon delirium to say, "I am very happy that Canada does not publish those caricatures. We do not need the Islamic reaction."

Agreed. We don't need *the* Islamic reaction. Or, accounting for language differences, *an* Islamic reaction. We need *many* Islamic reactions—among them applause, revulsion, dismissal, embarrassment, nonviolent protest and peals of laughter. As we see from the letters I've posted, Muslims hold a palette of views. Just not openly so. Our bad. If we really want to dispel hurtful stereotypes of Islam, then it's Muslims who must allow the off-color, oft-offensive opinions *within* our communities to flourish. It's Muslims who must brush off the dishonor of being stamped a "self-hater." It's Muslims who must stop comporting ourselves as a constituency of drones, thereby handing bona fide bigots the fodder to peg all Muslims as terrorists.

An essential step toward publicizing our diversity: Circumvent the bogus business of who "represents" and who doesn't. The culture critic Ian Buruma alludes to the racket that community representatives tend to run. In his essay "The Freedom to Offend," Buruma observes that

leaders of minorities are a bit like bosses of criminal gangs. Crime syndicates, organized along ethnic lines, often claim to represent the interests of recent immigrants who have nowhere else to turn in an unfamiliar country. But which second- or third-generation Italian-American or British-Chinese would want to be represented by the Mafia or the Chinese Triads?

Are mainstream Muslim leaders akin to mobsters? Not everywhere, yet too many reform-minded Muslims kowtow to them anyway. Which signals to non-Muslims—from politicians to publishers to police officers—that to "do" diversity is to assuage a cartel of mainstream spokespeople. But that's a parody of diversity. The fear felt by reform-minded Muslims contributes to it. If we don't grow the Andalusian cojones to be individuals, then we become accessories of Islamo-tribalists—and their Islamophobia.

———

Now for a note to non-Muslims, particularly aspiring global citizens. Petrified of being taken for provincial imbeciles, many of you feel a special responsibility to "respect" Islam. I put "respect" in quotations because when you write to me, that's the word you typically choose. It's also a word that throws you for a loop. David, a student who attends York University in Toronto, emailed,

> I'm a graduate of political studies focusing on Middle East politics, peace and conflict . . . I'm writing to you during a break in my class on "Islam Through the Ages" and I seek your advice on how to keep alive debate. . . . The vast majority of this class is Muslim. But the vast majority of those Muslims appear to be in here to make sure that they are properly represented and Islam is treated with the proper respect. . . . I'm hoping you can offer up some strategies for how I can ask my questions without having to worry about causing an uproar (which seems to happen every class or so) and/or without being disrespectful.

Let's say that I'm the Muslim student demanding respect. David has every right to tell me, *Religions and cultures don't talk. People talk on their behalf. When I, David, question your beliefs, Irshad, I'm questioning how you define ideas, not how God does. Your own scripture makes no bones about it: Only God knows the final meanings of all that Muslims profess. I'm not God and neither are you. So we can move forward with my questions for you, and yours for me.*

"Respect me, not just my religion," I might retort to David. Having heard this one umpteen times myself, I now appreciate that "Respect me" serves as a pitch-perfect dog whistle for "Don't challenge me." But indifference is the antithesis of respect. George Steiner, the scholar and writer, nails what I mean: "The way you honor a person is, you ask of him an effort." That kind of honor trusts in an individual's capacity.

With a clean conscience, then, David can reply, *Rest assured, Irshad, that I'm respecting you. By engaging with you, I'm respecting your mind, soul and substance. If I doubted that you've got any of these, I wouldn't waste my energy. If you still take refuge in defensiveness, though, you're suggesting that you're an automaton who's easily unhinged by questions. How are you respecting yourself?*

David's choice of clarity over delicacy might well generate the ruckus he'd hoped to avert. Fine. A no-nonsense love of humanity is always the right reason to stir the rancid pot of indifference. It will be a memorable educational moment that makes tuition worth (almost) every penny. Even so, David shouldn't get caught up in dark imaginings of an insurrection against him. More than a few Muslim students will breathe sighs of relief at hearing someone say what they think they can't. After watching *Faith Without Fear*, Layla wrote, "I cried because I thought I was alone in my questions and frustrations with mullahs who have interpreted Qur'an to control populations. . . . I like it when you ask the West to challenge us. That will make us grow. I WILL BECOME A BETTER MUSLIM, WHICH IN TURN MEANS A BETTER HUMAN BEING."

Layla should have dinner with Josée, a French-speaking Acadian who's brimming with questions and stewing over those who want to bleach questions from reality. "Last summer," she told me about her seaside holiday in Canada,

I saw a large number of women wearing the hijab. This included a girl of my daughter's age, 9 years old. It bothered me. Not because I don't agree with expressing faith, *au contraire,* I do it myself. It bothered me because there is always that question in the back of my mind: "Is it really a choice?" . . . But when I heard you on TV, I realized that what bothers me the most is not feeling free enough to simply ASK those questions.

What also scares me is when I hear Muslims (or any other religious people) tell me that I don't have the authority to discuss religion. When a person tells that to another person, it creates an even bigger gap between cultures because the person who is trying to understand is suddenly not able to express questions. It is also giving the authority to a certain group of people who have the power to explain and interpret religious books the way they want. Slowly, Muslims become THEM and we are the group called US. History has shown that THEM is the cause of all troubles, and has to be eliminated by US. We need more people brave enough to ask real questions. We don't need answers immediately, but questions are a necessity!

Josée and Layla have just done the work of high-minded scholars. They've warned us that fear of questions doesn't merely stifle individual growth, it conjures up suspicions about the Other that can mushroom into much worse. Where's our halcyon diversity then? Down the insatiable rabbit hole of relativism. I propose that we experiment with a rival to relativism.

Pluralism. As a pluralist, I happily live with many perspectives and truths, but I won't devolve into a relativist—someone who falls for anything because she stands for nothing. Unlike the relativist, the pluralist gets her questions off her chest. The pluralist makes judgments, fully aware that her judgments are provisional, and all the more so if she gives God the last word. But with or without God, the pluralist judges unapologetically, since her conclusions are interim and contingent on hearing new, more persuasive arguments. Thus the importance of exercising free speech.

Led by pluralism, here's how I deal with Josée's concern, the hijab: I choose not to wear it, and if another woman decides the opposite for herself, I won't stop her. But what I will do is express my judgment that choosing hijab makes her a billboard for the most chauvinistic aspects of Arab tribal culture. Far from protecting herself against the "Western" disease of sexualizing breasts and other bodily bits, she's fetishizing her *entire* body as genitalia.

"That's not what it's about!" rings out the hijabi's reply. "It's about modesty!" In theory, sure. But as a peace studies major pointed out while debating a Muslim on my Facebook page, "You are sadly mistaken if you think women who wear hijab, niqab and/or burqa are never judged on their looks." The student surveyed some of her male Muslim friends:

I asked them when a woman wears hijab, if they have interest in the woman who has the most beautiful face. All of them said, "Yes." I asked them when a woman wears niqab, if they find the woman with the most beautiful eyes, the most beautiful person. They all answered, "Yes." I then asked about the burqa-clad women. Who were the men most attracted to? Of course, the answer was the woman with the best silhouette.

Regardless of how much a woman covers herself, she is still being judged on how she looks. Do you socialize with many Middle Eastern women? They are notoriously hard on each other when it comes to how they look underneath the veil.

The Muslim didn't respond.

My tentative take on hijab: It's an emblem of faux modesty. Still, as a pluralist, I'm willing to change my mind. Bring on the evidence that men don't gawk at women who cover.

Some women tell me that by choosing hijab they're making a political point, not a spiritual one. "If the liberated West pities poor me," goes the argument, "then let the West see that I'm choosing my oppression!" But by marshaling hijab to make a public show of politics rather than a personal investment in faith, such women are exhibitionists.

I'm offending here, but I too am offended. I'm offended by the superficiality of combating Western prejudices about women by using Arab prejudices about women. As models of "progressive" politics, these women do a severe injustice to progress. Real progress doesn't drape itself in problematic definitions of honor; it dismantles those definitions.

Hijabis-by-choice insist on being appreciated for their minds, so the pluralist should honor them with questions. *How does your political point differ from that of young Western feminists who wear Playboy bunny pendants in order to reclaim female independence? Or African Americans who tattoo "nigger" on their skin in order to show the white man that they're proud of their putative chains? Aren't all of you acquiescing to somebody else's terms rather than firing up the imagination to create your own terms? Finally, how are you standing up for Muslim women who don't yet enjoy the rights that you do—the right, at a minimum, to choose?*

My hijab-wearing sisters, I expect nothing of you that I don't expect of myself and others. Consider my reply to Anonymous, the infuriated reader of a column I wrote after an Islamo-tribalist fatally shot Theo van Gogh, the Dutch filmmaker and commentator. Anonymous lambasted me:

You make it look like [van Gogh] was killed JUST because he criticized Islam. Why did you ignore that his "criticism" was extremely offensive, even to some non-Muslims, who found his dirty movie to be a complete disregard of Muslim feelings? Or was the killing of van Gogh a good chance to use it for your own cause, no matter how many facts you slay?

"Van Gogh's assaults left many Muslims feeling humiliated," I concurred.

But van Gogh said equally nasty things about Jews and Christians—and they refrained from slitting his throat. Would you argue that they should have killed him? In that case, do Muslim women who are routinely humiliated by Muslim men have the right to murder those men? If not, why the double standard?

No reply.

———

My liberal friends, you might judge the very notion of judging as illiberal, which would itself be a shoddy judgment. All the shoddier when gross criminality, including honor-based murder, cries out for moral clarity. The assumed safety of relativism is among the more tragic evasions of our time because it promotes passivity as a response to abuse of power. Worse, such passivity poses as activism. It's a lie that no liberal conscience ought to, or needs to, tolerate.

In *Moral Clarity: A Guide for Grown-Up Idealists*, the liberal philosopher Susan Neiman extols Prophet Abraham's example. When

God reveals plans to decimate the cities of Sodom and Gomorrah as His punishment for the sins of a few, Abraham tenaciously asks questions out loud. "Shall not the Judge of all the earth do right?" he protests (Genesis 18:25). Through a conversation suffused with moral courage, the prophet convinces the Almighty to go easier than He had intended. By appealing to God's capacity for compassion, Abraham does more than save lives; he spares people who aren't his "own," testifying to the universality of human rights.

Remember this when questioning Muslims and non-Muslims who act like the messiahs of multiculturalism. They'll be the ones launching the verbal missile "You can't comment because you don't represent." Borrow a response from the prophet of Judaism, Christianity and Islam, and intercept that missile with questions: *Why are you profiling me? You're telling me that because of my non-Muslim background I can't join this most public of public conversations. In effect, you're reducing me to my demographics instead of elevating us to shared values. Racial profiling shouldn't be done to Muslims. Why is it acceptable when done to non-Muslims?*

If a shifty reply flies your way, follow up with more questions: *Do you realize what you're saying by insisting that I can't comment because I don't "represent"? You're saying civilians can't interrogate human rights violations at Abu Ghraib or Guantánamo Bay because we don't live in the culture of the military. You're saying that working stiffs can't demand transparency from Wall Street because we don't belong to banking culture. You're saying that Muslims in the Middle East have no right to judge U.S. foreign policy because they're not "of" American culture. Do you buy this hooey? Nor do I. So why should I buy the same hooey steaming from a different pile—yours?*

However pungent the language, I'm not naive enough to believe that pluralists will have relativists on the ropes anytime soon. "I teach criticism," writes the New York University journalism professor Susie Linfield, "and I teach it to students who often don't like to make judgments, though they want to be critics." Such students, she notes, have "imbibed from their elders" that "not making judgments might be somehow connected to being a 'fair' person or a 'good' person, whereas I think it's connected to being a person who has renounced her own autonomy and is therefore unlikely to be either fair or good." The rabbit hole of relativism devours even those with professional ambitions to distinguish good from bad.

That's a wake-up call to ordinary individuals. Layla and Josée, David and Awais, Mohammad and Lise—their daily interactions will have to bring sanity to diversity, question by question. If that sounds like a slog, it may be all we've got. The historian of scams, Charles Mackay, saw individuals as the sole bulwarks against mass folly. People, he realized, "go mad in herds, while they only recover their senses slowly, and one by one." Question by question. Spurt by spurt of moral courage.

By opposing censorship, I don't mean that absolutely everything under the sun should be exposed to the sun's light—or heat. In these pages I've censored the name of the Sharia law student at Al-Azhar University who aligns himself with my message of ijtihad, or critical thinking. He denounces the prohibition on questions at his college. He shakes his metaphorical fist at the Jew-baiting and woman-veiling that surrounds him. He even proclaims his support for gays and lesbians. Given the atavistic environment in which he studies, disclosing his name would subject him to direct harm. For this reason too, I signed a contract with my Arabic and Farsi translators stipulating that I'll never release their identifying details.

In most contexts, however, we should aim for boldness—despite what might feel like impending harm. My Urdu translator, Tahir

Aslam Gora, chose to go public. A disturbing message then landed in his inbox from "Progressive Shia Muslim":

> stop it basterd. . . . we are not Taliban people but you and irshad are on our killing list. REMEMBER we are watching. . . . we will keep watching and some day we will get you. LAST THING ask pakistani publisher to take back book from the market. We are contacting ulma [clergy] and government to stop qabli qatal masanfa [woman writer who should be put to death].

Pakistani booksellers wiped their shelves of the Urdu translation, so it went up on my website. No harm, no foul. Better still, Gora remains blessedly breathing and won't back down. He agreed that I should post the threat on my site as a testimonial to what can be overcome when we accept that some things are simply more important than fear.

But neither of us anticipated the next call for censorship. Zahra wrote:

> On your website, I saw the death threat from a "Progressive Shia Muslim." I beg you to please take any angry signature down that says "Muslim." I myself am Shia and I feel that if someone looks at that email and sees "Shia," they will see other Shias like that. In a larger scope, they will see all Muslims like that.

"I find it revealing," I responded to Zahra,

> that you would expend your energy begging me to edit out the death threat. Instead, you could be writing an email through me to the person who issued the threat—explaining why, in your view, a "progressive Shia Muslim" cannot be progressive, Shia, or Muslim while inciting murder. Does it not occur to you that this would be a more pious response than pleading with me to san-

itize? Why is your conscience more troubled by what I'm doing than by what my aspiring assassin would do if he or she had the chance? Why are you more interested in spinning Islam's negative image than in helping to fix the reason for that image?

In February 2008, I finally got confirmation that Muslims have it in them to disapprove of death threats. On Al Jazeera International, David Frost interviewed me about reconciling Islam with free expression. My remarks stirred a fevered debate on YouTube. "Senadin" posted early on, "Kill this whore now." It didn't take long for "WarGuardian18" to dive in with a denunciation: "How dare my brothers and sisters call for the death of anyone! . . . Shame on you!"

The surprise, though, sprang from YouTube itself, where the death threat appeared and then abruptly evaporated. I would have allowed YouTube editors to restore the threat, waiving any liability on their part for the consequences to me. After all, every comment—pro and con freedom in Islam, pro and con the revival of ijtihad, pro and con survival for Irshad—contains precious hints about where young Muslims are at. By deleting the roughest edges of the debate, we become willfully dumb about what we're up against in attempting to reform Muslim mind-sets. Akbar Ladak, the young Muslim from India, says it plainly: "You cannot get reform without discussion, and you cannot have discussion without freedom of speech." YouTube's attorneys might greet this argument with a corporate guffaw. If so, it's just another indication that individuals, not institutions, will have to carry the pail of principle.

———

A professor at the University of London warned me that no good can come from putting principle above politeness. "If you're able to predict that something will upset sensitivities," he growled, "don't do it." For all his advanced degrees, this man has a shrunken moral universe. His preemptive politeness inoculates people against unspoken prejudices, but it also forecloses opportunities to defeat spoken prejudices.

If she'd followed the professor's advice, Hissa Hilal of Saudi Arabia wouldn't have recited a poem on the pan-Arab TV program *Poet of Millions*, calling out Muslim clerics for "terrorizing people and preying on everyone seeking peace." She wouldn't have described suicide bombers as "barbaric in thinking and action, angry and blind, wearing death as a dress and covering it with a belt." Surely she knew that her unsparing indictments would "upset sensitivities." Subsequent vilifications of her on the Internet proved it. But for all the upset, millions of Muslims witnessed a homemaker's moral courage in motion. She became the first woman to reach the show's final round.

If they'd taken the professor's blinkered counsel, the crew of *Slumdog Millionaire* would have stopped filming—or never started. These days, scarcely a week elapses in India without lawsuits or ambushes by groups grieving "misrepresentation." The Hindu People's Awakening Committee tried to ban *Slumdog*, in part because of a scene in which a Hindu girl falls in love with a Muslim boy. Does Danny Boyle, *Slumdog*'s director, need to teach our professor that offending Hindu fundamentalists with diabolically entertaining displays of pluralism might be the decent thing to do?

If he'd accepted the professor's instruction, Elie Wiesel wouldn't have championed intervention in the Bosnian genocide. As a young journalist in 1993, I remember being pained by global imperviousness to the suffering of Muslims in the former Yugoslavia. I then heard about Wiesel's audacity in front of President Bill Clinton. The U.S. Holocaust Memorial Museum had just opened, and Wiesel, a Holocaust survivor and Nobel peace laureate, joined Clinton onstage. Something—anything—must be done about the targetting of Muslims in Bosnia, Wiesel appealed to the president, angering some of his fellow Jews by capitalizing on this hallowed platform. But he told his detractors that "when men are dying, when innocent people are subjected to rape and torture, when cities are being transformed into cemeteries, Jews do not have the right to be silent." Two years later, the United States got involved in a UN mission to help save Bosnian Muslims from more massacres—a policy that had its genesis in Wiesel's willingness to offend.

To preempt upset is to preempt the emergence of today's Galileos, Gandhis and Ghaffar Khans, be they homemakers, filmmakers or peacemakers.

After the professor told me that I should avoid inflaming sensitivities for any reason, he let slip his profusely emotional agenda. "I sympathize with the murderous rage of Muslims," he said. Thud. That statement hit me like a brick because it attests to a fact nobody admits: Even when we think we're thinking, we're probably feeling. The more we mistake feeling for thinking, the more entrenched the culture of offense becomes. "I feel offended" takes on the stature of a substantive argument, making actual substance irrelevant. If you think (or feel) that I'm talking about how Muslims reacted to the Danish cartoons, you're only partly right. Frenzied debates about building mosques across America might be the new cartoon wars.

Anti-mosque activists constantly trump thinking with sloganeering, but multiculturalists have been just as emotional. Some multiculturalists feel so offended by anti-mosque squadrons that these feelings alone drive them to support more mosques—without prior thought as to what, exactly, they're supporting. Bob emailed me, "Here in Tennessee we have seen some rather ugly responses to a Muslim community expansion project. I found local citizens to be intolerant and un-American. So as a gesture of tolerance and Americanism, I donated to the mosque building fund."

Before pledging a penny, Bob should have taken a breath and asked the imam, *Where will the men's entrance be?* It's a discreet way of discerning whether this new mosque will replicate segregation, and thus whether Bob's antipathy for intolerant behavior will wind up tolerating, well, intolerant behavior. I'm not saying that Bob should cast his lot with the anti-mosque picketers. I'm saying he shouldn't give them the power to commandeer his brain by hijacking his heart. He ought to think for himself, even as he feels for Muslims.

Put differently, if you're offended, don't just react; engage your feelings of offense to examine the issues further. That's when unexpected opportunities can present themselves for meaningful diversity—that is, diversity of thought.

What about the granddaddy of all U.S. mosque projects: Park51, a multistory Islamic community center and prayer space to be erected at the edge of Ground Zero in New York? Let me be straight about my own emotions. I'm offended by its proximity to the graveyard of 9/11. I'm also offended that Imam Feisal Rauf, the cleric who once fronted Park51, played crass politics unbecoming a man of dialogue. He rebuffed accusations of insensitivity, although he made those very accusations about the Danish cartoons of Prophet Muhammad. In February 2006 the imam announced himself "appalled" by the drawings, calling their publication throughout Europe "willful fomentation" and "gratuitous." In the weeks that followed, almost no U.S. newspaper printed the caricatures.

Four years later, most Americans believed *him* to be guilty of willful fomentation, yet he and his retinue didn't empathize. Not once did they acknowledge that the feelings of these "appalled" Americans parallel how Muslims such as Imam Rauf felt during the cartoon debacle. Instead, he wrote off the concerns as Islamophobia. That bugged the bejeezus out of me.

For all the restless offense I felt, I stepped back and stilled myself. Questions arose. Does spinning our wheels steer us anywhere except deeper into the muck of tizzy? Does barren deadlock consecrate anything other than the culture of taking and giving offense? As I questioned myself, I discovered an opportunity for something more constructive than anger: accountability. Thanks to the provocative location of Park51, the nation will be scrutinizing what takes place inside. Americans have the opportunity to be clear about the contours they expect from any Islam practiced at this achingly contested site. Which means asking questions that stem from human values. *Will the swimming pool be segregated between women and men at any time of the day or night? May women lead congregational prayers any day of the week? May Jews and Christians, fellow People of the Book, use the prayer sanctuary for their services just as Muslims share prayer space with Christians and Jews in the Pentagon? What will be taught about homosexuals? About agnostics? About polytheists? About atheists? About apostasy? And, Where does one sign up for advance tickets for Salman Rushdie's lecture at Park51?*

These questions aren't gratuitous. I remain haunted by the three hundred Muslims who chanted "Death to Rushdie" on September 10, 2001. They gathered outside a theater in Houston to protest a visit by the author. One Muslim told reporters, "The fatwa is valid even if the Iranian government no longer supports it." Another sniffed, "We have not forgotten about him and his evil act." That man affiliated himself with Houston's Islamic Education Center. Education or indoctrination? The question deserves an honest answer. Through engagement that emphasizes questions such as these, Muslims and non-Muslims may very well make Ground Zero host to the most open, most democratic, most modern Islam ever. I think (and don't just feel) that this would be a fitting tribute to the victims of 9/11. It would turn the tables on the liberty-lashing culture of al-Qaeda and it would subvert the thought-less culture of offense.

———

Martin Luther King, Jr., I expect, would have been the first to ask searching questions of moderate Muslims such as Imam Rauf. In Islam today, moderates are like the diplomatic Christians of the 1960s who, behind drawn curtains, couldn't abide antisegregation activists. When moderate Christians sulked at the kerfuffles alleg-edly instigated by King, he shot back,

> We merely bring to the surface the hidden tension that is already alive. We bring it out in the open, where it can be seen and dealt with. Like a boil that can never be cured so long as it is covered up but must be opened with all its ugliness to the natural medicines of air and light, injustice must likewise be exposed, with all of the tension its exposure creates, to the light of human conscience.

King's conviction: In times of moral crisis, moderation is a cop-out.

Post-9/11, moderate Muslims wear the mantle of the "good guys." And many are, in fact, affable folks. But being nice, while an emotionally useful springboard to dialogue, means bupkes to reach-ing real milestones on the wide path of Islam. Wherever abuses of power are legion, rooting out corruption is never an act of modera-tion; it's a loving act of intense commitment.

In the next chapter I'll introduce a white woman from Georgia who pushed Southern moderates to see that racial segregation needed more than an incremental demise. She helped King adopt "the extreme way" as "the good way." This lady represented white and black, Northerner and Southerner, with transcendently human values. Let's take her cue. Ask for moral courage from moderate Muslims, and as we do, we'll develop moral courage in ourselves.

6

IN TIMES OF MORAL CRISIS, MODERATION IS A COP-OUT

Where's the love?

It's Valentine's Day. I'm encircled by moderate Muslim women and one of their non-Muslim feminist allies at the University of Illinois at Chicago. They've braved the worst blizzard of the winter to be here. For this, I'm grateful. To them, I'm just grating.

We're debating the urgency of stopping death by stoning—the pulverizing of women and men by fist-sized rocks, a twenty-first-century equivalent of burning at the stake. Amnesty International, the human rights watchdog, describes stoning as a "grotesque punishment" for transgressing the community's honor. It's "specifically designed to increase the suffering of its victims." In other words, your suffering doesn't begin once you're placed in a freshly dug dirt pit. Rather, stoning caps a pile-on of prejudices.

Especially if you're a woman, Amnesty reports. In much of Iran, for instance,

> women are not treated equally with men under the law and by courts, and they are also particularly vulnerable to unfair trials

169

because their higher illiteracy rate makes them more likely to sign confessions to crimes they did not commit. Despite this bleak reality, human rights defenders in Iran believe that international publicity can help bring an end to stoning. Courageous efforts are being made by their Stop Stoning Forever campaign, whose efforts have helped save five people . . . and led to another sentence being stayed . . . since it began in October 2006.

For all its internal teeth-gnashing about what to make of honor culture, Amnesty International calls on Iran to "immediately abolish" stoning.

But not the university-educated Muslim moderates who surround me. Not even their feminist associate. All insist that a moratorium—a *temporary* halt—will do. In the open society of the United States, they'll never face stoning mobs, so they can afford to be cavalier. What a waste of privilege. I try a different tack: "Suppose it's your sister who's sentenced to stoning. Unlike a ban, a mere moratorium can be lifted at any time. Is that good enough when the victim's your sister?"

"There you go again personalizing the issue," groans one of the students, whose comment confirms that she dwells in the distant world of theory.

"Personalizing? Personalizing?" I stammer. "No. I'm humanizing it."

As we prepare to go our separate ways, another student—her conscience apparently rumbling—asks, "What do you want from us?"

"To lead by example," I answer.

I wish I'd remembered the story of Joseph Darby, a U.S. soldier who exposed torture at Abu Ghraib. At twenty-four, Darby could have been a classmate of these women, but he didn't need the wisdom of years to know what mattered most. As his mother told journalists, her son "could not stand the atrocities he had stumbled upon. He said he kept thinking, what if it was my mom, my grandmother, my brother, or my wife." I doubt my detractors would have accused this serviceman of unfairly "personalizing" the U.S. Army's torture.

Then again, standing by in the grim face of torture—be it stoning alleged adulterers or hooking up detainees to electrodes—isn't exactly rare. The moderate Muslims only behaved as many U.S. soldiers and their commander-in-chief did. In response to news of the Abu Ghraib abuses, President George W. Bush minimized them as aberrant. But Darby, who felt on the margins much of his life, developed empathy. He witnessed a moral crisis, withstood death threats and went on to blow the whistle that much louder. He led by example.

In May 2004, the president apologized for the "abhorrent" violations suffered by some Iraqi prisoners. And in October of that year the U.S. Congress commended Joseph Darby for exemplifying moral courage. "The need to act in accord with one's conscience, risking one's career and even the esteem of one's colleagues by pursuing what is right is especially important today," read the resolution. A young reservist understood—and got official America to understand—what moderate Muslims and their "progressive" defenders still need to confront.

Lesson six: *In times of moral crisis, moderation is a cop-out.*

Tariq Ramadan, arguably Europe's most high-profile Muslim scholar, backs a moratorium on stoning because "by condemning you are not going to change anything." His alternative to demanding a permanent ban: deliberation among jurists. But since the Qur'an never mentions the stoning of women, what in God's name is there to deliberate about? The response, I predict, would be that deliberation among mostly male elders gives credibility to the conclusion. Yet how do we know they'll reach a rational conclusion about stoning? Couldn't those elders, like power brokers in any system, let geopolitics aggravate their emotions—and pollute their analyses of Islam's teachings?

This is, after all, how the Qatar-based theologian Yusuf al-Qaradawi came to endorse suicide bombings of Israeli civilians. The Qur'an expressly opposes suicide under all pretexts and implores Muslim combatants to have mercy on noncombatants. But al-Qaradawi figures that "Israeli society is militaristic in nature," rendering every citizen a soldier by default. Therefore, blowing up civilians becomes an unfortunate "necessity" and "necessity makes the forbidden things permitted." The clatter of politics sidelines the conscience of the Qur'an.

And not just for al-Qaradawi. His views have won over a critical mass of Muslim theologians who deliberated upon them. When the scripturally forbidden can get reappraised as "permitted" for nakedly opportunistic reasons, why should I believe that a discussion among jurists will end the stoning of women or men? How does Ramadan's moratorium ensure Islam's integrity? Who's the idealist now?

I wouldn't spill ink on Tariq Ramadan but for one fact: He inadvertently reveals the moral crisis among moderate Muslims today. To be sure, some commentators decry him as a crypto-Islamist, not a moderate. Ramadan is the grandson of Hassan al-Banna, founder of the Muslim Brotherhood. That's the Egyptian equivalent of the Afrikaner Broederbond, the secretive Protestant brotherhood that legitimized South African apartheid through racist readings of the Bible. Both have operated as cults. Both have subscribed to a Manichaean vision of fighting the filth in their midst, Jews being the contaminants for the Muslim Brotherhood, blacks for the Afrikaner Broederbond. In their heyday, both made violence a disinfectant.

Earlier, I wrote about Archbishop Desmond Tutu's friend Beyers Naudé, a son of the family that built the Broederbond. As an adult, Naudé rejected his father's views. By contrast, when I heard Ramadan recently being invited to renounce his grandfather's totalitarian sympathies, he equivocated. He spoke about the context that convinced al-Banna to side with the Nazis against European Zionists. He also requested "true quotations"—proper translations—of his grandfather's Arabic statements, without addressing what would be true or proper enough to inspire in him the moral courage of a Beyers Naudé. Such a dragnet of qualifiers leads many to bust Ramadan as an Islamist. But by contemporary Muslim standards, he's a moderate. Therein lies the larger problem.

Let me set the stage a bit more. For years, the Bush administration prohibited Ramadan from coming to America, postulating—without proving—that he has terrorist ties. In early 2010, Hillary Clinton's State Department finally issued Ramadan a coveted entry visa. Days later, he participated in a conversation at New York's Cooper Union, the venue where a Republican presidential hopeful named Abraham Lincoln inflamed the anger of Southern movers and shakers by speaking forcefully against slavery. Under the same roof, Ramadan sought to build bridges, promoting a common future between East and West.

Toward the end of the evening, he offhandedly remarked to a fellow panelist that "mainstream" Muslims would be "what you call orthodox." On this, Ramadan is dead right. There's scant daylight between moderate and orthodox Muslims today. For me, though, such a statement isn't a casual aside. It's a major piece of the puzzle about why Islam's moderates so often obstruct liberal democratic values: If most Muslims are moderate, then moderation is mainstream; and if mainstream is orthodox, then a moderate Muslim is an orthodox one.

In every religion, insularity, dogma and fear mark orthodoxy. Beyers Naudé reminds us of literalist Christianity's screaming injustices. Literalist Judaism spawns illegal settlers and an Israeli rabbinate that shafts women who want divorces from their husbands. But in Christianity and Judaism today, moderates have an inventory of complaints about the insularity, dogma and fear that rule their literalist brethren. In Islam today, it's the opposite: Insularity, dogma and fear stain the behavior of moderates themselves.

———

The Quilliam Foundation, a British counterterror outfit set up by former jihadis, offers food for thought. In its publication *Pulling Together to End Terror*, Quilliam exposes how profoundly in denial of their dogma mainstream Muslim leaders are. As only one example: "The Islamic Foundation, a Leicester-based think tank, continues to publish the works of Islamist ideologues, including the Pakistani journalist Mawdudi." It's worth examining what this guy stood for and how it affects your world and mine.

Scholars often compare Syed Abul A'la Mawdudi to Hassan al-Banna. Mawdudi established Pakistan's equivalent of the Muslim Brotherhood—a puritan religious party called the Jamaat-e-Islami. I stress "puritan." His dogma deems a minority sect within Islam, the Ahmadis, as infidels and thus kafirs. To this day, the Ahmadis face derision by moderate Muslims in the West and paroxysms of rage in Pakistan. One sacred Friday in May 2010, the Pakistani Taliban massacred nearly a hundred Ahmadi worshippers in two mosques.

While we're on the subject of kafirs, anyone who chooses to leave Islam is, according to Mawdudi, "a permanent plague spreading among the people and a source of fear lest also the other whole and healthy members of a society be permeated with his poison. . . .

Better to punish him by death and thereby put an end to his own and society's misery." Eerily similar to the motive behind honor killings of women, isn't it?

Neighborhoods in Britain may be awash in Mawdudi's words, but I've also picked up his propaganda from street-corner leafleters in downtown Toronto. It even circulates in New York's live-and-let-live hothouse, Greenwich Village. I've played the curious passerby in both places and inquired, "Is this mainstream Islam?" In each case the pusher blithely affirmed that it is. In *that* case, mainstream Muslims have some questioning to do. Because the glossy Mawdudi paperback that I got in Greenwich Village— *Towards Understanding Islam*—preaches the following under "Jihad": "In the language of the Divine Law," which Mawdudi's acolytes would enforce here on Earth,

> *this word is used specifically for the war that is waged solely in the name of God against those who perpetrate oppression as enemies of Islam. This supreme sacrifice is the responsibility of all Muslims . . . One who avoids it is a sinner. His every claim to being a Muslim is doubtful. He is plainly a hypocrite who fails in the test of sincerity and all his acts of worship are a sham, a worthless, hollow show of devotion.*

Ladies and gentlemen, meet God. Not.

The Greenwich Village proselytizers—village idiots, really—may be unaware of the immoderation baked into Mawdudi's mainstream Islam, but Faisal Shahzad knew about it. He's the young Muslim and naturalized U.S. citizen who tried to activate a car bomb in New York's Times Square in May 2010. Why would a seeming model of immigrant integration, riding the ups and downs of the American Dream, do such a thing? Retaliation for U.S. air strikes against the Taliban in Pakistan, came the immediate news. Later, however, Shahzad confessed to more inspirations. Among them: Mawdudi.

"What has happened to us?" pleaded Saira, a reader of mine in Toronto.

Why are so many Muslims using their potential to destroy so much of what our oft-forgiving, merciful and kind God has given to us, all of us? Does it really help anyone when another suicide bomber dies and their family is left behind? Why is so much energy spent on creating havoc and death instead of a better life? Why are we moderate Muslims not taking a stronger, defiant stand against all this madness, in the name of "Islam"?

Saira began to answer with her next insight:

Yeah, injustices have been done, country against country, no doubt about it. But are we going to hold onto that resentment and hate for the rest of our lives, at the expense of trying to create a comfortable existence for future generations?

Rarely have I come across such a full-throated call to replace attachment to grievance with capacity for growth.

Saira has hit on a conspicuous barrier to that growth: group identity. Moderate Muslims are so consumed with Western colonialism that they've diverted themselves from dealing with the imperialists *inside* Islam. It's the perfect recipe for high defenses against the Other and low expectations of ourselves. Rewind to the young Muslim women who scrummed me in Chicago. They couldn't bring themselves to condemn outright a death by stoning—not after two hours in which a packed room of students fumed about Western prejudices and policies—because the Viagra of group identity kicked in and kept their defenses up.

Moderate Muslims stumble into this trap all the time. Would an advocate of interfaith dialogue qualify as a moderate? If so, let me tell you something more about the New Jersey Muslim who wanted to be my censor. Not only did he itemize offensive sentences to be cut from *The Trouble with Islam Today*, he also demanded that I insert a different analysis of what ails Muslims. It's neither America nor Israel, I'd concluded in my book. Mostly, it's we Muslims. His edit: "American military occupation of Muslim lands is the real cause." On the page where I argued that Muslims' adherence to seventh-century Islam "is killing us," he amended, "Judeo-Christian fundamentalism is killing the world." Once more, high defenses against the Other and low expectations of ourselves.

Being "distracted by one's own defensiveness," says the Columbia University scholar Akeel Bilgrami, makes Muslim moderates easy pawns of Muslim absolutists. Think Mawdudi. Or Khomeini. Or even Idi Amin, the military dictator of Uganda. A reader named Adnan emailed me, "Continue to be a factotum of Anglo-Saxon arrogance and hostility. . . . It is a pity that Idi Amin didn't finish off you and your family." Why does Adnan root for Idi Amin, who notoriously slaughtered tens of thousands of his fellow Muslims? Because Idi Amin loathed the white man. Adnan has let himself be taken hostage to a grinding, blinding grievance against only one version of imperial callousness—the "Anglo-Saxon." The butcher of color gets a pass.

Akeel Bilgrami chalks up the moderate Muslim's elevated defenses to a fear that criticizing other Muslims "would amount to a surrender," the ultimate abdication of group honor to a contemptuous West. But, Bilgrami astutely clarifies, the *reverse* holds true:

The final triumph for colonizers is the Muslim habit of denying and deflecting our internal dysfunction. Denial and deflection strip Muslims of the ability to be introspective and therefore free. In the process, moderate Muslims throttle the very moderation to which they claim they're devoted.

Muslims in eastern Europe bolster Bilgrami's argument. During the Nazi occupation, entire Muslim villages in Albania sheltered Jews. The Albanian prime minister, Mehdi Frashëri, gave a secret order to fellow believers: "All Jewish children will sleep with your children, all will eat the same food, all will live as one family." Frashëri belonged to the Bektashi, a sect of Islam whose members had been persecuted by Mustafa Kemal Atatürk, founder of the Republic of Turkey. In the early 1920s, Atatürk expelled the Bektashi, who established their new base in Tiranë, Albania.

Twenty years later, the Bektashi of Albania organized an underground movement to keep Jews hidden not only from Hitler's National Socialists but also from Mussolini's National Fascists. Bektashi Muslims could have let their Turkish traumas bully them into becoming picayune. They chose differently. Even today, after decades of Communist repression, a Bektashi leader in Albania refuses to let injustice against his people undercut his capacity for humanity. "God is in every pore and every cell, therefore all are God's children," he propounds. "There cannot be infidels."

Not every Muslim villager stood firm with Jewish citizens and refugees. Elida Bicaku recalls that some in her town capitulated to their fears of the Germans and Italians, demanding that Jews go away. So her "devout Muslim" grandfather and father left the village to live with Jews in the mountains. Their moral courage became necessary despite an Albanian code of honor that emphasized responsibility for the Other. Which shows, once again, that cultures don't make choices. Individuals do.

Safwan, a reader of mine in Morocco, passionately brings the point home to mainstream Muslims. "We are only victims if we choose to be," he posted in a chat room for moderates.

Yes the U.S. and the West have [done] and are doing some hypocritical and unfair deeds but what about us? What about our conception of Islam, of a "Muslim" society, of our "Muslim values"? Do we have the key to knowledge and righteousness just because we are Muslims? And what is Islam? Do we practice it the right way? What is the right way? Should we be preaching to others? Ask yourselves these questions first. That is what ijtihad is advocating, a questioning of our values and practices as rational individuals.

As if to complete Safwan's thought, Akeel Bilgrami urges genuine moderates to acknowledge the obvious: A reactionary agenda, carried out in Islam's name, "is something we have uncritically and indiscriminately embraced out of demoralization and defeat, often allowing it to dominate our political actions, and it has gotten us nowhere." Moderates should learn to say that it's "up to us to work towards [our] reform . . ."

If you want meaningful moderation in Islam, then turn for more lessons to the world's largest Muslim-majority country, Indonesia. (Prophet Muhammad recommended that Muslims go as far as China for knowledge. My inner ijtihadi reinterprets "China" as "Indonesia." Same time zone.)

In April 2008, I flew to Jakarta to launch my book and film at the national library. Hundreds of students showed up, among them Islamists and transsexuals. They spoke their minds. They disagreed. In between the verbal sparring, guitarists strummed, poets recited and dancers kicked up their Javanese heels. Nobody low-balled the tensions; they treated tension as a necessity in democracy—the hallmark of true moderation.

As far as I know, everyone left the launch safely. That includes the most vocal transsexual, who proudly announced in front of Islamists that, postsurgery, she'd fought for the right to wear hijab (known in Indonesia as *jilbab*). She won that fight. We respectfully disputed each other's interpretations of the headscarf, and that's as it ought to be in a pluralistic society. I felt overwhelmingly grateful for three things: that we could openly reason with each other, that we did so with civility, and that a former "he" could be a "she" with relative security and unflinching integrity in a mainly Muslim nation governed by a secular constitution. My uncovered head spun at the layers of diversity.

Indonesians could have drowned themselves in acid baths of bile over being colonized. From 1800 to 1942, most of them lived under some form of Dutch rule, followed by about fifty years of dictatorship by their own strongmen. In 1998 a period of experimental democracy—or *reformasi*—began. Islamo-tribalists latched on to their new freedoms and got busy, as did their Saudi benefactors. Today, the Indonesian archipelago of seventeen thousand islands and hundreds of ethnicities struggles with Saudi cultural imperialism. Islamist banners hang from poles arduously pounded into the ground. An influx of money has paid for the extra muscle—staying power is the message.

Here, too, Islamists try to outlaw the minority Ahmadis. And restrictions on women's clothing are rising, particularly in cities and towns where tourists from the Arabian peninsula congregate. In Aceh, a province that has never integrated fully into the secular Indonesian state, politicians passed a 2009 law to permit stoning. In 2010, two women "caught" selling rice at a stall over the fasting hours of Ramadhan found themselves being caned before hundreds of spectators.

Yet plenty of Indonesians also see that the tightening Saudi noose has to be resisted, and their vibrant civil society counters this latest version of colonialism. During my visit, Hindun Annisa taught a cavernous auditorium of students that "when theologians talk about Islamic history, they're talking about Arab history." The students instantly understood. Annisa later escorted me to a *pesantren*, or Islamic boarding school, where visible joy, a makeshift basketball court (adorned with a Chicago Bulls backboard) and my conversations with the girls painted for me a fresco of Muslim faith.

Annisa's mother runs the pesantren. As we spoke, I couldn't help but think that she and her daughter embody the values of R. A. Kartini, an early twentieth-century pioneer of Indonesian women's rights. Kartini borrowed concepts from European feminists and adapted them to her people's conditions. Every April, Indonesia officially celebrates Kartini Days. I timed my visit for that occasion, witnessing on national TV and in print an affection for Kartini that resembles America's annual salute to Martin Luther King, Jr. In each case, the transformative power of uplift is being hailed over the enfeebling habits of victimhood.

If moderate Muslims elsewhere devote themselves to that transformation—from group victimhood to individual agency—they'll seriously contribute to leaching corruption out of Islamic practices. But without this interior change, their moderation will be moderate in theory alone. In reality, the defensive moderate will legitimize the militant. For now, then, the Islamic ideal of moderation has to be achieved by reforming moderates themselves. A word of warning: In saying something's askew with Muslim moderation today, prepare to be labeled as extreme as Osama bin Laden. A word of encouragement: When branded an extremist, you'll find yourself in more august company than Osama bin Laden.

"I must admit that I was initially disappointed in being so categorized," Martin Luther King, Jr., told the "white moderates" who judged his nonviolent actions as extremist. Moderates wanted to slow down the segregation train—pursue a moratorium, if you will—rather than stop the train in its tracks. "Shallow understanding from people of good will is more frustrating than absolute misunderstanding from people of ill will," King reflected. Contemplating it further, though, he

> gained a measure of satisfaction from being considered an extremist. Was not Jesus an extremist for love—"Love your enemies, bless them that curse you, do good to them that hate you, pray for them which despitefully use you, and persecute you." Was not Amos an extremist for justice—"Let justice roll down like waters and righteousness like an ever-flowing stream." Was not Paul an extremist for the Christian gospel—"I bear in my body the marks of the Lord Jesus." Was not Martin Luther an extremist—"Here I stand; I cannot do otherwise, so help me God." And John Bunyan—"I will stay in jail to the end of my days before I make a butchery of my conscience." And Abraham Lincoln—"This nation cannot survive half slave and half free." And Thomas Jefferson—"We hold these truths to be self-evident, that all men are created equal." So the question is not whether we will be extremists, but what kind of extremists we will be. Will we be extremists for hate or for love?

King could have been talking to Muslims today when he emphasized that "the nation and the world are in dire need of creative extremists." Destructive extremists need not apply.

———

I want you to meet one of the creative extremists who made an indelible impact on King. Lillian Smith, a white Georgian, wrote the blockbuster 1944 novel *Strange Fruit.* (Her title, coined in 1930s New York by a Jewish high school teacher and popularized in song by Billie Holiday, refers to lynched blacks dangling from trees.) I first came across Smith in King's "Letter from Birmingham Jail." He named a handful of white Southerners who "have grasped the meaning of this social revolution and committed themselves to it." Tucked between mentions of men and women I'd heard of was King's nod to someone I hadn't: Lillian Smith. I looked her up.

In 1956, years before King would encourage white moderates to become "creative extremists," Smith brought that idea to black civil rights activists in Montgomery, Alabama. By "dramatizing that the extreme way can be the good way, the creative way, and that in times of ordeal it is the only way, you are helping the white South find its way, too," she explained. Smith practiced not noblesse oblige, nor benevolent pity, but mutual liberation. With every breath of her authorial voice, with every platform afforded her, she made the case that black civil rights would free white oppressors from their own crippling anxieties. But her fellow liberals remained lukewarm about taking on the South's culture of honor and the segregationists it supported.

In 1944, a generation ahead of the civil rights sit-ins, Smith penned an open letter. The title: "Addressed to White Liberals." In it, she declared segregation

> *a menace to the health of our culture and our individual souls. For segregation as a way of life— or shall we say a way of death— is cultural schizophrenia, bearing a curious resemblance to the schizophrenia of individual personality. It is chilling to note the paranoid symptoms of those among us who cling to segregation: their violence, their sensitiveness to criticism, their stereotyped defenses, their inability to identify their overesteem of themselves*

with the emotional needs of others, their reluctance to reach out and accept new ideas, their profound desire to withdraw from everything hard to face, everything that requires of their personalities further growth. . . .

We who do not believe in segregation as a way of life must say so. We must break the conspiracy of silence which has held us in a grip so strong that it has become a taboo. We must say why segregation is unendurable to the human spirit. We must somehow find the courage to say it aloud. For, however we rationalize our silence, it is fear that is holding our tongues today. A widespread denial of a belief in segregation and all it implies will shake this way of life to its roots. Each of us knows this in his heart. In the beginning was the Word and today the Word is powerful. To remain silent while the demagogues, the Negro haters, the racists, the mentally ill, loudly reaffirm their faith in segregation and the spiritual lynching which their way of life inflicts, is to be traitorous to everything that is good and creative and sane in human values.

Smith's moral courage helped rupture the walls of a Southern culture coarsened by group honor, a culture whose elites preserved segregation by invoking tradition. Sound familiar?

She denounced the pantomime of moderation as being no answer to moral crisis. "What do people mean when they use that fuzzy word, moderation?" Smith mused. "What makes the word so hypnotic?" She upbraided liberals for "working harder to be moderates than they are working to meet the crisis. They are driving straight down the middle of the road with their eyes shut and you know what happens in traffic when you do that." You turn yourself into roadkill. Or you turn others into roadkill. "Magazines with mass circulation are timid about 'offending the white segregationists,'" Smith wrote. "And this is very sad: to see our people, our proud, free people grow afraid to speak out and to act according to their conscience." Sound familiar?

Above all, Smith decried relativism. She compared habitual thieves with the habitually honest, asking, "Are they equally harmful? Or equally good? Those who think so have abandoned the concept of morality and the concept of quality and sanity in human affairs." She then cautioned against the ripple effect of relativism:

> *While the moderates are staying silent, the bad extremists are shouting at the top of their lungs. And because it is so difficult for the young white Southerner to hear anything good and creative said, because he sees so little courage, so little valor among his elders, he is losing his beliefs in the good, creative, brave way of life. One young man said to me recently, "I'd risk anything for something I believed in. I just don't think I believe in anything much, anymore."*

That's why Smith drew so much optimism from black activists. "You are giving young white Southerners hope," she assured them.

> *You are persuading some of them that there is something worth believing in and risking for. You are stirring their imaginations and their hearts—not simply because you are brave and running risks but because you know that the means we use are the important thing: the means must be right; the means must be full of truth and dignity and love and wisdom.*

In sum, "This is how the creative act works: it always helps somebody else besides you." On that score, Smith can be utterly trusted. In 1960, African American college students conducted the first sit-in in Greensboro, North Carolina. Their stated inspirations? Sociologist Gunnar Myrdal, Mahatma Gandhi—and Lillian Smith. She expected of the students not puerile idealism, but personal responsibility. Smith insisted all along that to lead by example, blacks must "discard *their* suspicions of whites, *their* need to hate other people, *their* need to feel persecuted [her italics]." With that, she foresaw the modern civil rights movement as a human mission.

Even when approaching the twilight of her life, Smith leapt into the future again. "Our big problem is not civil rights," she suggested in 1963, "but how to make into a related whole the split pieces of the human experience, how to bridge mythic and rational mind." Reconciling the mythic and the rational: strikes me as the paramount purpose in an era seething with cultural, religious and ideological dogmas. That era is ours.

———————

As Lillian Smith and Martin Luther King, Jr., asked of America's Southern moderates, Muslims and non-Muslims must raise our expectations of Islam's self-declared moderates. That means working up the moral courage to ask them questions: *As you castigate the West, do you also repudiate Islam's own segregationists—those who divide humanity between the kafir and everyone else?*

If you condemn the Ku Klux Klan, then you should have no hesitation—none, nada—in seeing the Taliban in the same light. In fact, they're near replicas of the knife- and rope-packing lynch mobs that terrorized Jim Crow America. The historian Taylor Branch sketches this scene from the steamy Georgia summer of 1946:

> *Mobs assassinated no fewer than six Negro war veterans in a single three-week period. . . . One of those six veterans died when a group of hooded men pulled him, his wife, and another Negro couple out of a car near Monroe, lined the four of them up in front of a*

ditch, and fired a barrage that left a reported 180 bullet holes in one of the four corpses. In the aftermath, state investigators in Monroe complained that "the best people in town won't talk about this" . . .

Compare that terror to what Farhat Taj documented about the Pakistani Taliban in May 2010:

This is not the first time that the Taliban have chopped off hands. On dozens of occasions in the past, they have amputated men, flogged people and hung up dead bodies on trees. And now this past week, they literally blew up two alleged spies by attaching explosives to them and triggering them—in a public place. Of course, this has the effect of causing extreme fear and dread in the local population which obviously has no choice but to see all this happen in silence.

"Washington helped create the Taliban," moderate Muslims constantly tell me as if to stop the conversation. Yes, Washington did help create the Taliban, and because of that colossal blunder the Cold War isn't over. But does this sorry reality excuse moderate Muslims from discrediting the dogma on which the Taliban feasts? Not in the least. Since moderates are driven to distraction by the colonizers of Muslims, they've got even more incentive to get noisy about the Taliban: Washington doesn't rule the fear-ridden tribal area that Farhat Taj writes about. It's "under de facto control of the Taliban," she confirms, "along with al Qaeda foreigners." Foreigners. *Get outta here. Will moderates denounce intrusive foreigners from any address—or just those foreigners from a Western address?* Another question for all of us to ask in the name of a durable peace.

———

The Taliban only top the litany of Islam's segregationists. We can't let moderates overlook the genocidal militias of Darfur, Sudan, whose expertise in ethnic cleansing and enslavement would humble the good ol' boys of antebellum Georgia. A destructive extremist such as bin Laden blames "Crusader invaders" to fortify the defenses of moderates, but Mona Eltahawy, the clear-eyed Muslim reformer I introduced in chapter 2, sees through bin Laden's deceptions. "Muslims are killing Muslims in Darfur," she chronicles. "This is no Israeli occupation or U.S.-led invasion." A journalist who punishes her passport even more than I do mine, Eltahawy has collected stories from around the world and compiled an authoritative mosaic. "The sad fact," she concludes, "is that more Muslims today are dying at the hands of Muslims than by acts of Israelis, Americans, or any other perceived enemies—whether it's from almost weekly suicide bombings in Pakistan, intra-Palestinian fighting, or sectarian violence in Iraq."

Three researchers backed up her conclusion in December 2009. Reviewing Arabic-language news sources, they found that from 2004 to 2008, 85 percent of al-Qaeda's victims were Muslims, with the number hitting 98 percent from 2006 to 2008. In a report for the Combating Terrorism Center at West Point, they also disproved the standard assumption that Muslims get slaughtered only where America invades. "Outside the war zones of Afghanistan and Iraq," the analysts showed, "99% of al-Qa'ida's victims were non-Western in 2007, and 96% were non-Western in 2008." In other words, al-Qaeda doesn't need the barbarity of the United States to take its own barbarity out on Muslims.

Why shouldn't we expect moderates to stand up as fervently for civilians who are harmed by Muslim violence as those damaged by Western violence? Don't Muslim lives count as much when they're snuffed out by other Muslims? Are we to gauge the value of human beings according to who extinguishes them? Still, informing moderates about al-Qaeda foreigners (or the mincemeat they make of Muslims) won't necessarily ensure honest discussion. Knowledge doesn't guarantee rationality. To bridge the mythic and the rational, we need to open *hearts* in addition to minds.

A European student recently tested this point. She posted a message in my Facebook forum:

> Would appreciate your advice. The Student Union at our university will be twinned with the Islamic University in Gaza. I am very much against this, as the university in Gaza receives both funds and moral support from terrorist organizations whose leaders speak about the need to kill all Jews, Christians and even moderate Muslims. . . . I don't know what to do, as all the Europeans with whom I have spoken just don't get it!! I know the referendum will pass—we have no chance—but I want to fight against this as much as I can.

Here's what I knew: If it's Gaza, Hamas has its hands in the till. And of the multiple reasons to repudiate Hamas, one must surely be that its charter accepts slavery under Islam. It tells the slaves of Muslims that they may battle Zionists without their masters' permission. Hamas, therefore, tolerates bondage by Muslims while clamoring for emancipation from non-Muslims.

The romantic sides of some European students would have fancied any chance to express solidarity with Muslims, who are routinely assumed to be the victims and never the perpetrators of imperialism. So, I advised my Facebook friend,

> Ask supporters of this referendum how it's "anti-imperialist" to twin with a university that receives funds from those who would kill moderate Muslims. Use the language of anti-colonialism to show that what the referendum

defenders are doing goes exactly against their rhetoric of human rights. You'll find that many agree with you, and some might even be encouraged to speak up because you're explaining your concerns in a language—the language of anti-imperialism—that they understand.

Three days later, she posted the counterargument from skeptics: "They say that we're doing this for the students at the University of Gaza and not for Hamas, ignoring how they are (in most cases) closely intertwined." Three weeks on, the student posted once more: "After a very hard week (in which I was even called a Nazi), WE WON! And as you said, many people identified with us. I had a Pakistani girl come up to me and say that she voted NO. . . . I was amazed. I learned a lot."

We've arrived at a second way to expect better from moderates. On the meter of emotional awkwardness, this one's a doozy. But widening the path of Islam requires more of us to ask questions of the religion itself—not just of the tribal culture that has colonized contemporary Muslim psyches.

As I mentioned earlier, while filming *Faith Without Fear*, I interviewed Osama bin Laden's former bodyguard. Ahmed Nasser, a Yemeni citizen, had undergone his government's vaunted deprogramming initiative and the authorities trotted him out as a counterterrorism success story. But with a broad smile and every intention to train his five-year-old son in martyrdom, Nasser gloated to me that he remains convinced of the need for violence. "Jihad was practiced by the prophet himself and by his companions as well," Nasser instructed. "Some of them fell as martyrs. So the prophet and his companions are our role models."

In a video filmed ahead of the 2005 London transit bombings,

Mohammad Sidique Khan stated that "our religion is Islam—obedience to the one true God, Allah, and following the footsteps of the final prophet and messenger, Muhammad. . . . This is how our ethical stances are dictated." Khan made this pronouncement before saying a syllable about Western foreign policies.

Mohammed Bouyeri, the Dutch-born Muslim who fatally shot Theo van Gogh, stoically confessed that he operated from religious conviction. He knew that bullets would be enough to do his victim in, yet he also whisked out a blade to decapitate the corpse. Brandishing the blade reenacted seventh-century tribal warfare. Even the note that Bouyeri stabbed into van Gogh's body, scrawled in Dutch, had the unmistakable rhythms of Arabic poetry.

Moderate Muslims blanch at the thought of exploring their religion's role in terrorist strife. They deplore violence committed in Islam's name, but reflexively recite that "Islam has nothing to do with it." In their denial, moderate Muslims cede responsibility for interpretation, effectively telling terrorists-in-waiting: "You guys get to walk away with the show. We're not going to come back at you with bold and competing reinterpretations. Because if we did, we'd be accepting that religion has something to do with the violence. Since Islam is perfect, we can't go there."

Islam is what Muslims make it. Just as Christians and Jews have reinterpreted the troubling passages of their scriptures for new centuries, Muslims have to do likewise. That's not rewriting the Qur'an; it's updating interpretations of existing words. Islamo-tribalists may decree their interpretations as the only true ones, but their arrogance breaches the Qur'an's unambiguous reminder that God alone has the full truth, and it dupes too many of us into believing that just one approach can hold water. For both reasons, reinterpretation is a noble endeavor—all the more when certain verses are cited to service killing sprees.

As it stands, the most that moderates do is put awkward Qur'anic verses "in context," entombing interpretation in a seventh-century tribal time warp. In a British TV documentary, Tariq Ramadan sits down with Muslims to discuss a Qur'anic verse that's invoked by many who regard Islam as a religion of hate: "Fight and slay the pagans wherever you find them, and seize them and beleaguer them" (9:5). The Muslims examining this passage, Ramadan tells us, "are quick to see that these words should not be taken out of context." Says one of them, "If we read the preceding verse, we can see immediately that the position is defensive. The verse tells us, 'Fight those who fight you in the path of Allah.' So it is necessary to have been attacked and therefore to be a victim in the first place." Ramadan looks on approvingly. He informs us that "these verses speak about the situation before battle, which threatened the survival of the first Muslim community. It can't be seen as a general permission to kill all non-Muslims."

But how does his analysis depart from what terrorists claim? In Yemen, Ahmed Nasser insisted to me that wars of Western imperialism have victimized the twenty-first-century ummah, which is why "I have committed myself to protect Muslims everywhere." We've seen this movie before. Ramadan's answer to Nasser's position? "The message of the Qur'an is quite clear: that it's wrong to kill civilians." We've seen this movie before too. It hasn't exactly influenced Yusuf al-Qaradawi, the theologian who decided—to the applause of his peers—that Muslims can legitimately target Israeli *civilians*. Nor does Ramadan's focus on civilians move Nasser. He turns it inside out by saying that Muslim women and children are the civilians who need defending against infidel forces. Therefore, as the seventh-century Muslim community did, "fight those who fight you in the path of Allah."

The verse could be reinterpreted altogether. We could recognize that today more Muslims are being maimed, imprisoned, tortured and murdered by Muslims than by anyone else. In order to "fight those who fight you in the path of Allah," Muslims would have to repel the colonizing schemes of fellow Muslims. This is what Mohammad Sidique Khan, Faisal Shahzad and other anti-imperialist jihadis ought to have heard about showing "solidarity" with the ummah. Muslim-on-Muslim violence is the backbone of a narrative that deflates jihadi grandstanding. It's a counternarrative that deals in reality while doing justice to a loving God. Moderate Muslims need to share this counternarrative with the young men and women of their communities. The rest of us need to expect them to share it.

Moderates could reset their moral compass in at least one other way. Don't just steam about non-Muslims; spotlight Muslims who demonstrate that internal reform is itself anti-imperialist. Tell the story of Abdul Ghaffar Khan. Educate your children about Rana Husseini, the Jordanian journalist who's blowing the cover off honor-based crimes in her society. Take pride in the Stop Stoning Forever initiative. Spread the word about the Iranian Women's One Million Signatures Campaign for Equality. And notice that each of these freedom fighters chooses nonviolence.

Iran's reformers remind us of the choices that anti-imperialists have—wherever they live. You've probably heard of twenty-seven-year-old Neda Agha-Soltan, often known simply as Neda, who died in the streets of Tehran while protesting her country's rigged 2009 election. Her assassination, orchestrated by the Iranian state, rocketed around the world through video recorded on mobile phones. Neda's murder almost instantly came to symbolize the injustice being confronted by Iranian patriots. But it's her behind-the-scenes decisions that unveil the larger scope of the choices she made. Neda's faith and intellect motivated her to study Islamic philosophy at Azad University. After two terms, she quit. Neda "used to say that the God they are teaching us at these universities is different from the God I worship," her sister remembers. "A professor taught them about a vengeful God, but Neda said, 'This is not my God. The God I worship is a compassionate and loving God.'"

On the first anniversary of the protests, I read about more examples of everyday resistance in Iran. "The son of a prominent official told a friend he would no longer accept money from his father because the father worked for the government, which the son considered corrupt," *The New York Times* reported. "While many people are disappointed" that the regime has survived, the story ended,

others say the year of pain and sacrifice is paying off. "People have absolutely gained something, a certain degree of individual independence," said a 20-year-old medical student. "They began to decide for themselves that they would go out to protest, to follow the news. This is something that has happened for everybody. In different areas of their lives they are losing patience and are not likely to say anymore that they will put up with things."

All of these players are battling Islam's power-abusers by owning their responsibility for uplift. They're not standing by while Muslim jurists, as susceptible to grubby politics as American or Israeli policymakers, reach verdicts on behalf of everyone else. They're taking it upon themselves to reshape Islam in practice. Their resistance is anything but passive.

————

Frankly, I'm not certain that all the pugnacious verses of the Qur'an can be reinterpreted for our century. But maybe every such passage doesn't need to be actively rethought if the Qur'an's pluralistic verses can be publicized to a critical mass of Muslims. Nobody can know until more of us try. I *am* certain that it won't nurture the faith of freedom-hungry Muslims when moderates, in their defensiveness, resort to the sellout card.

After the 2005 London bombings, I delivered a radio commentary crediting mainstream Muslims for their condolences to the victims and condemnations of the criminals. But, I continued, "too many imams would rather deny that the Qur'an plays any role in this mess." I chose the example of Imam Feisal Abdul Rauf, the prominent New York City cleric. In my commentary I kept him anonymous, fearing that my point could be weakened by accusations of an ad hominem attack. Referring to the imam as "gentle" and "decent," I then dissected the press release that he issued after the London upheaval. It said that according to the Qur'an, "Whoever kills a human being, it is as if he has killed all mankind" (5:32).

"Not quite," I said with regret. "The full verse reads, 'Whoever kills a human being, *except as punishment for murder or other villainy in the land*, shall be regarded as having killed all mankind [my italics].'" For the London jihadis, I went on, "villainy in the land" describes the boot prints of U.S. soldiers in Iraqi soil. This otherwise humane Qur'anic passage gives all jihadis an escape hatch that starts with "except." What, I asked, are we to do with that loophole? At the time I didn't clue into the robust counternarrative —that "villainy in the land" can describe actions by al-Qaeda and the Taliban. In my commentary, I articulated this as a "next step": Moderate Muslims should join moderate Jews and Christians "in acknowledging the nasty side of all our texts . . . Let us be honest with each other, even as we're struggling to be fair with each other."

The following week, a Muslim acquaintance emailed me. Peeved that I'd "go after moderate Muslims," she curtly counseled me to "wash laundry in the backyard." I recount this experience for one reason. As a Muslim who's secure in my faith, I can manage the well-rehearsed politicians of identity, but how about the Muslim whose faith hangs by a thread? Are tired accusations the best she can look forward to when she dares to be candid?

I'm thinking about Saba, a college student with a conscience and a conundrum:

As the public relations officer in our Muslim Students' Association (MSA), I have had the opportunity to influence many people about Islam, especially the misconceptions that non-Muslims may have. . . . Unfortunately, my greater concern now revolves around Muslims' own misconceptions. After joking with a few of the MSA guys, I loudly exclaimed, "Well, my opinion counts just as much as yours," to which one of my male friends quietly replied, "not according to the Sunnah." He was of course referring to the need for two female witnesses to substitute for one male witness (Quran 2:282).

Regardless of what this line may have meant in the context of 7th century Mecca, it is clear that many men still take it to mean that a woman's voice is actually inferior to a man's. . . . How am I supposed to counteract this negative image of women when our own doctrine seems to support the idea of submissive and deficient females?

Icy allegations of betrayal will delay the fresh insights that Saba might inject into Islam as it can be lived. The militant's lack of moral scruple desecrates a merciful God, but the moderate's lack of moral courage does too. We don't have to limit ourselves to those pallid choices: lack of scruple versus lack of spine. Faith is capable of abundance.

To challenge the weaseling politics behind moderation, more of us have to be aware—and wary—of three pronounced tendencies in any conversation about Islam.

First, whenever a militant Muslim commits an egregious act while incanting religious inspiration, moderates incant a version of "This isn't Islam." In November 2009, Major Nidal Malik Hasan opened fire on his U.S. Army comrades in Fort Hood, Texas. He shouted, *Allahu Akbar*—"God is greater"—as he let loose. Asra Nomani, a countercultural Muslim, went public about the unsettling aftermath: "There is this mantra from Muslim organizations: 'Major Hasan does not represent Islam.' Well, that doesn't deal with the reality that, yes indeed, Major Hasan followed an interpretation of Islam that is prevalent in the community. This is real."

When moderates run from this reality, they raise suspicions about Islam, which fulfills their self-serving prophecy that all questions for moderates must be born of bigotry. We have to remind moderates of a simple truth: You can't have constructive conversations on the run.

Sometimes, the reminder actually works. In April 2007, I attended an event for Islamic Awareness Week at Simmons College near Boston. A married couple gave the presentation, alongside the wife's father. Afterward, a Muslim student in the audience asked the female presenter why so much silence shrouds the crime of stoning. "I think it's utopian to believe that Muslims can speak out," the presenter replied.

"It's not utopian," the student maintained. "It's our responsibility."

"Then," the presenter allowed, "one of the most important things we can do is *du'a* [prayer]."

"Du'a is lovely," the student responded, "but your answer is a huge cop-out."

The speaker's father complained that "we moderates never get media attention." Perhaps embarrassed by her father's non sequitur, or perhaps pushed to a place of moral maturity, the presenter admitted that "we have to stop blaming others before we look at ourselves." Her husband, echoing the Qur'an's plea for personal responsibility, added that "we have to change ourselves."

Falak, a reader of mine, vindicates my faith in having higher expectations of moderates. "I grew up as a Muslim woman in the Middle East and moved to Canada, marrying a non-Muslim Canadian," she emailed to me.

In practicing Islam, living our daily lives and listening to the usual BS about the "evil" West, I found myself reciting the same lines as many Muslims of the post 9/11 era: These are fanatics (not REAL Muslims) who have strayed from the right path. . . . You know what I've realized since? That these were religious and educated Muslims from privileged backgrounds who did it. They found something somewhere that absolved them of the act of killing.

Falak pledged to "impart a more balanced faith" to her daughters.

The second tendency to be vigilant about: We routinely accept that the height of Muslim accountability is the denunciation of violence, period. But in fact there's something more to be done. In the wake of the Fort Hood shooting, the mainstream Council on American-Islamic Relations (CAIR) put out a press release stating, "We condemn this cowardly act in the strongest terms possible and ask that the perpetrators be punished to the full extent of the law. No religious or political ideology could ever justify or excuse such wanton and indiscriminate violence." As a condemnation, CAIR's is better than a poke in the eye, but the "strongest terms possible"? No. CAIR would need to acknowledge that a certain interpretation of Islam might have tipped the scales for Major Hasan, and if that's the case then Muslims must engage in some reinterpretation.

A few months into the investigation, U.S. Attorney General Eric

Holder sat before members of Congress. He, like the public, knew by then that Major Hasan surfed Islamist websites and communicated with a radical imam, a Yemeni American who promulgates hatred. Holder fielded repeated questions about the role of Islamism in instigating the shooting but couldn't allow himself to consider any such role. "Whaddya expect?" some readers will scoff. I expect more. Because Holder himself purports to expect more—at least of the American conversation about race. He famously characterized his fellow citizens as "a nation of cowards" for ducking tough dialogue on racial matters, and he was spot-on. But when it comes to the conversation about Islam, Holder's making the same old mistakes. He—and we—should make new mistakes.

Have I lost every last marble? Aren't the stakes too apocalyptic to risk more missteps? Not if the stakes involve a peace worth having. In October 2006, moderate Muslim "authorities and scholars" drafted an open letter to their Christian counterparts. Entitled "A Common Word Between Us and You," the letter speaks glowingly of reconciliation, but sets an important condition for Christians to earn Muslim love: Don't start a war with Islam. Reasonable, until you think about it.

Any gesture, including a humanitarian one, can be interpreted as hostile to Islam depending on the political agenda of the one doing the interpreting. Would NATO intervention to end genocide in the Muslim-majority country of Sudan have amounted to starting a war with Islam? Violent jihadis could have made it so. Then they could have cited the war-with-Islam rationale as their excuse for terrorism, leaving moderate Muslims to blame Western foreign policies for producing terrorists. It's stupefying—and stupefyingly predictable. By playing on these terms, moderate Muslim thinkers validate this strand of militancy. And by not assiduously questioning them about it, Christian thinkers return the favor. The Christian responses I've read to "A Common Word" have strained to sound glowing about harmony, uttering barely a peep about the rickety premise behind the Muslim letter's concept of peace.

In calling out the fuzziness of this dialogue, I aim for honesty and clarity, and that's what we've got in the final question I recommend when discussing Islam with moderates. The question goes like this: *I'm not wondering about the theory of Islam, which I trust is beautiful, but I am wondering about the practice of it. What element of Islam, when followed in the real and imperfect world, leads to pain— and why?* It's a question designed to cut through the third tendency: that moderates talk about Islam in the abstract. This tendency breeds banalities such as "Islam is peace." When skeptics hear that cliché, they often take it as a sign of Muslim duplicity. Fact is, though, many moderates sincerely believe that Islam is peace. What they're saying is, "Islam *means* peace." What they're *not* saying is, *Just because a word means something doesn't guarantee that reality lines up.*

With a wink and a grin, I remind the scowling moderates in my audiences that "Irshad means guidance. Yet you're clearly convinced that by examining the trouble within Islam today, I'm misguided. Similarly, Islam means peace. But we have the evidence that it often doesn't turn out that way. Which is it, then? Is the meaning of a word all that matters? If so, you'd have to admit that I'm blessed with God's guidance. If not, you'd have to admit there may be aspects of Islam, in practice, that we need to adapt to the twenty-first century." The scowls don't lift. But eyebrows do. And interior dialogues get under way, a helpful precursor to exchanges between and among people.

I've just laid out three tendencies to take note of, then to push back on, keeping in mind that to love and honor others is to have faith in their capacity to grow. Human beings, however, are gullible when it comes to our emotions. Fear can snooker us into deciding that questions only make matters worse, especially in an already polarized environment. That's why the questions I ask—and ask you to ask—reject the artificial divide between Islam and the West. My questions reimagine the public discussion so that Muslims and non-Muslims can find shared purpose in human values. As the reformist scholar Khaled Abou El Fadl writes, "Muslim thinking has remained either pro-West or anti-West instead of focusing on a far more important question: Is Muslim thinking in the modern world pro-human or anti-human?"

To be pro-human, we'll need to snap out of the illusion of neutrality. Lillian Smith taught that in a context of obscene practices such as lynching and stoning, it's belligerent to take a kindly distance. Neutrality cements brutality, and it throws honest-to-God reformers under the bus.

————

Miss Lillian had to be sneaked onto the grounds of a university in the U.S. South because of her unpopularity among whites. Yet, throughout her battle against the bloodcurdling cries of cross-burners, the "singsong voices" of segregationist politicians and the "gentle backdoor cruelties" of moderates, she proclaimed herself "pro-Southern." She held out hope that "underneath all our troubles, our blindness, there is a good South a-growing, a creative people who are beginning to lift themselves out of their old defensiveness and are coming to terms with the world they live in. . . . Yes, I am pro-Southern."

Likewise, I am pro-Islam. In *Al-Fatiha*, the opening passage of the Qur'an and the hallmark prayer of all Muslims, those who have gone "astray" are characterized by the very word used elsewhere for those who have abandoned hope. To hope, then, is to trust in Allah's grace—His permission, protection and love, so I can strive for a better effort from myself, and for the betterment of more than myself. Which means that as I walk the wide path of Islam, even death threats become fodder for creative freedom. Anonymous emailed me:

Roses are Red
Her Blood is Redder.
God wants her DEAD
And we promise Him We'll get her.

My reply:
I've just chatted with God;
He doesn't recall asking you to murder.
Maybe you misheard Him
When He said: "Hmmm . . . Hurt her?

"No, fools," He clarified,
"That's not the way;
Think and engage,
Or don't bother to pray.

"For I gave my creatures a gift.
It's called free will.
You might hate how it's used,
But it's not yours to kill."

Anonymous responded:
So when my brothaz explode,
They're using free will.
You can speak against it,
But hey, it's not yours to kill.
Gotcha BITCH.

My follow-up:
Gotcha? Not yet.
You forgot one fact:
When your "brothers" detonate,
They kill others with that.

If they harmed only themselves
I wouldn't complain.
But they steal free will from many more,
That's a whole different game.

It's clear that they're thieves.
I must ask: What are you?
An accomplice? A Muslim?
Is there no line 'tween the two?

Anonymous again:
Nice poem, whore.
But it won't Save you
Only ALLAH will,
And guess what? He HATES you.

Me now:
Is it God who hates me?
Or Is it you?
Just because roses are red
Doesn't mean violets are too . . .
Gotcha, gangsta.

Anonymous didn't write back. And I'm more alive than ever.

7

LACK OF MEANING IS
THE REAL DEATH THREAT

A cheerleader for al-Qaeda and a spin doctor for George W. Bush walk into a war. Which one walks out with integrity? The flippant response is "Neither!" But it wouldn't be true. I'll explain why through a challenge I received from a Muslim man named Amin. He'd been reading of a Muslim woman, Malika, who blogged about Islam's "duty" to destroy the West. Until recently, Malika carefully operated within the laws of her country, Belgium, and proudly accepted public vilification for her beliefs. Amin figured that Malika met all three conditions of moral courage: speaking truth to power, speaking it within her community and expressing herself for a greater good. So, he asked, isn't this jihadi blogger an agent of the values that I promote?

In my reply, I asked Amin a few questions. What "truth" does this woman speak? She rants about Western intrusions, but says squat about the fact that in Pakistan, Sunni militants use Shias for target practice. That in Afghanistan, Qur'an-quoting warlords gang-rape Muslim girls. That in Lebanon, Palestinians scrape by on odd jobs because they're barred from buying property, let alone becoming professionals. That in Israel, Katyusha rockets launched by Hezbollah tear through the homes of Arab Muslims. Add these truths to Malika's; then we'll talk.

Next, I reminded Amin, moral courage requires us not only to speak truth, but to speak it to those who demand uncritical fealty. In an open society, it doesn't take gargantuan backbone to spout off about the nefarious West. To have moral courage, Malika would have to tell her jihadi brethren the truth about how Muslims lacerate each other.

Finally, what "greater good" is she striving for? Obviously, it's not the protection of Muslims worldwide. I held out an olive branch to Amin. Blogging about Muslim-on-Muslim crimes isn't the only way that Malika could serve a greater good. The $1,100 monthly welfare check that she got at the time from the Belgian government hinted at another choice: She might donate a portion of her dole to Iraqi war widows, who collect a maximum of $40 per month. Surely they could use the help of a sister. I then suggested that Malika's responsibility rises when we consider one more reality: Many of Iraq's women have been left without husbands thanks to Western troops, yes, but thanks also to Muslim insurgents imported from foreign lands—the non-Iraqis whom Malika eggs on in her blog.

Perhaps, I proposed, she should learn from Scott McClellan, a former press secretary to President George W. Bush. After quitting his post, McClellan wrote a bestselling book about the deception that infests Washington, D.C. In June 2008, he committed to sharing his royalties with families of Iraq war victims, whom he said he'd injured with the misinformation he'd been given—and handed out—while in the White House. That day, McClellan transcended tribe to exude moral courage.

Through his example, he affirmed that whatever Malika's history of hesitations or wholesale silences, she can make new choices now. Any of us can. To have meaning is to know that my choices carry consequences. And if my choices have consequences, then choosing anew can never be "too little too late." When I accept that my choices are consequential, I'm alive to my meaning—and to my capacity for helping others realize theirs.

Muslims may need this last lesson in order to choose moral courage, but all citizens of democracies need it too. As people with the permission to be individuals, we're preposterously lucky. Yet without more of us exercising our individuality and integrity, our luck is just that: fortunate, not foundational. It's cruise control in place of self-awareness and asking questions. We know what besets societies that coast on blind faith.

Lesson seven: *Lack of meaning is the real death threat.*

———

Why do I live to widen Islam's path? More to the point, why would I die for it? My daredevil expedition might seem obtuse—not only because I've got no idea if it will succeed, but also because whatever affects the outcome can't fully be forecast. Think about all the information we don't yet have. As China acquires superpower status, will the communal bent of its culture obliterate, truncate, toggle between or harmonize with the individuality permitted by my democratic culture? Growing numbers of Chinese women are surgically reconstructing their hymens so they'll be presumed virgins when they marry. The Arab honor code finds a friend in this phenomenon. With China ascendant and its values fanning out in who-knows-what ways, will Muslim women's fight for sexual authenticity go limp? Or will it somehow be invigorated?

On a different note, the Congressional Budget Office states that in my lifetime, interest on America's debt will exceed the country's entire defense budget. Good news or bad news for recalibrating U.S. foreign policy? Good news or bad news for finding alternatives to Saudi oil? Good news or bad news for healing partisan chasms and honoring human priorities? All of the above, I think.

When the world as I know it feels as if it's unspooling, there's calm in these few certainties: I have a mission. I've chosen it. My choice infuses it with personal commitment that no faraway political maneuver, however inept or underhanded, can sap. And because this mission tries to give back to my society the freedoms that my society has given to me, I'm blissfully at one with the aims behind my choices. Robert F. Kennedy would have called them "ultimate moral aims." They reflect "the realities of human faith and of passion and of belief; forces ultimately more powerful than all the calculations of our economists or of our generals."

After the assassination of Martin Luther King, Jr., his widow made a startling remark about how he valued his existence. "My husband often told the children that if a man had nothing that was worth dying for," Coretta Scott King remembered, "then he was not fit to live." King could demand so much of himself, in part, because of his Christian devotion to life everlasting. But in his willingness to die for justice, King also drank deep from the well of American feminism.

Forget the 1960s; I'm referring to the 1830s, when a coterie of Christian women convened to strategize against slavery. "This is a cause worth dying for," one of them announced in New York, home to the first Anti-Slavery Convention of American Women. Any standoff with their opponents threatened to boil over into a brawl, but the women stood anyway. The following year, in Philadelphia, thousands of men swarmed their meeting site, shattering windows before torching the premises. Bear in mind, these women came together not to demand *their* equality but to insist on the full, nonnegotiable humanity of black people. By living with ultimate moral aims—and steeling themselves to die for the same—they did more than enliven the campaign for abolition; they discovered a voice for themselves.

And they did it by widening the path of Christianity. Imagine voting on this resolution: "The time has come for woman to move in that sphere which Providence has assigned her, and no longer remain satisfied with the circumscribed limits with which corrupt custom and a perverse application of Scripture have encircled her." Corrupt custom. Perverse application of scripture. No longer satisfied. It's a resolution tailor-made for today's Muslim reformers.

"This statement," reveals Helen LaKelly Hunt in *Faith and Feminism*, "is the first public call for women's rights in America." It wasn't premeditated to be, but that's how creative extremism works, spinning off into yet more meaning for yet more of humanity. Only a decade after their antislavery convention, five of the female organizers pledged to hold a women's rights conference. One of them, Elizabeth Cady Stanton, pushed the envelope further, raising the right of women to vote. Even her allies cackled: *Dream on.* So she did.

Stanton pulled in Frederick Douglass, the former slave whose loyalty to individual liberty extended well beyond "his" people. Douglass didn't fear being told to butt out of women's business, not after white women had butted into the business of abolishing the enslavement of blacks. If women could see their family as all of humanity, so could he. The moral courage these misfits exemplified gave meaning to democracy, and to the duties of living in one.

To me, they epitomize the hope for transcendence—the freedom to choose your purpose over everybody else's politics. Your conscience grants you this freedom. Don't seek permission from your family. Or from your culture. Or even from your head. "We are always connected to inspiration, but we do not perceive it because our minds are filled with all kinds of haphazard thoughts," writes Sultan Abdulhameed.

If you have a dominant purpose in life, your mind looks for and collects information related to fulfilling your purpose. If there

*is no purpose, your mind absorbs all kinds of random informa-
tion and images from the surroundings. . . . When someone's
mind is filled up with a thick layer of junk, he or she is not able to
perceive the messages coming from deeper awareness.*

Notice that listening to your conscience simplifies choices, even as it
multiplies them.

I can hear some of you responding, "Terrorists act on their consciences too. Their choices have consequences and, man, do they ever
milk meaning from that." But it's one thing to take up destructive
extremism as if all that counts is the afterlife; quite another to be a creative extremist who strives for a life of lasting value. "To create a life of
lasting value requires being different from the herd," Abdulhameed
explains. "It requires having your own mind; it requires marshalling
your time and resources for your purpose." Well, doesn't that description capture Osama bin Laden? Not so much. Bin Laden may have
poured his days and dollars into violent jihad, but as an Islamo-tribalist
he subsisted on groupthink—the opposite of differing from the herd.

By contrast, the Muslim reformer Abdul Ghaffar Khan broke out
of groupthink. He championed freedom of belief—having your own
mind—and pursued that principle nonviolently, itself evidence of his
own mind. Whereas bin Laden lived to expunge the individual's
choices, Ghaffir Khan lived to expand them. He produced a life of *lasting* value by putting transcendence within reach of future generations.

———

That's assuming future generations don't give up on the future. If
many Muslims have trouble expressing their individuality, many
non-Muslims have trouble caring enough to express it. They often
demean themselves, with freedom decaying into what Lillian Smith
deemed "Nothingness."

Why are we so blind to each disaster as it begins slowly, slowly, and then rushes toward us! Is it complacency? But what causes this kind of complacency, so unreal, so without substance? Why are we suppressing anxiety, denying danger? Why apathy when we desperately need moral energy? Why flabby spirits when we need iron strength?

With liberal democracy losing global influence to Communist demagoguery, Smith asked these questions in 1963. In 1964, Abraham Maslow published *Religions, Values, and Peak-Experiences*, an odyssey into the human need for transcendence. Like Smith, Maslow palpitated with questions that are central to the health of free societies:

Which well-known artists or writers today are trying to teach, to inspire, to conduce to virtue? Which of them could even use the word "virtue" without gagging? Upon which of them can an "idealistic" young man model himself? . . . He has nothing very inspiring or affirmative to suggest that we fight for, much less die for.

Maslow and Smith could have been speaking for Ed Husain, the ex-jihadi I quoted in chapter 4. Remember how he became a destructive extremist? Among the unremarkable, off-the-radar factors: "Nobody had the courage to stand up for liberal democracy without qualms," Husain told us about the administrators of his British college. When he and his merry band of beards "were holding events against women and against gay people, where were our college principals and teachers, challenging us?"

In the rabbit hole of relativism.

To dig out, we can't be ashamed of talking openly about transcendence and the choices it entails. Better, I believe, to embarrass ourselves with buckets of meaning than to demean ourselves with Nothingness. Because Nothingness isn't benign. It's an invitation to mock tolerance, a vacuum of values that cannier ideologies swoop into. In *Moral Clarity*, Susan Neiman confronts the stakes: "If our need for transcendence isn't satisfied by the right kind of ideals, we may turn to the wrong ones." Enough of us already have, but the shabby consequences of that choice can be reversed—with higher expectations of ourselves, and therefore with new choices.

On one of my book tours, I had an upbeat conversation with a Dutch journalist. Yet in her follow-up email, she faltered into a debilitating pessimism. "Passivity is our greatest enemy," she said of Europeans. "We lack everything we need to solve our problems: courage, determination, action, cooperation, love of progress, imagination. Anyhow, as long as people like you don't lose their freedom of speech, we're at least intellectually safe." I felt hosed, two inspirational hours fizzling into a paean to the very defeatism this European reviled! Irony doesn't always enchant.

Still, I can't single her out—or Europeans, for that matter. I don't have the stomach to count the number of times I've been encouraged to "keep going," only for the pep-talkers to decide that their piece of the action means zilch. Or, if it does have consequences, the backlash will hurt more than they can endure. They assume that unbridled backlash is all they can look forward to. Wrapping up lunch in a desolate New York diner, a colleague leaned in and whispered to me, "If I said what you say, my friends would practically stone me to death." She already knew her choices have consequences, but she demeaned those choices by anticipating only the worst. On top of it all, she lowered her voice as if the entire world were eavesdropping on her fears—in an empty eatery.

Why do so many of us, even when blessed with freedom, underestimate our capacity? The answers may be as near as the words in a dictionary, those humdrum tools with which we frame our dreams and desires. One psychology study found that of 558 English-language words for our emotions, 62 percent are downers. They drag us into doubt. (Is English less positive than other languages?) "Across the board, we seem wired to focus on the negative," say Chip and Dan Heath, authors of *Switch: How to Change Things When Change Is Hard*. "A group of psychologists reviewed over two hundred articles and concluded that, for a wide range of human behavior and perception, a general principle holds true: 'Bad is stronger than good.'" As another example, "People who were shown photos of bad and good events spent longer viewing the bad ones." Doesn't sound like much of a choice, does it, if we're "wired" toward bleakness? But a choice it is. Tendency doesn't mean destiny.

Which is where the "switch" comes in. We can make the conscious choice to preoccupy ourselves with something other than the problems—namely, the solutions. When I told young Muslims that no publisher in the Arab world would translate my book, a raft of them lobbed back a solution: Translate it yourself and post it online. Voluminous downloads later, I appreciate more than ever a question that *Switch* recommends we keep asking: "What's working, and how can we do more of it?" It's a question that requires a little less fixation on the mountain before us (the problem) and a little more learning from the individuals who are imperfectly but doggedly scaling it (the solution).

Reyana, a reader of *The Trouble with Islam Today*, could be the poster child for this principle. "I'm so happy that someone finally has the guts to stand up to the so-called scholars and imams of today," she exhaled to me via email.

I was at a point when I was really feeling lost, but after reading your book, I've gained love and faith for Islam again. I've never been able to understand organized religion. It's been hammered into my head since childhood that being a good person isn't enough . . . that hell has more women than men in it. As if we don't suffer enough on earth—let a man give birth just once! Or that you will go to hell if you disobey your husband. Puh-leeze!! Being an independent Muslim woman of the 21st century, I always felt suffocated by the rules and regulations of institutional Islam. I'm now in the process of weeding out the culture. I no longer feel suffocated. If anything, I feel free, and this is the Islam that I will pass on to my children. I'm also having a huge effect on the way my husband sees Islam.

Reyana enthuses not just about learning to love Islam by peeling away tribal culture, but also that "someone" demonstrated to her that it's possible. "Ideas do not influence [people] deeply when they are taught only as ideas and thoughts," observed the psychologist and philosopher Erich Fromm. Instead, the impact of an idea increases when it "appears in the flesh." Reyana isn't eccentric in testifying to Fromm's insight. Nearly every day for several years, I've gotten flashes of proof that my personal choice to practice moral courage illuminates choices for others:

My family and I are Muslims. I am a professor of literature. My wife is a physician. Your stand has made my life easier to bear because ever since 9/11, I have been deeply troubled by my adoptive faith. You make it easier for me to figure out what to say to my kids.   —Alamin

I'm an anthropologist doing research with Muslim women living in the slums of Kolkata, India. During my last trip there, I showed some of the women your website and they started reading *The Trouble with Islam Today* in Urdu. One woman, Amina, runs a small NGO that operates a free school for children, and she immediately incorporated your work into her classes on Islam. Her comment on reading your ideas: "This is exactly what I have been saying!" They now read and discuss your work together.   —Lorena

I must confess that I haven't finished reading your book yet because within the first 100 pages it became clear that there is a place for me in Islam, so I converted and picked up the Qur'an. I was turned away from Islam when I lived in Saudi Arabia as a child. Ijtihad was the missing piece that brought me home. Come in thirst. Go in peace.   —Davi

I am a Norwegian-born Muslim. . . . As an adult, I moved to London to take a degree in marketing. I decided never to go back to the hell of my family life, which included a violent father and a community that hated me because I had a Norwegian boyfriend who I saw every day. . . . I moved back to Norway after two years when my boyfriend proposed and I accepted. Now, thanks to your book, I feel Islam is my path and I try to inter- pret it in my own way. Of course, my family turned their back on me. But you know what? I don't care anymore. The Qur'an encourages us to find our own path. I have, thank God, and I am very happy.   — Fatima

When I was 18, I was in Pakistan surrounded by my elders. It was the largest gathering of the male members of my extended family that I had ever been at. Talk centered around world politics, the plight of Muslims, education, etc. Eventually, one of my father's uncles asked me what I was thinking. I opened my mouth and said, "You know who the biggest enemies of Islam are? Muslims." The silence was quite deafening. That day, I shat- tered something that all the king's horses and all the king's men couldn't put back together again. I was branded "to be watched" and the preaching began and continues to this day. My parents wish to remote-control me no matter where I am. Irshad, just knowing you're out there fighting the good fight makes me feel more alive.   —Khalid

I have always been thinking about setting up a school for women and children in Bangladesh. Your book is inspiring me to seriously start implementing that project.

—Shamim

My girlfriend is a VERY faithful Christian. The closer to her I grow, the more I realize that my parents would ultimately like to see me with a Muslim girl, not because [Muslims] are any more intelligent, kind, or warm, but because they possess the same religious credentials. I want to thank you for expressing so eloquently what very many young Muslims have been afraid to. . . . I feel relief to know that it is not wrong to think with a liberal mind about Islam.

—Mohammad

I live in Malaysia and I just finished reading your book. Earlier in my life, when I first started my work, I also felt that Islam as practiced needs reformation. . . . Maybe the path to heaven is more certain if we improve ourselves in our relationship with God and with our fellow man and woman. Your voice for ijtihad and reform encourages people like me who before this dare[d] not be so loud in our opinions.

—Azam

I'm also *damned* for being the flesh (to use Erich Fromm's words) behind certain ideas. You've read denunciations of me throughout this book. Yet the fact that people relate to people is a fact that can open hearts too. Wrote a reader named Nas:

I've lived in England throughout my 30 years of life. During that time, I have vigorously defended my faith and my culture against the Paki-bashers that pervade English society. It was my husband who first told me about you—a traitor in our midst. I was lent your book about a month ago so I could find out what we devout Muslims were up against. The title made me furious and the picture of you nauseated me; a typical wannabe-white MTV presenter bimbo with right-on trendy liberal credentials. . . . Then I sat down to read.

I then went to your website to find out more. And I read. The ideas left me stunned. The beauty of the vision of Islam that you present leaves me in tears. . . . I still find it difficult not to instinctively justify the (often barbaric) behavior and beliefs of Muslims against the white infidels or try to deflect the responsibility. But I see now that by doing so, I only harm our faith and the possibility that it might sit in harmony with the world's other great religions.

More importantly, as my son and daughter grow up and ask me about life, the universe and everything, I'll encourage them to read not only the Qur'an but every other book they can get their hands on. To research, learn for themselves and challenge all the ideas that are put before them. Most of all, to think.

––––––––

Learn from Nas, Khalid, Reyana and the rest. Living the possibilities of change is the surest way to convey those possibilities, whether to your children, to your parents or to your spouse. You're not posing as a prophet, waiting for Allah to select you with Olympian drama. God has already vested faith in each of us by sending human beings into the material world, where we can touch and teach others.

All are chosen; a few of us recognize our choices and act on them. This Islam doesn't interrogate you about whether you've got faith in Allah. It replaces fear with freedom by asking: *What are you doing so that Allah can have faith in you?*

Guided by gratitude for God's faith in us, we can reciprocate by having faith in ourselves no less than in Him. Faith in ourselves lets us choose from the multitude of openings for serving humanity. (Might this be an allegorical meaning of *The Opening*, the title of the Qur'an's first chapter?) The openings vastly outnumber the individuals willing to fill them. Go ahead, then. Step into the vacancy that calls your name. Personify the ideal. You have the permission, and possibly even the obligation.

Emory University's Abdullahi An-Na'im speaks stirringly about the obligation involved. "Moral courage should not be as rare as Bobby Kennedy was saying," he asserted in our March 2008 discussion. "I am not a martyr. I want to live a good, productive and creative life. For that, I need to have everyone around me willing to make moral courage unnecessary. The more all of us do what little we can, the less each of us has to do to keep everybody happy and safe."

"The more all of us do": He's not talking here about supreme sacrifices. He's talking about daily choices that amount to creating a routine of moral courage—routine enough that it doesn't need to feel like boldness at all. In *Courageous Resistance*, researchers show that ordinary humans have this capacity. "Over time," they write, "people's attitudes toward authority as well as their orientations toward others become habitual and self-reinforcing. Defiance of illegitimate authority and helping others become part of routine practices. Each action allows people to progress to greater forms of defiance and to increase the amount of help they offer to others." Holocaust rescuers, for instance, "were ordinary people who habitually cared about and for others."

Key word: habitually. Affirms Richard J. Leider in *The Power of Purpose*, "Nothing shapes our lives as much as the questions we ask—or refuse to ask—throughout our lives." What we repeatedly wonder, or avoid wondering, eventually becomes yet another habit with repercussions. Let me show you how my own habit of asking questions out loud has come in handy for practical reasons as much as for spiritual ones.

In late 2007, I caught a whiff of the systemic corruption that would soon throw the global economy into a nosedive. The whiff wafted from the fact that my investment advisers began mouthing technicalities. I suspected they no longer knew what they'd been commissioned to sell. In a face-to-face meeting, I told my advisers that while I'd like to trust them, I can't trust the system. They laughed dismissively. "We've got the best information," one assured me. His partner nodded, "The system is sound." I brought my concerns to their manager, who tried to endear himself to me rather than address my questions. Had I become paranoid? I gave my advisers a last-ditch test: Please explain what you're marketing to me in language that a high school student would understand. They couldn't.

In the spring of 2008, as worldwide financial tumult burbled, I phoned my advisers. "This is going to be a tough discussion," I warned them, explaining that after months of asking questions and receiving only chortles and charm, I'd chosen to take my business elsewhere. A habit of asking questions made it obvious to me that just as religious dogma shouldn't be insulated from inquiry, neither should financial dogma. I didn't consider it a matter of "courage" to question. It was a matter of integrity.

My questions wouldn't reverse the world's financial implosion; they only gave my former advisers a brief pain in the ass and handed me a small win. Yet "small wins" can have the utmost significance. Describing them as "stable building blocks," the Cornell University psychologist Karl Weick uses an analogy that any high school student would understand: "Your task is to count out a thousand sheets of paper while you are subject to periodic interruptions. Each interruption causes you to lose track of the count and forces you to start over. If you count the thousand as a single sequence, then an interruption could cause you, at worst, to lose a count of as many as 999." But small wins "are like short stacks. They preserve gains, they cannot unravel [and] each one requires less coordination to execute."

Vitally, small wins give us the building blocks of confidence, or faith, in ourselves. I can contribute to, but I can't control, whether politicians implement comprehensive financial reform. Nouriel Roubini, a New York University economist once ridiculed for predicting the crisis, suspects that U.S. politicians won't touch real reform because they fear being slurred as socialists. Spineless? You bet your devalued bottom dollar. Beyond your personal control? Ditto. But the small win? Far more within your control. What investment adviser would call you a socialist for asking questions about your own money? Even if she does, who gives a flying sickle?

Educators increasingly agree. According to Garth Saloner, dean of Stanford University's Graduate School of Business, MBA students must learn to ask, "In whose interest am I making the decision?" Does that question ring a bell? It almost replicates what Unni Wikan, the Norwegian anthropologist, teaches us. If multiculturalism entices you to bite your tongue about honor killings, Wikan wants you to ask: *When I respect custom, what does that do to the weaker members of the group?*

One social worker can't control the integration policies (and politics) of his country's government, but what he can immediately do is ask questions of himself: *Whose agenda am I serving by returning this Muslim girl to her family when she has run away from their culturally sanctioned violence? By escaping the household, isn't she telling me that she chooses a set of values different from her parents'? If I send her back to where I assume she "belongs," aren't I misconstruing belonging for ownership? Aren't I then empowering people who think they own this girl's spirit? Is their identity the same as her integrity?* Through such questions, a human life could be delivered from bondage—and from premature death.

Karl Weick, the psychologist, sees small wins as "miniature experiments." You can't engineer outcomes but, like a scientist, you can create opportunities to discover new outcomes. Scientific culture is said to sustain three things: "the sense of individual wonder, the power of hope, and the vivid but questing belief in a future for the globe." To me, that sounds like spirituality. "The most beautiful and deepest experience a man can have is the sense of the mysterious," Albert Einstein rhapsodized. "It is the underlying principle of religion as well as all serious endeavor in art and science. He who never had this experience seems to me, if not dead then at least blind."

Recently, *The New York Times* profiled a professor of physics who declared himself "euphoric" at challenging a near-scriptural truth in science. "For me, gravity doesn't exist," Erik Verlinde stated flat out. "We've known for a long time [that] gravity doesn't exist. It's time to yell it." The gravity of that pronouncement didn't escape the reporter:

> It's hard to imagine a more fundamental and ubiquitous aspect of life on the Earth than gravity, from the moment you first took a step and fell on your diapered bottom to the slow terminal sagging of flesh and dreams. But what if it's all an illusion, a sort of cosmic frill, or a side effect of something else going on at deeper levels of reality?

Verlinde hatched the opportunity to address that question— and he hatched it out of a circumstance beyond his control. He'd been robbed at the end of a holiday in the south of France. Hanging back for a replacement passport, Verlinde let the unexpected free time incubate fresh thinking. His eureka moment arrived on Day 3. "What has he been drinking?" jested his brother, Herman. "It's interesting how having to change plans can lead to different thoughts." But only if you permit the possibility. Did Verlinde worry about blaspheming against the elders of physics? "I don't see immediately that I am wrong," he said. "That's enough to go ahead."

As it is for the Dalai Lama. In an age of identity politics, the conscience of Buddhism flaunts his heretical side by making an adventure out of exile. Booted from Tibet by Chinese authorities, the Dalai Lama rejoiced, "Now we are free." His biographer, Pico Iyer, explains:

> He could bring democratic and modern reforms to the Tibetan people that he might not easily have done in old Tibet. He and his compatriots could learn from Western science and other religions, and give back to them. He could create a new, improved Tibet— global and contemporary—outside Tibet. The very condition that most of us would see as loss, severance and confinement, he saw as possibility.

Granted, the Dalai Lama is more enlightened than most. But, fellow Muslims, you don't have to be a Mu-Bu (Muslim Buddhist) or Bu-Mu (you get it) to inch toward personal meaning. You can just declare *talaq*—"I divorce thee"—to the patrollers of Muslim authenticity.

Take strength from Taj Hargey, whom we encountered in chapter 2. Among other crimes against conformity, Hargey officiates interfaith marriages for Muslim women. Smeared by mouthpieces of mainstream Islam in Britain, he won a libel case in April 2009. Afterward, Hargey published a firecracker of an editorial in *The Times* of London. "I hope," he wrote, "that my public vindication in the courts will embolden more progressives, dissenters and particularly thinking women to put their heads above the parapet. . . . We need a reformation that saves Islam from foreign-inspired zealots." But, Hargey cautioned, "because this reformation is still in its infancy, the reactionary clergy and its supporters [are] doing everything to strangle it."

Where other reform-minded Muslims detect a nightmare, Hargey discovers opportunities to widen the path of Islam. He helps me appreciate that in thinking for ourselves, we're not abandoning the community; we're choosing to express ourselves more honestly within it.

Embracing ijtihad isn't about leaving Islam, but about staying with integrity. Faith allows us—actually, it implores us—to experiment. The Qur'an is studded with overtures to think, reason, examine, reflect, dissect and think again, with the safety net of the final truth being God's. Hence the liberty, duty and humility behind asking our questions. Ijtihad is faith at its fullest.

I know that a lot of us fear making mistakes and that fear, being a negative emotion, has more power than hope. That's why you have to be conscious of God's love in order to choose hope. I'll reiterate a point from chapter 1. Research by Umar Faruq Abd-Allah suggests that, to early Islamic scholars, "every person performing ijtihad receives a reward when mistaken, not by virtue of the error but because of obedience to God in fulfilling the command to undergo the labor of ijtihad." (Again: You're free to download Abd-Allah's entire paper, "Innovation and Creativity in Islam," from my website.) As long as your errors don't oppress others in turn, your efforts demonstrate to God that He didn't waste breath on you. In good faith, each of us can experiment.

———————

I'll start us off: What is "to pray"? As Sultan Abdulhameed notes, "A remarkable fact is that the Quran does not recommend a format for prayer. The Quran insists that people should pray but consistently avoids prescribing a method for doing it." Sadly, "the idea that prayer could be spontaneous or joyful" has become "almost heretical." Tell me about it.

In *The Trouble with Islam Today*, I explained my choice to communicate with God in English, not Arabic, and through unstructured daily dialogue, not rote ritual. Knowing myself better than somebody else's rules could know me, the practice I've chosen restores my intimacy with Allah. As soon as word got out that I don't follow the five-times-a-day, on-your-rug-to-pray drill, another word got out: kafir.

To be fair, not everyone is that trite. Abdullah, a member of the public, emailed back-to-back questions to me: "So u call urself a muslim, do u? Out of curiosity, how many times a day do u pray?" I replied, "10, 12, sometimes 15. You?" Hearing nothing in response, I re-sent my answer. Maybe Abdullah didn't know what to do with it. Judging by the tone of his email, he was chomping at the bit to hear me say that I pray fewer than the traditionally allotted five times daily—if at all. But *more*?

My own mother subscribes to the myth that serious prayer doesn't lend itself to experimentation. A scene in *Faith Without Fear* has Mum driving as we're discussing the issue. We approach a stop sign.

Mum: You don't pray at all.

Me: No, that's not true. I do—

Mum: You pray in your own way.

Me: I pray in my own way. Exactly.

Mum: Yeah, well, you know what? Look at these traffic lights. We can say, "Oh well, I drive my own way." But there are rules in life. There is a stop sign, and if you don't stop, the police catch you. . . . "Well, there were no cars," you say. And the police will say, "I really don't care whether the cars were there or not. It says stop— you need to stop." So God has laws too.

As for expressing gratitude, "that's besides the prayers," Mum corrects me. She soon finds a spot in a cluttered parking lot, and she knows why: Allah rewards *true* prayer.

At screenings, I've watched Muslims perk up at my mother's reference to traffic regulations. Her metaphor comes straight out of the Ronald Reagan handbook on potent rhetoric: Enlist your surroundings to enhance your message. Muslims are only human to swoon over this style of communication. But according to the Qur'an, we don't have to accept only one style of prayer.

In an email to me, a Muslim convert named R.L. said that for eight years, she tried to follow convention. That "experiment," as she described it,

allow[ed] me to see where my faith is and is not. I identified with your documentary in so many ways, especially your discussion with your mother about inner prayers. I have had the same discussion numerous times with my daughter. She has learned the "rules" from her father, and she asks me all the time why I don't "pray." I tell her the same thing you told your mother. And I feel confident in my views. After 8 years of reciting words in a foreign language and bowing and prostrating in ritual sequence, I can tell you that my only closeness to God came from knowing that I was trying to do what was right. When I gave myself permission to do what I felt was right without the imposition of somebody else's rituals, I finally found a true, unshakeable relationship with my creator. . . . The time has come for peace in our generation and our children's.

A lover of the Qur'an expands on R.L.'s understanding that peace in our generation begins with peace in ourselves. "In learning to pray well, you have to reform your view of what God is like," Sultan Abdulhameed contends. "If the word 'God' creates fear in you, it is likely you utter words of prayer in a fearful manner. Your prayer then produces more fear in you."

My latest form of prayer: Every morning when I'm not traveling, I shuffle to the bursting bookcases in my apartment, coffee cup in hand, and pluck out a title at random. Typically, I read two or three pages at the beginning of the book, then several more in the middle. For the first gauzy minutes of my day, I'm awakened by, and to, ideas, which then become a prism through which to reflect on the rest of my day.

So each morning brings two gifts: a new lens and a sturdy reminder that while God alone possesses truth, individuals may create opportunities to pursue it. I don't know how Mum will feel about this, but I've retrieved my childhood prayer rug and oriented it to the bookcases. I take Allah's inaugural command to Prophet Muhammad—"Read!"—as a command to all believers, as well as a command to read all beliefs. When I submit to it, in moments both solitary and silent, my Muslim faith is most sure of its foundations.

More of us, everywhere, yearn to experiment in good faith. From "an anxious and depressed Muslim" in Britain, I've received a "fearful thumbs up. Thumbs up because your questions rage in my mind. Fearful because by asking these things, we may be forsaking our religion." But why must the choice be losing or keeping religion? Why not a third choice: transforming our understanding of religion by reforming ourselves?

I can't say it enough: No religion speaks for itself. Its practitioners speak on religion's behalf. Not just by words, but also by deeds. Not just by action, but also by inaction. Not just by choices made, but also by choices relinquished.

"Do I fully consider myself a Muslim?" asked Sarah, a reader born and raised in the United Arab Emirates. "I don't know. A sizeable amount of being a Muslim to me is what I've known to be 'truth' through cultural practices, not what causes me to stop in my tracks and feel the presence of divinity." She's one of countless people, Muslim and not, who fight with themselves to graft a manufactured identity onto personal integrity. No need. If the identity doesn't fit, reimagine it. That's what Fatema, Sarah's fellow Emirati from chapter 2, has done. And Fatema's faith seems far more resilient (more redolent too) than the insecure orthodoxies of those who spew "kafir!" at her.

————

Insecurity craves company, so if you walk the wide path of Islam— or almost any religion—you'll be targeted by verbal bomb-throwers. Their improvised emotional device is the Who-The-Hell-Are-You hand grenade. "I regard myself [as] a Moderate Muslim," Imran emailed to me. "I am an American citizen who works for the government. I do not know much about my faith but I do know this much, it's the best one out there. I heard your so-called message to the Muslims and the first thing that came in my mind was 'Who the hell are you?'"

Love to burst his bubble: Historical progress abounds with the seamstress who would become a Rosa Parks. Socrates, who never claimed to produce the answers, did produce a student known as Plato. Not bad for a self-educated hound of wisdom. Spinoza exerted a lasting influence on the radical notions of individual liberty and religious tolerance, yet he worked for years as a grinder of glass. Einstein toiled as a patent clerk. Who the hell were they?

Now reflect on Isabella Hardenbergh, the American slave who bolted from her master's plantation and changed her name to Sojourner Truth. She rose to renown as an abolitionist as well as a feminist, but she never stopped dodging the Who-The-Hell-Are-You hand grenades. Once told that the sting of her speeches amounted to flea bites, Sojourner bit back, "Lord willing, I'll keep you scratching." Another time, she pointed to a Christian minister who derided women's rights:

"That little man in black there . . . He say women can't have as much rights as men, 'cause Christ wasn't a woman! Where did your Christ come from?" The crowd went wild. "From God and a woman." She then shot a withering look toward the minister and boomed, "Man had nothing to do with him."

The Who-The-Hell-Are-You hand grenade is disarmed the moment you love your individuality. Sojourner's "courage to claim her God-given rightful place began when she declared: '*I am*'—self-owned, self-defined, and self-asserted," affirms the feminist Christian Helen LaKelly Hunt. When you're a self-owned individual, you can be many things at once, which in turn benefits the communities you identify with because you're adding nuance to how they're perceived. You're also growing those communities from within by showing that there's more than one way to belong to them.

I can't think of a finer example than Rana Husseini. In the opening pages of her memoir *Murder in the Name of Honor*, Husseini announces, "I am an Arab Muslim woman intent upon living in a sound society where all members benefit from justice, regardless of rank, religion, race, or gender." Her statement of intention tells the critics that she doesn't need to be an "expert" in religion, history or anything other than her conscience. Husseini's individuality serves as her north star.

Above all, individuality helps you transcend dogmas of your own because your sense of self doesn't hinge on a single label or the supposedly static truth it represents. Sahan, one of my readers, takes this to heart: "As a queer, Arab and Muslim, it seems I've been going against the current all my life. . . . Maybe some of us can see ahead and light the way better than someone who is entrenched in tradition. Maybe we are the ones forced to look at the norm from the outside."

Being an enthusiast of ijtihad, I don't oppose tradition; I oppose the thrusting of tradition on those who wish to choose their tribe, their community, their "we." On that front, Sahan would be pleased to hear we have friends in traditional places. At a 2007 conference, an Iraqi cleric approached me after I spoke. He'd read the online Arabic translation of my book. As I braced myself for a verbal flogging, he said that the merciful God will forgive him for approving of a lesbian and the omnipotent God must have created me that way for a reason. Then he grinned: "The Almighty knows best." More proof that humility can accompany individuality—in this case, a mullah's.

Still, such exchanges will be few and far between as long as the hand grenades fly fast and furious. And right now, they're raining down. I feel the onslaught not just from Muslim conservatives, but also from non-Muslim conservatives, religious and secular. In the past few minutes, even as I write, another diatribe has landed in my inbox. "Islam sucks," proclaims someone who signs off as "Our American Family, USA." The harangue reads:

"allah" (non-existent) sucks. Mo the false prophet Warlord sucks. The Koran—a Declaration of open-ended warfare against the Infidel—sucks. Get it? Brava Wafa Sultan, Hirsi Ali, Brigitte Gabriel, Nonie Darwish, and Bat Ye'or. You, Manji, are NOTHING compared to them. You're still a moon-god worshipper . . .

I forgive this grenade-hurler. Voltaire, for one, made scalding generalizations about Jews, seething that they "are, all of them, born with raging fanaticism in their hearts." If a hero of European rationality could be so irrational, it stands to reason that a champion of the "American family" could too. Yes, I have higher expectations, but of myself before anyone else. Thus the need to forgive.

Less forgivable to me is this increasingly common confusion:

Some who want to wipe Islam off the map assume that their agenda actually supports Muslim reformers. I asked a self-described "secular Jew" in my Facebook forum to share her view of reform in Islam. She responded, "Chuck the whole thing." I told her she's part of the problem that she presumes to be against. This woman defines all of Islam in the same dogmatic terms as destructive Muslim extremists do. Her Who-The-Hell-Are-You hand grenade would tar me as "Muslim-lite." By trivializing the wide path of Islam, she makes Islamo-tribalists even more credible.

Others indulge in semiconscious games. More than once, Christians have assured me that I'm not a true Muslim because I advocate reform, yet those very Christians condemn Muslims who won't reform. The luminous logic: You're a fake Muslim if you reconcile Allah, liberty and love, but you're an evil Muslim if you don't. Only my moon-god can parse that one for me.

Until then, I'll be blunt: Islam-haters are no allies of faithful Muslim reformers. Tipped with ulterior motives, their hand grenades blast Muslim reformers into retreat.

But the most stealthy silencers of all? The Who-The-Hell-Are-You hand grenades flung by Muslims in the form of this crisp sentence: "You're not a scholar." Ka-boom, baby. Or this sentence from Muslims who can't argue with the scholars you do quote: "They're not *real* scholars." In my experience, reform-minded Muslims let such papier-mâché ploys smash our confidence. This, too, can change.

At an event on my Indonesian book tour, a woman from the local Islamist political party stood up to dispute the idea of democratizing ijtihad. If she needs her teeth fixed, she reasoned, she goes to a dentist. If she needs a heart transplant, she turns to a surgeon. Muslims aren't qualified to think for themselves so religious scholars must wield the spiritual scalpel for us.

Another Indonesian gave the best countercultural response I've ever heard. "Medicine," he explained to the Islamist,

has an expression—"first do no harm." When dentists and doctors harm people with their diagnoses, they can be sued for malpractice. So if you're going to compare religious scholars to medical professionals, Muslims should have the right to sue scholars when their conclusions harm people. In effect, Irshad Manji is doing this by exposing their damage in the court of international public opinion.

He both cracked up and shook up our audience. And, niftily, I picked up on a new sin: mullah malpractice.

A year later, this time in India, I felt the freedom that comes from ditching defensiveness. A film director—and evangelical atheist, I soon realized—hosted a private screening of *Faith Without Fear*. Not two minutes after I strode into the party, he started on me about faith being a fool's errand. At the end of our boisterous evening, worn out as a rag doll, I shrugged that "my faith is my integrity. It's important for me to be able to sleep at night."

"I'm very happy you can sleep at night," he teased. "My question is, When will you wake up?"

I burst into a belly laugh. His quicksilver wit captivated me, and my sullen exhaustion made way for sudden exuberance. We gave each other an affectionate parting hug. The next day I celebrated the Hindu festival of colors, Holi, with the atheist, his Muslim wife and interfaith couples as far as the eye could see.

Throughout these pages, I've extolled the virtue of raising expectations—of ourselves, first and foremost. The danger of doing so isn't lost on me: Higher expectations can skid into wounding disappointments, all the more when we expect higher of others. In June 2009, Tariq Ramadan and I had a train wreck of a debate about free speech and human rights in Oslo. The tone became so noxious that I couldn't neglect *that* as an issue either. "Something has threatened you this morning," I said to Ramadan mid-debate, "and I don't quite know what it is."

"Women," he replied. I suspect that Ramadan felt I'd blindsided him by bringing up his endorsement of only a moratorium on stoning—a stance for which he believes he's being persecuted. Irretrievably emotional by now, our discussion degenerated into a swap of daggers. Each of us skulked off the stage, grimacing.

Later spotting Ramadan eating his lunch alone, I pulled up a chair and told him that I regretted how our debate had unfolded. He appreciated the outreach, and we ended the frosty dialogue by agreeing that "you can love human beings; you don't have to love their minds." A thoroughly reasonable principle—one that could be a motto for reform in any community: *To question each other's ideas is not to deny each other's humanity.* What could be less complicated?

Yet what could be more ambitious? On the twentieth anniversary of Khomeini's fatwa against him, Salman Rushdie told me, "The trouble with fear is that it's not susceptible to reason. You can say to people, 'Here are seventy-two reasons not to be afraid' and they'll say, 'Yeah, but I'm still scared.'" In the same conversation, though, he gave evidence that even amid tangible peril, individuals can—and sometimes will—rise to the occasion. At the height of the fatwa frenzy, Rushdie says, he watched

the incredible courage of ordinary people. There were anonymous phone calls to publishing companies; secretaries being told, "We know where your children go to school." There were attacks on people working in bookstores. There was the pipe bomb. . . . And those people responded to that determined not to be cowed. So I found myself not only in a storm of hostility, but also in a demonstration of human beings behaving at their absolute best. Actually, I remember that now with greater force than the other things. What we learned, to put it at its simplest: If we do like this, we can actually defeat the threat.

"The threat" doesn't stop at terrorism; the threat against living freely manifests itself daily in our fears of racking up the small wins that make for habits of moral courage. In each chapter, I've proposed strategies, tactics and resources to transcend the threat. Whether you're presenting your parents with Imam Khaleel Mohammed's interfaith marriage blessing, or lobbying your local school (and madrassa) to teach the story of Abdul Ghaffar Khan, or writing your political representatives to fund campaigns against honor crimes, or asking specific questions at a dinner-table conversation about Islam, you're exercising freedom and expanding it for others.

I have three more tips to get you going on the path *now*.

First, visit irshadmanji.com and sign the petition for secular values, being sure to include your city and country. "The fact that this must be considered an act of bravery is a bitter reality," one backer emailed me. But ever since the petition went up, only a handful of backers have developed cold feet and asked to be removed. Another supporter expressed the concrete value of choosing to sign: "It makes the struggle a little more real for someone like me, who's not in the public eye and taking the heat."

Second, decide what you're willing to take heat for if you have to. Here are five statements for you to complete. They'll make you think about whether you believe anything passionately enough to risk backlash over it:

+ What I love about my community is . . .

+ I disagree with my community about . . .

+ If I say what I think, the worst that can happen is . . .

+ If I say what I think, the best that can happen is . . .

+ Should I say what I think? I've decided that . . .

Through my website, readers have not only filled in these statements, they've also let me use their answers to teach my students about how people around the world are taking the journey to moral courage. A Tunisian man, for example, wants to improve "civic-mindedness" in his country. His commitment is more urgent than ever, now that Tunisians have revolted for democracy and inspired other Arabs to follow their lead.

Responding to the five moral courage statements, an American Muslim envisions her community adapting "the Amish concept of Rumspringa," which would allow youth "some time to experience life outside of Islam and then choose what's best for them." An Israeli Jew "differs wildly" from her family of religious settlers and seeks to be less tongue-tied in their presence. A member of the U.S. military loves her liberty "with a passion indescribable"—to the point of pursuing equality for gay and lesbian soldiers in the barracks and not just in law. A British bloke wishes to turn around the "close-minded, ignorant [and] unethical" among his fellow queers. A single mother in California gushes, "When I am learning, I am alive. It has been my defining moment, being back in school." True to her word about loving to learn, she attended one of my college lectures about Islam and stayed long after to ask questions. To this day she dreams of awarding tuition to women who value "self-discovery" over "shame."

This exercise will clarify your sources of meaning. The better you know yourself, the better you'll understand what defines your honor, and the more conscious your choices will become about how to serve beyond your immediate self. Do you recall the Sharia law student in Egypt who intends to be a "reformist" imam? He voiced that intention by finishing the five moral courage statements.

Finally, feed your countercultural energies by inviting friends for homemade *chai* tea. To sustain your journey toward moral courage, you'll need support. As Sultan Abdulhameed confirms, "It is essential to be in the company of friends who are patient and encouraging when we falter and rejoice when we succeed, not the company of those who are critical of our efforts and jealous when they see us grow." This means maturing beyond the tribe of your birth to assemble the team of your choice.

That's pretty much what happened in the mid-1800s, when five American abolitionists got together for tea. They resolved to build on their successes by agitating for women's equality too. Their tea party, and many more to follow, evolved into a "free space"—a place where reformers could talk without fear of being overheard by their antagonists. In the mid-1900s, civil rights advocates replicated free spaces in church basements, where they often socialized, brainstormed and planned action. John Lewis, now a U.S. congressman, says that such spaces inculcated "habits of free thinking" that overcame "a whole sense of self organized around fear."

Muslims and non-Muslims can create free spaces to nourish each other's moral courage— and do so over spiced Indian tea called chai. Fragrant with cardamom and cinnamon, chai seems to make every challenge sweeter. Or at least more digestible. I speak from experience: As I wrote this book, my friends and colleagues helped me work out my dilemmas over chai. Wanting to re-create those opportunities online, I introduced my Facebook community to the idea of "chai chats"—regular, real-time conversations in which they could ask me anything to advance their moral courage. And in planning the chats, another thought emerged: I'll publish my chai tea recipe at the back of this book so that readers can hold chai chats with their own friends.

Knowing that my schedule won't permit me to answer every new question that comes through my website, I'm offering a delicious incentive to transform your book clubs into free spaces. If you and your fellow readers come up with ideas to further your journey to moral courage, I might pop into your free space by Skype to learn from you. Visit irshadmanji.com to talk with my team about the possibility.

———

You don't have to consider yourself a certified leader; just consider yourself allowed and equipped to grow. Let me illustrate with one last example that hits home for me. While putting the final touches on this book, I learned that my younger sister, Fatima, has breast cancer. At the time, she was carrying her third child. Only forty-eight hours before the diagnosis, an ultrasound showed her the baby—its shape and size and arms and legs. Nobody could have predicted that cancer would creep in and complicate her elation.

Nobody, that is, except my devoutly Muslim mother. Mum didn't anticipate what Fatima told us, but she agonized about whether she'd upset God and brought on her daughter's affliction. "Maybe I missed too many morning prayers," Mum confided to me in anguish. This from a woman whose own physical ailments make it rough to do anything as she once could.

My anxiety reached a new high. Already I worried for Fatima, her husband and their two precocious toddlers. I worried for my older sister, Ishrat, whose patience with Fatima, Mum and me holds us together. I worried for my mother, who's made her three girls the center of her life. Mum's personality radiates optimism, but I've come to see it as a sunny fatalism. Beneath her vivacious smile is the unremitting dread of losing one of us. She's a mother. I get it. Still, I cringed when she said that God might be punishing her through Fatima's cancer. Mum's fear of God bred despair—and her despair wouldn't help my little sister's chances of survival.

I needed Mum to realize that a different grasp of God is possible. Whatever caused Fatima's cancer, be it the pregnancy, the environment, or something else that science would eventually explain, God's love assures us of one thing: Every problem contains opportunities for understanding ourselves. By understanding ourselves, we understand why our Creator has faith in each of His creatures to lift up another—in Mum's case, her youngest daughter. More than a responsibility, self-knowledge is an opportunity to live up to God's faith in us.

When I suggested to Mum that God believes in her, she went temporarily mute. (If you knew my mother, you'd know that such silence could only be temporary. The apple doesn't fall far from the tree.) Like many religious people, Mum assumed that a "relationship" with the Divine must be marked by a one-way flow of belief, from creature to Creator. But I reminded her of the verse in the Qur'an that I most adore: "God does not change the condition of a people until they change what is inside themselves." It's a sign of reciprocity—a relationship in the genuine, two-way sense.

Maybe, I told her, God loves His creatures so much that He hasn't made us mere subjects; maybe He wants us to be agents too. In that case, doesn't a relationship with God imply mutual confidence, yours in Him as well as His in you? Use the misfortune of cancer, I urged, to show that you're accepting the invitation to grow. Ask yourself daily, "What am I doing so that my Creator can *continue* having faith in me?"

The question intrigues Mum, so much so that we talk about it in almost every phone conversation. I'll take her thoughtful response as a small win, and I love and honor my mother enough to believe that she's capable of achieving more of them. Given what's riding on the small wins, we can't begin to measure their meaning.

IRSHADDERING CHAI TEA

This recipe makes five cups of chai, which is perfect for two talkative people because you'll have to negotiate who gets the fifth cup. Chai is too rich and fun a drink to get uptight about, so I won't give you precise measurements. But I guarantee that the final product is going to be scrumptious thanks to the ingredients, regardless of how much of them you use. Feel free to try different amounts of cinnamon and cardamom while brewing, as well as varied dollops of sugar and milk while serving. Soon enough, you're bound to hit your sweet spot. To discover it, you'll need:

- A medium-sized saucepan
- 3 tea bags (orange pekoe or any black tea; decaf is fine)
- 1 to 2 cinnamon sticks
- A handful of unshelled cardamom seeds
- Milk or cream
- Sugar

Fill the saucepan about three-quarters full of water and throw in a sprinkling of cardamom seeds. Bring to a boil. Meanwhile, break a cinnamon stick or two into smaller pieces and add to the water.

Once it's all boiling, turn the heat down a bit and put in the three tea bags. I prefer bags that are perforated so the flavor flows out readily, but regular tea bags will do.

Simmer for a few minutes, depending on how strong you like your tea.

Now you're ready to serve it with milk and sugar. If you're lactose-intolerant, skip the milk altogether. And if you're like me, you'll use cream instead of milk.

Remember: You'll be experimenting the first few times so don't worry about getting it right. I encourage you to surf the web for other recipes if you want additional ingredients. "Irshaddering chai tea" could be just the beginning for you.

ACKNOWLEDGMENTS

In the Author's Note at the beginning of this book, I thanked my teachers: members of the public who've contacted me in every way imaginable. Now, at the end, let me recognize them once more. Their comments and stories have rooted this book in reality checks— some of which are seldom voiced out loud. They've put the "public" in "public service."

Beyond my correspondents, a few people deserve to be singled out for having the guts to travel this journey with me—and to enhance my understanding of it. Deep gratitude goes to my colleagues at New York University's Robert F. Wagner Graduate School of Public Service, especially Dean Ellen Schall, the administrative dean Tyra Liebmann, and the academic dean Rogan Kersh. Katharine Rhodes Henderson, President of Auburn Theological Seminary, signed up for the journey, too. "This is a calling," she told me. "I get it." Better still, she got behind it. I'm equally proud of my friends at the European Foundation for Democracy, foremost among them the executive director Roberta Bonazzi. Then there are donors to the Moral Courage Project and its sister campaign, Project Ijtihad, who've also given their time and tears.

I'm indebted to my editors, particularly the brave and brilliant

Anne Collins. Another of my editorial coaches, Susan K. Reed, swooped in at a moment of self-doubt, while Leslie Meredith guided me to the finish. Along the way, research assistance came from multiple minds, chiefly Ismail Butera, Diederik van Hoogstraten, Arnold Yasin Mol, Roi Ben-Yehuda, Raquel Evita Saraswati, Sonal Gor, Karys Rhea, and Ivan Rodriguez.

My students at New York University have boosted my faith in the capacity that each of us has to cultivate moral courage and to share it with others, including our families. Which brings me to my own family. Mum, Ishrat and Fatima show me the face of God's grace. In thanking them for their love, I thank Allah for His.

RECOMMENDED READINGS

These are the books from which I've directly quoted. You can find many more sources—both academic and journalistic—in my footnotes, posted on irshadmanji.com.

Abdulhameed, Sultan. *The Quran and the Life of Excellence.* Denver, CO: Outskirts Press, 2010.

Appiah, Kwame Anthony. *The Honor Code: How Moral Revolutions Happen.* New York: W. W. Norton, 2010.

Barzun, Jacques. *From Dawn to Decadence: 500 Years of Western Cultural Life, 1500 to the Present.* New York: HarperCollins, 2000.

Bondurant, Joan V. *Conquest of Violence: The Gandhian Philosophy of Conflict.* Berkeley, CA: University of California Press, 1965.

Branch, Taylor. *Parting the Waters: America in the King Years, 1954–63.* New York: Simon & Schuster, 1988.

———. *At Canaan's Edge: America in the King Years, 1965–68.* New York: Simon & Schuster, 2006.

Chmiel, Mark. *Elie Wiesel and the Politics of Moral Leadership.* Philadelphia: Temple University Press, 2001.

de Botton, Alain. *Status Anxiety.* New York: Pantheon Books, 2004.

Drakulić, Slavenka. *Café Europa: Life After Communism.* New York: W. W. Norton, 1997.

Easwaran, Eknath. *Nonviolent Soldier of Islam: Badshah Khan, a Man to Match His Mountains.* Tomales, CA: Nilgiri Press, 1999.

El Fadl, Khaled Abou. *The Great Theft: Wrestling Islam from the Extremists.* New York: HarperSanFrancisco, 2005.

El Fadl, Khaled Abou, et al. *The Place of Tolerance in Islam.* Boston: Beacon Press, 2002.

Faulker, Robert K. *The Case for Greatness: Honorable Ambition and Its Critics.* New Haven, CT: Yale University Press, 2007.

Fromm, Erich. *On Disobedience: Why Freedom Means Saying "No" to Power.* New York: Harper Perennial Modern Thought, 2010.

Gershman, Norman H. *Besa: Muslims Who Saved Jews in World War II.* Syracuse, NY: Syracuse University Press, 2008.

Greenberg, Kenneth S. *Honor & Slavery.* Princeton, NJ: Princeton University Press, 1996.

Harris, Jennifer and Elwood Watson, eds. *The Oprah Phenomenon.* Lexington: University Press of Kentucky, 2007

Heath, Chip and Dan Heath. *Switch: How to Change Things When Change Is Hard.* New York: Broadway Books, 2010.

Herman, Arthur. *Gandhi & Churchill: The Epic Rivalry That Destroyed an Empire and Forged Our Age.* New York: Bantam Books, 2008.

Holmes, Richard. *The Age of Wonder: How the Romantic Generation Discovered the Beauty and Terror of Science.* London: Harper Press, 2008.

Hunt, Helen LaKelly. *Faith and Feminism: A Holy Alliance.* New York: Atria, 2004.

Husseini, Rana. *Murder in the Name of Honor: The True Story of One Woman's Heroic Fight Against an Unbelievable Crime.* New York: Oneworld Publications, 2009.

Inabdar, Subhash C. *Muhammad and the Rise of Islam: The Creation of Group Identity.* Madison, CT: Psychosocial Press, 2000.

RECOMMENDED READINGS

Jamison, Kay Redfield. *Exuberance: The Passion for Life.* New York: Alfred A. Knopf, 2004.

Karahasan, Dževad (Slobodan Drakulić, trans.). *Sarajevo, Exodus of a City.* New York: Kodansha International, 1994.

Kelsay, John. *Arguing the Just War in Islam.* Cambridge, MA: Harvard University Press, 2007.

Kennedy, Randall. *Sellout: The Politics of Racial Betrayal.* New York: Pantheon Books, 2008.

Khorasani, Noushin Ahmadi. *Iranian Women's One Million Signatures: Campaign for Equality—The Inside Story.* Bethesda, MD: Women's Learning Partnership, 2009.

King, Jr., Martin Luther. *Why We Can't Wait.* New York: Harper & Row, 1964.

Klausen, Jytte. *The Cartoons That Shook the World.* New Haven, CT: Yale University Press, 2009.

Krause, Sharon R. *Liberalism with Honor.* Cambridge, MA: Harvard University Press, 2002.

Leider, Richard J. *The Power of Purpose: Creating Meaning in Your Life and Work.* San Francisco: Berrett-Koehler, 1997.

Loveland, Anne C. *Lillian Smith: A Southerner Confronting the South.* Baton Rouge: Louisiana State University Press, 1986.

Mackay, Charles. *Memoirs of Extraordinary Popular Delusions and the Madness of Crowds.* New York: Farrar, Straus and Giroux, 1974 (reprint of 1852 edition).

Maslow, Abraham H. *Religions, Values, and Peak-Experiences.* Columbus: Ohio State University Press, 1964.

Mawdudi, Sayyed Abul A'la. *Towards Understanding Islam.* Islamic Circle of North America, 1986.

Mernissi, Fatema (Mary Jo Lakeland, trans.). *Islam and Democracy: Fear of the Modern World.* Cambridge, MA: Perseus, 1992 and updated 2002.

Moïsi, Dominique. *The Geopolitics of Emotion: How Cultures of Fear, Humiliation and Hope Are Re-Shaping the World*. New York: Doubleday, 2009.

Neiman, Susan. *Moral Clarity: A Guide for Grown-Up Idealists*. Orlando, FL: Harcourt, 2008.

Oren, Michael B. *Power, Faith and Fantasy: America in the Middle East, 1776 to the Present*. New York: W. W. Norton, 2007.

Packer, George, ed. *The Fight Is for Democracy: Winning the War of Ideas in America and the World*. New York: HarperCollins, 2003.

Rushdie, Salman. *The Satanic Verses*. New York: Picador, 1988.

Saeed, Abdullah, and Hassan Saeed. *Freedom of Religion, Apostasy and Islam*. Burlington, VT: Ashgate Publishing, 2004.

Schlesinger, Arthur M. *The Disuniting of America: Reflections on a Multicultural Society*. New York: W. W. Norton, 1998.

Smith, Lillian. *Killers of the Dream*. Garden City, NJ: Doubleday, 1963.

Smith, Lillian (Michelle Cliff, ed.). *The Winner Names the Age: A Collection of Writings*. New York: W. W. Norton, 1978.

Shweder, Richard, et al., eds. *Engaging Cultural Differences: The Multicultural Challenge in Liberal Societies*. New York: Russell Sage Foundation, 2002.

Thalhammer, Kristina E., et al. *Courageous Resistance: The Power of Ordinary People*. New York: Palgrave Macmillan, 2007.

Thoreau, Henry David. *Walden; or, Life in the Woods*. Boston: Beacon Press, 1997 (reprint of 1854 edition).

Tripathi, Salil. *Offence: The Hindu Case*. London: Seagull Books, 2009.

Tutu, Desmond M., and Mpho Tutu (Douglas C. Abrams, ed.). *Made for Goodness: And Why This Makes All the Difference*. New York: HarperOne, 2010.

Wahba, Mourad, and Mona Abousenna, eds. *Averroës and the Enlightenment.* Amherst, NY: Prometheus Books, 1996.

Whitaker, Brian. *What's Really Wrong with the Middle East.* London: Saqi Books, 2009.

Wikan, Unni. *Generous Betrayal: Politics of Culture in the New Europe.* Chicago: University of Chicago Press, 2002.

Yuksel, Edip, et al., trans. *Quran: A Reformist Translation.* Self-published/Brainbrow Press, 2007.

INDEX

INDEX

INDEX

ABOUT THE AUTHOR

Winner of Oprah Winfrey's first "Chutzpah Award" for boldness, Irshad Manji teaches moral courage at New York University's Robert F. Wagner Graduate School of Public Service. She is also a scholar with the European Foundation for Democracy. Her previous book, *The Trouble with Islam Today: A Muslim's Call for Reform in Her Faith*, earned international recognition and inspired Manji's Emmy-nominated PBS film, *Faith Without Fear*. *The New York Times* has called her "Osama bin Laden's worst nightmare," while *The Jakarta Post* in Indonesia, the world's largest Muslim country, has identified Irshad Manji as one of three women creating positive change in contemporary Islam. Learn more at irshadmanji.com.